D1737038

THE FATHERS
OF THE CHURCH

A NEW TRANSLATION

VOLUME 32

THE FATHERS
OF THE CHURCH

A NEW TRANSLATION

SAINT AUGUSTINE

LETTERS

VOLUME V (204-270)

Translated by

SISTER WILFRID PARSONS, S.N.D.

THE CATHOLIC UNIVERSITY OF AMERICA PRESS
Washington, D.C.

NIHIL OBSTAT:

JOHN A. GOODWINE

Censor Librorum

IMPRIMATUR:

✠ FRANCIS CARDINAL SPELLMAN

Archbishop of New York

June 15, 1956

Library of Congress Catalog Card No. 64-19948

ISBN 8132-0032-6

Copyright © 1956 by

THE CATHOLIC UNIVERSITY OF AMERICA PRESS, INC.

Second Printing 1977
Third Printing 1981

WRITINGS
OF
SAINT AUGUSTINE

VOLUME 13

CONTENTS

INTRODUCTION

THE REMAINING LETTERS (204-270) of St. Augustine
with which this volume concludes, form an unassorted
group, not so theologically technical in tone and
more likely to interest the general reader. The last dated
letter is No. 231, and the remainder of the collection com-
prises those for which no reliable date can be assigned.

Letters 204-231 show an Augustine still fighting a sharp
battle with heresy, dealing the death blow to Donatism,
repulsing the rear-guard action of Pelagianism, and sometimes defending himself against his own ecclesiastical brethren by whom his arguments on grace, free will, and predestination were not always favorably received. In Italy, in
Sicily, and especially on the Island of Lerins in southern
Gaul, there was lively opposition to his rigorist views, ranging
all the way from a simple difference of emphasis to an open
acceptance of quasi-Pelagian ideas (225, 226). Even in
Africa he had to contend with misinterpretation on the part
of Abbot Valentine and the monks of Hadrumetum (214-
216).

Problems of Church discipline continued to trouble him
to the end of his life. In 209 he appeals to Pope Celestine to
uphold his disciplinary action against Anthony of Fussala,

an auxiliary bishop who had been suspended from his diocese but not deprived of his rank, and who had appealed to
Rome. Augustine is torn between remorse at having consecrated so young and so unsuitable a man and compassion
for the people of Fussala who were the victims of his tyranny
and rapacity. In 219 Augustine joins other African fathers
in an appeal to two Gallic bishops for clemency to a repentant
monk. In 213 we have the official report on the action taken
by the Bishop of Hippo in naming Eraclius as his coadjutor
with right of succession. According to the custom of the
times, he submits his proposal to his flock, and the clerk
who takes down the proceedings records with minute and
serious care the exact number of times the people shouted
assent. The intensity of their approval ranges from five
times for 'That's right, he deserves it!' to thirty-six times for
'Thanks be to God! Praise to Christ!' An echo of the volume
of sound comes to us as each succeeding paragraph begins
with 'When silence was restored.' One of his suffragans,
Honoratus, Bishop of Thiave, deeply alarmed by the ominous
advance of the barbarians in Africa, had written what must
have been a desperate plea for permission to seek safety in
flight, justifying himself by certain Scriptural quotations.
Augustine writes him a long letter (228) in which he distinguishes between clergy and laity when it is a question of
flight from danger, insisting that so long as any of his flock
have not removed to a place of refuge, the bishop is obliged
to stay and minister to them. He reminds him that in times
of danger the churches are always thronged with people
seeking solace in prayer and the sacraments, and points out
the disastrous results when the shepherd becomes a hireling
and flees. With patience and tact he urges Honoratus to
imitate the Good Shepherd who lays down His life for His
flock, and to follow the more heroic course even if it leads
to martyrdom.

Two letters to public officials form a contrast as strong as the characters of the two men. To Count Boniface his final letter (220) contains a fearless rebuke for the instability and frequent lapses from Christian virtue which had brought him so low. Because of his absorption in his disreputable intrigues, Africa, which he was sworn to defend, had fallen farther and farther into enemy hands, with calamitous results for Church and for people. As usual, however, Augustine does not leave his correspondent in the depths, but tries to lead him gently back to the path of duty and fidelity to his Christian profession. Two letters to Count Darius (229, 231) two years later are in a conciliatory, not to say a respectful, tone. This official had been sent to arrange for peace—unfortunately a vain hope—and had, moreover, scholarly tastes and a high admiration for the Bishop of Hippo. He asks for a copy of 'that work of yours, entitled *Confessions*,' and receives not only the volume requested, but several others, together with a request for an honest opinion on them and a little homily on the dangers of vainglory.

Probably the best-known and the most controversial of the letters is No. 211, commonly called the "Rule" of St. Augustine. It is addressed to a convent of nuns who had set up an unseemly disturbance against their Superior. This was Mother Felicitas who had succeeded Augustine's sister upon the latter's death, and there is a broad hint that the real source of the strife was a new chaplain; so much to that Augustine wonders why they are not demanding his removal rather than their reverend Mother's. In some manuscripts this letter is entitled: '*Objurgatio contra Sanctimonialium dissensionem et post increpationem earum regularis informatio.*' This seems to indicate—especially the word *regularis*— that the Sisters were already living under a Rule, but were falling short of perfection in several points. These points are taken up in order: fraternal charity, observance of the common 'life, renunciation of worldly rank, prayer and psalmody (but no prescribed forms), mortification of the flesh, care of the sick, modest apparel (there was no uniform dress), custody of the eyes, modesty of demeanor outside the convent, fraternal correction, care of the wardrobe and of the body, forgiveness of injuries, respect and obedience toward superiors. These add up to what a religious of the present day would call a directory or set of recommendations or spiritual counsels; that is, not the religious rule itself, but helps to its observance. There is no mention of vows, religious exercises, reception of the sacraments, work, silence, order of the day, or government of the community, all of which form the core of a formal religious rule. It seems likely, therefore, that there must already have been a Rule, possibly an unwritten one, which this letter was written to elaborate. However, the fact remains that Letter 211 is always spoken of as the Augustinian Rule.

Beginning with Letter 232 is a collection of thirty-nine letters listed as Class IV. These are letters for which no clear indication of time can be found and which, therefore, cannot be assigned to a fixed date. They were all written after Augustine became bishop, and a few can be given time limits. Letter 232 can be placed between 399 and 408 because of the reference to laws against idolatry; in the exchange with Pascentius (238-241) Augustine admits that he is inferior in age to his correspondent; while elsewhere (250, 259, and 269) he refers to his advanced age. In the Introduction to Volume 33 of their *Patrology,* the Maurists announce that they have arranged these letters by order of subject, putting first those against the enemies of the Christian faith, then those referring to points of conduct, and, finally, certain letters of courtesy. These latter touch on various human problems and are generally brief and personal. In them Augustine often reveals the deep kindness of his heart. He writes to Ceretius (237) who was being impressed by some Priscillianist interpretations of Scripture, tearing their pretentions to shreds and ridiculing their attachment to an apocryphal hymn of Christ which they claimed was composed by our Lord Himself. He has a sharp wrangle with Pascentius over *homooúsion,* which brings in the whole Arian controversy. Posidius had asked advice on a risky subject (for African bishops) : what to do about women's dress, cosmetics, and earrings. In Letter 245 Augustine advises against overhasty action and makes a distinction between harmless and illicit adornment of the person. He thinks that married women try to beautify themselves to please their husbands, but he doubts that husbands are taken in by pink or white paint on the face or that they regard it as an improvement. As for un-married women, they have no right to please anyone but God. Letters 252-255 unfold the story of a girl, a ward of the Church, and therefore under Augustine's authority, who was sought in marriage by a pagan. The proposal had come, surprisingly enough, not from the young man, Rusticus, but from a bishop named Benenatus who professed to see some advantage in the match. The girl, naturally, had not been consulted at all; there is a hint that she was too young to know her own mind, but that she had expressed a desire to enter the convent. There is no clue to the end of the story. Seleuciana in Letter 265 wants to know when St. Peter and the other Apostles were baptized, because a Novatian heretic had claimed that they had not been. This was a subtle inquiry even for Augustine's subtle mind, but as usual he found an answer. Letter 268 gives us an early account of a well-established Church custom—that of taking up a collection. Augustine had gone surety for one Fascius who had taken sanctuary in the church to escape imprisonment for debt. After promising to pay later, he disappeared. The Bishop had to ask his flock to make up the sum which otherwise would have to come out of the church treasury. We are not told the sum collected.

Letter 269, perhaps Augustine's last, has a sad note. He has to refuse an invitation to the dedication of a church. He might have come if it had been at some warmer season; he might have disregarded winter's cold if he had been younger, but the cold of winter and the cold of age together are too much for him.

Roman civilization in Africa survived Augustine by only a few months, but, though Africa fell and Rome fell, Augustine's work has lived on. Today he is as powerful a figure in the Church as he was in the fourth and fifth centuries.

In bringing this work to its conclusion the translator would like to express her gratitude to the libraries of Harvard University and Trinity College, Washington, for the long-time loan of texts of the Letters of St. Augustine.

LETTERS

204-270

Translated by

SISTER WILFRID PARSONS, S.N.D.
Emmanuel College
Boston, Mass.

204. *Augustine gives greeting in the Lord to the noble lord, his honored son, Dulcitius*[1] *(420)*

I must not make light of the request in which you showed your desire to be instructed by me on how you should answer heretics whose salvation, in the mercy of the Lord, is the constant preoccupation of your zeal. Although great numbers of them understand the benefit[2] conferred on them, which gives us the greatest pleasure, some of them, ungrateful to God. and men, goaded on by a wretched fury, think to frighten us by their acts of self-destruction—when they cannot decimate us by their murders—seeking either joy for themselves by our deaths or sadness for us by theirs. But the mad aberration of a few men ought not to interfere with the salvation of such numbers of people. It is not only God and prudent men who are aware of our sentiments toward them, but even they themselves know it, although they are our bitterest enemies. They may think we can be frightened by their self-destruction, but they have no doubt that we do fear their eternal loss.

---

1 A tribune and executor in Africa of the imperial decrees against the Donatists.

2 The benefit of being released from fear of reprisals on the part of their sectaries when they returned to Catholic unity.

Now what are we to do, seeing how many, with the help of the Lord, find the way of peace, through your instrumentality? Surely, we neither can nor ought to hold them back from this impulse toward unity, through fear that some, utterly hard and cruel to themselves, may destroy themselves by their own will, not ours. Indeed, we should pray that all who carry the standard of Christ against Christ and boast of the Gospel against the Gospel may forsake their wrong way and rejoice with us in the unity of Christ. But since God, by an inscrutable yet just disposition of His will, has predestined some of them to the ultimate penalty, undoubtedly it is better for some of them to perish in their own fires, while an incomparably greater number are rescued and won over from that deadly schism and separation, than that all should equally burn in the eternal fires of hell as a punishment for their accursed dissension. The Church mourns their loss as holy David mourned the loss of his rebellious son[3] about whose safety he had given orders with anxious love. He grieved over his son's death, with tearful utterance, although it was the penalty of a wicked impiety; but as his proud and wicked spirit departed to its own place, the people of God that had been divided by his tyranny recognized their king, and the completeness of their reunion consoled the grief of the father for the loss of his son.

Therefore, noble lord and honored son, we do not blame you for thinking that such men at Thamugadi[4] should first be warned of the decree, but for saying to them: 'You know that you are to be put to a well-deserved death.' They thought, as their reports show, that you had threatened to kill those who were arrested, not understanding that you spoke of the death they wanted to inflict on themselves. For you did not receive the right of life and death over them by any laws, nor

3 2 Kings 18.9-12; 28-33.
4 Modern Timgad, in Numidia.

was it laid down in the imperial decrees that they should be put to death when the execution of the decrees was imposed on you. It is true that in the second decree of your Charity you declared what you intended. In thinking that their bishop should be addressed by letter you showed most humanely the restraint of mildness put on officials by the Catholic Church, even on those appointed by the power of a Christian emperor to correct errors by fear or by persuasion, but you addressed him in more complimentary terms than was fitting for a heretic.

As to your wanting me to give rebuttal to his reply, I imagine you thought this ought to benefit the citizens of Thamugadi, so that his false doctrine, by which they were being led astray, might be refuted somewhat more completely. But I am now extremely busy; besides, I have refuted this kind of nonsense in many other works of mine. I have proved countless times, both by debate and by writing, that they cannot have the death of martyrs because they have not the life of Christians, since it is not the pain but the purpose that makes a martyr. We have taught also that free will is given to man on such terms that punishments for grave sins are most justly enacted by divine and human laws, and that it concerns religious kings on earth not only to deal with adulteries and murders or other crimes of this kind, but also to restrain acts of sacrilege with fitting severity. Those are very wrong who think that we receive their sectaries just as they are because we do not rebaptize them. How can they be received just as they are when they are heretics, and bcome Catholics by coming over to us? From the fact that sacraments once given may not be repeated we must not conclude that hearts that have gone astray should not be converted.

In the matter of the frenzied deaths which some of them inflict on themselves, which commonly make them hateful

and horrible even to many of their own whose minds have
not been seized by this madness, we have often answered
them according to the Scripture and Christian reasoning, as
it is written: 'He that is evil to himself, to whom is he good?'[5]
At least let him who thinks it advantageous and allowable
to kill himself kill his neighbor also, since the Scripture says:
'Thou shalt love thy neighbor as thyself.'[6] But when no
laws or lawful authorities give command, it is not lawful to
kill another, even if he wishes and asks for it and has no
longer the strength to live, as is clearly proved by the
Scripture in the Book of Kings, where King David ordered
the slayer of King Saul to be put to death,[7] although he
said that he had been importuned by the wounded and
half-dead king to kill him with one blow and to free his soul
struggling with the fetters of the body and longing to be
released from those torments. Therefore, since everyone who
kills a man without any authorization of lawful power is a
murderer, anyone who kills himself will not be a murderer
if he is not a man. I have said all this in many ways in many
other sermons and letters of mine.

But, I must admit, I do not recall ever having answered
the objection based on the incident of Razias,[8] one of the
ancients. Embarrassed by the extreme scarcity of examples,
after having at one time and another delved into all the
authorities of the Church, they boast of having found this
person in the Book of Machabees, as if it were a precedent
for the crime of self-destruction. However, let this argument
suffice for your Charity and for prudent men generally to
refute them: If they are ready to apply to the life of Christians
the examples of all the deeds of the Jewish people taken from

5 Eccli. 14.5.
6 Matt. 22.39; Mark 12.31; Luke 10.27; Lev. 19.18.
7 2 Kings 1.1-16.
8 2 Mach. 14.37-46.

their writings, then let them apply this one, too. But if there are in their books numerous exploits of men who are truthfully praised in their writings, which are either not appropriate to this time or were not right even when done at that time, this is indeed such a one which Razias committed against himself. Since he was in high esteem among his own, and was most zealous in the Jewish religion, which the Apostle says is but loss and dung[9] in comparison with Christian justice, and since for this reason this same Razias was called the father of the Jews, what wonder if an overweening pride found its way, so to speak, into the man so that he chose to die by his own hand rather than suffer the indignity of slavery at the hands of an enemy, after having enjoyed such eminence in the sight of his countrymen?

Deeds like that are usually praised in pagan literature. But, although the man himself is praised in these Books of the Machabees, his deed is merely related, not praised, and it is set before our eyes as something to be judged rather than imitated; not, of course, to be judged by our judgment but by the judgment of temperate doctrine, which is conspicuous also in those same ancient books. Obviously, Razias was far from those words which we read: 'Take all that shall be brought upon thee, and in thy sorrow endure, and in thy humiliation have patience.'[10] Therefore, he was not a man of wisdom for choosing death, but of impatience in not bearing humiliation.

It is written that he chose to die nobly and manfully, but was it necessarily prudently? Nobly, of course, that he might not become a captive and lose the liberty of his rank, but manfully because he had such strength of mind on which he relied in order to destroy himself. When he could not accomplish this with the sword, he threw himself headlong

---

9 Phil. 3.8.
10 Eccli. 2.4.

from the wall, and, being still alive, he ran to a steep rock and there, almost bloodless, grasping his bowels with both hands, he cast them upon the people, and thereupon sank down exhausted and died. These are great deeds, but not necessarily good ones, for not everything which is great is good, since there are also great evils. God said: 'The innocent and just person thou shalt not put to death.'[11] If, then, he was not innocent and just, why is he proposed for our imitation? But, if he was innocent and just, why is the slayer of the innocent and just, that is, of this same Razias, thought thereupon to be worthy of praise?

This will have to be enough for the present to fill up my letter. I do not want to be garrulous. But I owe this kind of ministry of charity to the people of Thamugadi, since they have suggested to me, both by your request and by my honorable and dear son, Eleusinus, who held the office of tribune among them, that I should make such a reply to the two letters of Gaudentius, bishop of the Donatists, and especially to the later one which he thinks he has composed according to the sacred Scriptures, that nothing will seem to have been overlooked.

205. Augustine to his beloved brother, Consentius[1] (420)

There are some whom we see with our bodily eyes but do not know, because their life and aims are unknown to us; there are some whom we know but do not see, whose charity and affection are known to us, and among these we count

---

11 Exod. 23.7.

---

1 Cf. Letters 119, 120. If the recipient of this letter is the writer of 119 and the recipient of 120, it is strange that Augustine does not refer to the former letter. This Consentius is identified with the one to whom the *Contra mendacium* is dedicated. He lived in Spain among Priscillianists and was planning to go to Africa.

you. For that reason we greatly long to see you that you may be among those whom we both see and know. For those who, though unknown, are presented to our eyes are not only undesirable but even scarcely endurable, unless the beauty of the inward man appears in them by some outward signs. Those whose mind has become known to us, as yours has, before they made a bodily appearance are the ones we have known long since, but whom we long to see, so that what the eyes behold may give us a much more joyful and intimate enjoyment of the friend whom we already know within. Perhaps God will grant this, too, to our prayers, when events around us are quieter and safer, so that your visit may be the result of sincere charity rather than of troublesome necessity. For the present, let me answer, as best I can with the Lord's help, the points you sent me for solution in another manuscript in addition to your letter.

You ask whether the Lord's body has bones and blood or other marks of flesh. Suppose you added the question whether he has garments, would the topic not be widened? Why is it that we can scarcely think of things not deteriorating when we know they are subject to deterioration in the usage of daily life, even when certain proofs of divine miracles have already been given us from which it is possible to imagine greater marvels? For, if the garments of the Israelites could last without wearing out for so many years in the desert, and the hides of dead animals could continue undestroyed for so long a time in their shoes,[2] surely God can extend the quality of incorruption in certain bodies for as long as He wills. I think, therefore, that the body of the Lord is the same now in heaven as it was when He ascended into heaven. When His disciples doubted His Resurrection, as we read in the Gospel, and thought that what they saw was not a body but a spirit, He said to them: 'See my hands

---

2 Deut. 29.5.

and my feet; handle and see; for a spirit hath not flesh and
bones as you see me to have.'[3] Thus He was felt by their
hands while He was on earth; thus He was withdrawn from
their sight when He went into heaven. Then an angel's voice
was heard saying: 'He shall so come as you have seen him
going into heaven.'[4] Let faith be present and no question
will remain, unless, perhaps, an objection might be raised
about His blood, because when He said: 'Handle and see, for
a spirit hath not flesh and bones,' He did not add 'blood.' Let
us, then, not add the question about what He did not add to
His words. In brief, if you agree, let the question be ended,
for perhaps some tiresome investigator, taking advantage of
this question of blood, will press us and say: 'If blood, why
not phlegm, why not both yellow and black bile, by which
four humors the science of medicine teaches that the nature
of the flesh is kept in balance?' But whatever anyone adds,
let him beware of adding corruption, lest he corrupt the
soundness and purity of his own faith.

Human weakness uses its acquaintance with things experienced to measure divine works which are beyond its
experience, and thinks it has made quite a keen remark when
it says: 'If there is flesh, there is also blood; if blood, the
other humors are there, too; if the other humors are there,
corruption is necessarily there.' In the same way it would
say: 'If there is flame, it is hot; if it is hot, it burns; if it
burns, then it burned the bodies of the three men thrown into
the fiery furnace by the wicked king.'[5] If, then, no one who
has the correct idea of divine works doubts that a miracle
was wrought on these three men, why should we not believe
that He who prevented those bodies from being consumed by
the fire also prevented His body from being consumed by

3 Luke 24.37-39.
4 Acts 1.11.
5 Dan. 3.19-24; 91-94.

fire or famine or disease or old age or any other of the forces by which corruption usually breaks down human bodies? But if anyone says that incorruption against the fire was not added to the flesh of the three men, but that the power of destruction was taken away from the fire itself, why do we fear that He who took away the ability of fire to destroy could not make flesh which could not be destroyed? For, if we understand that change to have been in the fire, not in the flesh, it is much more remarkable, for at one and the same time it did not burn the bodies of the men, so as to be able to hurt them, but it burned the wood in the furnace so as to make it hot. But those who do not even believe these marvels have too great a disbelief in divine power, and our present talk is not with them nor to them; those who do believe may certainly conjecture from them the answer to what they seek with faith. So, the divine power is able to remove whatever qualities He wills from that visible and palpable nature of bodies, while some qualities remain unchanged; so He is able to add an unwearying strength to mortal members, preserving the characteristic marks of their form, even when they have died because of the corruption of mortality, so that mortal appearance is there, but wasting disease is absent; motion is there, but fatigue is not; the ability to eat is there, but the necessity of hunger is not.

The question raised by the words we read in the Apostle: 'Flesh and blood will not possess the kingdom of God,'[6] is solved in the manner you mentioned, by saying that under the name of flesh and blood we are to understand the works of flesh and blood. But, inasmuch as the Apostle was not speaking of works, but of the mode of resurrection, and was analyzing that question by discussing it, it is better in that passage to take flesh and blood as used in the sense of corruption of flesh and blood. For, if the word flesh means

---

6 1 Cor. 15.50.

activity, why should it not also mean corruption, as in the passage: 'All flesh is grass,' for here that corruptibility is indicated, and it continues: 'and all the glory of the flesh as the flower of grass; the grass is withered, the flower is fallen.'[7] Does this agree with that flesh and blood of which it was said: 'Handle and see, for a spirit hath not flesh and bones as you see me to have?' For how could it wither and fall, when it is written that 'Christ rising from the dead dieth now no more; death shall no more have dominion over him?'[8]

Look again, then, at that statement of the Apostle and consider it as a whole. As he was trying to argue convincingly for the resurrection of the dead with men who said there was no resurrection of the dead, he first adduced the Resurrection of Christ as an example, and among other arguments which he used he asked himself this question: 'But some man will say: How do the dead rise again? or with what body will they come?', that is, what kind of body? Then he brings in the analogy of seed and says: 'Senseless man, that which thou sowest is not quickened except it die first. And that which thou sowest, thou sowest not the body that shall be, but bare grain, as of wheat or of some of the rest. But God giveth it a body as he will, and to every seed its proper body.'[9] According to this, therefore, he said: 'thou sowest not the body that shall be,' for wheat will come only from wheat, but because no one sows the leaf or the stalk and the manifold layers covering the chaff of grain, with which, notwithstanding, the seed comes up; for that reason he says 'but the bare grain,' wishing to show from this that if God can add what was not in the bare grain, how much more can He make over what was in the body of man.

However, what he adds to this refers to the difference in

---

7 Isa. 40.6-8.
8 Rom. 6.9.
9 1 Cor. 15.42-44.

condition of those who rise again, occasioned by the different degrees of glory in the faithful and in the saints. 'Not all flesh,' he says, 'is the same flesh, but one is the flesh of men, another of beasts, another of birds, another of fishes. And there are bodies celestial and bodies terrestrial; one is the glory of the celestial, another of the terrestrial; one is the glory of the sun, another the glory of the moon and another the glory of the stars. For star differeth from star in glory; so also is the resurrection of the dead.'[10] This is the tenor of all these examples: if the kinds of flesh—though all are mortal—differ from each other according to the varieties of living beings; and if bodies—though all are visible—differ according to the diversities of place, so that 'one is the glory of the celestial, another of the terrestrial'; and if, in lofty places—though all are celestial—they differ from each other in brilliance of light, it is not be wondered at that in the resurrection of the dead there will be a difference of rewards.

From this he comes to that characteristic held in common by all flesh which rises to eternal life and he says: 'It is sown in corruption, it shall rise in incorruption; it is sown in dishonor, it shall rise in glory; it is sown in weakness, it shall rise in power; it is sown a natural body, it shall rise a spiritual body.'[11] From these words of the Apostle it surely is not allowable to think that our bodies will rise to a better state than the body of Christ, which is proposed as an example which we ought to look upon with faith and hope for through His grace. Consequently, the Body of Christ could not possibly rise in corruption if ours, as we are promised, are to rise in incorruption; it could not rise without glory, if ours will rise in glory; but what glory could there be where there is still corruption? It is too senseless to believe that that Body was sown in weakness, that is, put to death, and rose in weakness,

10 1 Cor. 15.39-42.
11 1 Cor. 15.42-44.

when our body is sown in weakness but rises in power; and when the same Apostle says of Christ: 'Although he was crucified through weakness, yet he liveth by the power of God',[12] who would be so wise in his foolishness as to believe that Christ's Body was sown a natural body and was raised up a natural body, if ours is sown a natural body and will rise up a spiritual body?

It is clear, then, and we cannot doubt that the Body of Christ, which could be pierced with nails and lance, although it did not see the corruption of rottenness in the tomb, of which it is written: 'Thou wilt not give thy holy one to see corruption,'[13] is now wholly established in incorruption, and that what was sown in the ignominy of passion and death is now in the glory of eternal life; that what could be crucified through weakness now reigns with power; and what was a natural body, since it was derived from Adam, is now a spiritual body, since it is inseparably joined to spirit. For when the Apostle wished to adduce the testimony of Scripture on the natural body, he quoted that passage found in Genesis: 'If there be a natural body,' he says, 'there is also a spiritual body; as it is written: the first man, Adam, was made into a living soul,' or 'into a quickening spirit.'[14] You recall, I am sure, how it is written: 'And God breathed into his face the breath of life and man became a living soul.'[15] But of animals it was said: 'Let the earth bring forth the living creature.'[16] We understand, then, that the natural body is said to be like the other animals because of the dissolution and corruption of death; it is daily renewed by food, and when the bond of life is broken it is dissolved; but the spiritual body which is now with the spirit is immortal.

---

12 2 Cor. 13.4.
13 Ps. 15.10.
14 1 Cor. 15.44,45.
15 Gen. 2.7.
16 Gen. 1.24.

It is true that some think that the body will become spiritual by changing the body itself into spirit, and that whereas man was composed of body and spirit, both will be totally spirit, as if the Apostle had said: 'It is sown a body, it will rise a spirit.' But what he said was: 'It is sown a natural body, it will rise a spiritual body.' Therefore, as the natural body is not a living principle, but a body, so we ought to think that the spiritual body is not a spirit, but a body. Moreover, who would dare to think that Christ's Body either did not rise a spiritual body or, if it rose a spiritual body, was no longer body but spirit, although He refuted this idea in the disciples by saying to them when they saw Him and thought they saw a spirit: 'Handle and see, for a spirit hath not flesh and bones as you see me to have?' Therefore, that flesh was a spiritual body; yet it was not a spirit, but a body, never again to be loosed and separated from the soul by death. Such was the natural body as it was made alive by the breath of God when 'Man became a living soul,' destined to pass from a natural to a spiritual body without the interruption of death, a reward which God would have given if it had preserved its innocence and if transgression of the first command had not inflicted the penalty of sin committed.

Hence, the Lord Christ came to us through us, when the just found us sinners, covered, so to speak, with our lowliness, but with no taint of our sin. He appeared to us in a natural body, that is, a mortal one, although if He had willed, He could have come first in an immortal body. But, because it was fitting for us to be healed by the humility of the Son of God, He descended to our weakness, and by the power of His Resurrection He showed us the merit and reward of our faith. Therefore, the Apostle goes on to say: 'The last Adam [was made] into a quickening spirit.'[17] Whether we are to understand as the first Adam him who was formed from the

17 1 Cor. 15.45.

dust in the beginning, and as the last Adam Him who was born of the Virgin, or whether both are completed in each man, so that the first Adam would be man in a mortal body, and the last Adam the same man in an immortal body, He nevertheless wished this difference to be apparent between the living soul and the quickening spirit: that the former is a natural body, the latter a spiritual one. In the natural body the soul lives, indeed, but it does not quicken it so as to ward off corruption, whereas in the spiritual body, since 'he who is perfectly joined to the Lord is one spirit,'[18] it so quickens it that it makes it a spiritual body, putting off all corruption and fearing no separation.

Thus, the Apostle continues: 'Yet that was not first which is spiritual but that which is natural; afterwards that which is spiritual. The first man was of the earth, earthly, the second man from heaven, heavenly. Such as is the earthly, such also are the earthly; and such as is the heavenly, such also are they that are heavenly. Therefore as we have borne the image of the earthly, let us also bear the image of him who is from heaven.'[19] What is the meaning of 'such as is the earthly, such also are the earthly,' except that they are mortal from a mortal man? And what is the meaning of 'such as is the heavenly, such also are they that are heavenly,' except that they are immortal through one who is immortal: the first through Adam, the second through Christ? The Lord who was heavenly became earthly that He might make heavenly those who were earthly; that is, from immortal He became mortal by 'taking the form of a servant,'[20] not by changing the nature of the Lord; that He might make immortal those who were mortal by imparting the grace of the Lord, not by retaining the offense of the servant.

18 1 Cor. 6.17.
19 1 Cor. 15.46-49.
20 Phil. 2.7.

Therefore, when the Apostle was arguing about the resurrection of the body and was teaching that our bodies from being corruptible will become incorruptible, from contemptible will be glorious, from weak strong, from natural spiritual, that is, from mortal they will become immortal, he concluded his argument by saying: 'Now this I say, brethren, that flesh and blood cannot possess the kingdom of God,' and lest anyone should think that he had defined this according to the flesh, he clarified what he had said by adding: 'Neither shall corruption possess incorruption,'[21] as if to say: 'When I say flesh and blood shall not possess the kingdom of God, I mean corruption shall not possess incorruption.' Therefore, in this passage, by the expression 'flesh and blood' he wishes us to understand the corruption of mortality.

Finally, as if someone had said to him: 'How will it be flesh and not be flesh?—for obviously it will be flesh because the Lord said after His Resurrection: 'Handle and see, for a spirit hath not flesh and bones as you see me to have,' but it will not be flesh, because 'Flesh and blood cannot possess the kingdom of God'—he explains what he said by adding: 'Behold, I tell you a mystery. We shall all indeed rise again'— or, as some Greek versions have it, 'We shall all indeed sleep,'—'but we shall not all be changed.'[22] The words that follow show whether he meant this change to be for worse or better: 'In a moment,' he says, that is, in a point of time that cannot be divided[23]—'in the twinkling of an eye,' that is, with the utmost speed; 'at the last trumpet,' that is, at the last signal which will be given for the final completion, 'for the trumpet shall sound and the dead shall rise again incorruptible and we shall be changed.'[24] There is, then, no

21 1 Cor. 15.50.
22 1 Cor. 15.51.
23 He uses the words 'in atomo.'
24 1 Cor. 15.52.

doubt that we must understand this change to be for the better, because all, both just and unjust, will rise again, but as the Lord says in the Gospel: 'And they that have done good things shall come forth unto the resurrection of life, but they that have done evil unto the resurrection of judgment,'[25] calling eternal punishment judgment, as He says in another place: 'He that doth not believe is already judged.'[26] Therefore, those who are to rise to judgment will not be changed to that incorruption which cannot suffer the corruption of pain, which is that of the faithful and the saints, but they will be tortured by an everlasting corruption because 'their fire shall not be quenched and their worm shall not die.'[27]

What, then, is the meaning of that distinction, 'and the dead shall rise again incorruptible and we shall be changed,' except that all shall rise again incorruptible, but of these the just shall be changed to an incorruption which no corruption can possibly hurt? Hence, those who will not be changed to that incorruption will rise incorrupt, it is true, in the wholeness of their bodily parts, but subject to corruption in the suffering of pains, when they shall hear: 'Depart . . . into everlasting fire, which was prepared for the devil and his angels.'[28] From this 'evil hearing the just shall not fear.'[29] But when he speaks of that transformation of the just and says: 'We shall be changed,' as if we were to ask how that will come to pass and what the nature of that change will be, he goes on and says: 'For this corruptible must put on incorruption and this mortal must put on immortality.'[30] I think there is no doubt that this saying is consistent with his other words: 'Flesh and blood shall not possess the kingdom

---

25 John 5.29.
26 John 3.18.
27 Isa. 66.24.
28 Matt. 28.41.
29 Cf. Ps. 111.7.
30 1 Cor. 15.53.

of God,' because in that state there will be no corruption or mortality of flesh and blood, and it is in reference to these qualities that he speaks in this passage of flesh and blood.

On this point I will set down something here by way of example, which has just occurred to me. Where it is written: 'Lest perchance he that tempteth should have tempted you and our labor should be made vain,'[31] the Devil is understood as the subject, since God does not tempt anyone, as Scripture says in another place: 'But he tempteth no man';[32] yet this statement is not contrary to the other which says: 'The Lord your God tempteth you.'[33] The difficulty is solved by giving different meanings to the word 'temptation,' because the temptation of deception is not the same as the temptation of trial, and in the first sense the Devil is the only tempter, but in the second God does tempt us. In the same way, when we say: 'Flesh will possess the kingdom of God,' and 'flesh will not possess the kingdom of God,' let the meaning of this term be distinguished and there will be no difficulty, since flesh as substance, in the saying: 'A spirit hath not flesh and bones as you see me to have,' possesses the kingdom of God; but flesh taken in the sense of corruption will not possess it, and this is shown by the sequence of phrases: 'Flesh and blood shall not possess the kingdom of God,' to which these words are straightway added: 'Neither shall corruption possess incorruption.' I think we have discussed this point sufficiently.

You will not be troubled by your question whether the features of bodies are formed separately by God our Creator if you understand the power of divine operation, as far as the human mind can understand it. For, how can we deny that God works now in all the things that are created, when the Lord says: 'My Father worketh until now?'[34] And that rest

---

31 1 Thess. 3.5.
32 James 1.13.
33 Deut. 13.3.
34 John 5.17.

which occurred on the seventh day is to be understood as applying to the creation of nature, not to the government of the things created. Therefore, when the universe is governed by the Creator and all things come to birth according to their kind at the predestined places and times, God works until now. For, if God does not now form them, how can we read: 'Before I formed thee in the womb, I knew thee,'[35] and how can we explain: 'But if the grass of the field which is today, and tomorrow is cast into the oven, God doth so clothe,'[36] unless we are to believe, perhaps, that the grass is clothed by God, but bodies are not formed by God? For, when He said 'clothes' He shows clearly that He means present operation, not past ordinance. There is also that other passage of the Apostle about seed which I quoted above: 'Thou sowest not the body that shall be, but bare grain, as of wheat or of some of the rest, but God giveth it a body as he will.'[37] He did not say 'gave' or 'ordered,' but 'gives,' that you may know how the Creator applies the effective power of His wisdom to the creation of things which come into existence daily at their appointed times. Of this wisdom the Prophet said: 'It reacheth from end to end mightily and ordereth'—he did not say ordered—'all things sweetly.'[38] It is a great thing to know even superficially how transitory and temporal things are created not by transitory or temporal acts of the Creator, but by His eternal and unchanging power.

On that question which you thought should be raised, whether all the baptized who may go out of the body without repentance, entangled in various crimes, may attain pardon at some time, I have written a book[39] of considerable

35 Jer. 1.5.
36 Matt. 6.30.
37 1 Cor. 15.37,38.
38 Wisd. 8.1.
39 *Faith and Works.*

length, and if you care to copy it you will probably not look for anything further on the subject.

You want also to learn from me whether the breath which God breathed into Adam was the same as his soul. I answer briefly: Either it was or the soul was created by it. God speaks of the soul by the Prophet Isaias when He says: 'Every breath I have made,' which the following words explain adequately, for they continue: 'On account of sin have I struck it lightly,'[40] that is, 'it' refers to the same breath and the rest, which can only be understood of the human soul. In this matter we must be especially careful not to believe that the soul, made by God, or any particle of it, is the nature and substance of God, as is His only-begotten Son, who is His Word, as if that nature and substance by which He is God, whatever it is, could be changeable, which no one who feels that he has a soul can fail to feel that the soul is.

While I was dictating the above, the bearer who was awaiting a favorable wind to sail kept hurrying me. So, if on reading it, you find anything confused and inelegantly said, or if you see that the whole letter is so, attend to the doctrine and pardon the language.

206. *Augustine gives greeting in the Lord to Valerius,*[1] *his deservedly distinguished and eminent lord, and his very dear son (c. 420)*

Whenever people ask me to recommend them to your kindness and protection, I feel that I am making a wrong judgment of your compassion toward those in need of help and

---

40 Isa. 57.16,17. (Septuagint).

1 Cf. Letter 200.

of your kindness toward us, if I do not do so. Therefore, I do it most readily for the ministers of Christ who have charge of the Church of which I rejoice that you are a co-heir and son, and I do not hesitate to recommend them to your Excellency, deservedly distinguished and eminent lord, and very dear son in Christ. Consequently, when my holy brother and fellow bishop, Felix,[2] asked me to do this, surely I ought not to refuse, and so I commend to you a bishop in need of the help of a man in high position. Do for him what you can, since the Lord has given you power to do much, and I know that you are most desirous of His rewards.

207. Augustine gives greeting in the Lord to his saintly brother and fellow bishop, Claudius[1] (421)

In the ardor of your brotherly zeal for me, you sent me, of your own accord, without my asking you, the four books of Julian[2] which he has written against one of mine, so I have thought that I could do nothing more appropriate than to let you read first the answer[3] I made so that you may judge whether I have answered him correctly and appositely. Someone or other had written to the noble and God-fearing man, Count Valerius, some extracts from these four books against that same book of mine, which he knew that I had written for him. When these notes came into my hands through the careful attention of that eminent man, I lost no time in adding a second volume to the first, in which, to the best of

---

2 Mentioned in the lists of bishops in Letters 175, 176.

1 Probably an African bishop.
2 Julian of Eclanum took over the active leadership of the Pelagian heresy after the disappearance of Pelagius. These four books, no longer extant, contained an attack on Augustine's *De nuptiis et concupiscentia,* which he had sent to Count Valerius. Cf. Letter 200.
3 The second book of *De nuptiis et concupiscentia.*

my ability, I refuted all those fallacies. But now, after a more careful examination of the books themselves, I have discovered that the writer who made the extracts from them did not set everything down as it is read in these books. Consequently, it might appear to Julian, or anyone else of their sect, that I had lied, because it is certain that these four books could not be recognized as identical with the extracts which were taken from them and sent to the above-mentioned count. Therefore, whoever reads that second volume of mine, addressed, like the first, to Count Valerius, will know that in some points I have not answered Julian, but the man who selected the passages from his book, and did not set them down as he found them, but felt that he should make some changes, probably thinking in that way to make his own what was manifestly another's work. But now, as I believe the copy sent by your Holiness is more authentic, I see that I must answer the author himself, who boasts that he has disproved my one book by his four books, and who continues to scatter his poison everywhere against the faith. So, I have made a start on this work by the help of the Saviour of 'little and great,'[4] and I know that you have prayed for me that I may finish it, as well as for those to whom I believe and hope a work of this kind will be helpful. Wait, then, for my reply; the beginning of it will follow this letter. May you flourish in the Lord, and remember me, most saintly brother.

---

4 Apoc. 19.18.

208. Augustine gives greeting in the Lord to the lady Felicia,[1]
his daughter justly cherished and honored among
the members of Christ (423)

I do not doubt that your mind has been troubled because
of your own faith and the weakness or wickedness of others,
although the Apostle, filled with the marrow of charity, confesses and says: 'Who is weak and I am not weak? Who is
scandalized and I am not on fire?'[2] For this reason, being
distressed and anxious for your salvation which is in Christ,
I have thought it advisable to send your Holiness this letter
of consolation or exhortation, since you have become very
close to me in the body of our Lord Jesus Christ which is
His Church and the unity of His members; you are loved
as an honorable member in His body, and you live with us
by His Holy Spirit.

Hence, I advise you not to be too deeply disturbed by
these scandals, because their coming was foretold so that,
when they came, we might remember that they had been
foretold and might not be greatly troubled by them. The
Lord Himself thus foretold them in the Gospel: 'Woe to the
world because of scandals! For it must needs be that scandals
come, but nevertheless woe to that man by whom the scandal
cometh.'[3] And who are those men if not those of whom the
Apostle says: 'seeking the things that are their own, not the
things that are Jesus Christ's'?[4] Therefore, there are some who
occupy the pastoral chair in order to care for the flock of
Christ, but there are others who sit in it to gratify themselves
by temporal honors and worldly advantages. These are the

---

1 A Christian virgin who had been scandalized at the life of some
    prelate, probably Anthony of Fussala, also a former Donatist. Cf.
    Letter 209.
2 2 Cor. 11.29.
3 Matt. 18.7; Luke 17.1.
4 Phil. 2.21.

two kinds of pastors, some dying, some being born, who must needs continue in the Catholic Church itself until the end of the world and the judgment of the Lord. If there were such men in the times of the Apostles, whom the Apostle lamented as false brethren when he said: 'Perils from false brethren,'[5] yet whom he did not proudly dismiss but bore with them and tolerated them, how much more likely is it that there should be such men in our times, when the Lord speaks openly of this time of the world which is nearing its end, saying: 'Because iniquity hath abounded the charity of many shall grow cold!' But what follows ought to console and encourage us: 'He that shall persevere to the end,' He says, 'he shall be saved.'[6] Now, as there are good and bad shepherds, so also among the flocks there are good and bad. The good are signified by the name of sheep, while the bad are called goats. But they feed, mingled equally together, until 'the prince of pastors shall appear,'[7] who is called the 'one shepherd,'[8] who, as He promised, shall 'separate them as the shepherd separateth the sheep from the goats.'[9] He has commanded us to gather them together, but for Himself He has reserved the task of separating them, because He who cannot err is the one who ought to separate. As to those proud servants who have lightly dared to separate before the time which the Lord has reserved for Himself, they ought rather to be separated themselves from Catholic unity, for how can those who are tainted with schism have an untainted flock?

Our Shepherd urges us, then, to remain in unity; not to abandon the Lord's threshing floor because we are offended by the scandals of chaff; but rather, as good grain, to

---

5 2 Cor. 11.26.
6 Matt. 24.12,13; 10.22; Mark 13.13.
7 1 Peter 5.4.
8 John 10.16.
9 Matt. 25.32.

persevere to the end, to the time of winnowing, and by the strong weight of our charity to bear with the lightness of the straw.[10] In the Gospel He speaks to us of good shepherds,[11] and tells us not to place our hope even in them because of their good works, but to glorify the 'Father who is in heaven'[12] who made them such; and He speaks of bad shepherds whom He wished to signify by the name of Scribes and Pharisees, whose teaching is good, but whose conduct is bad.[13] Of the good shepherds He speaks thus: 'You are the light of the world. A city seated on a mountain cannot be hid; neither do men light a candle and put it under a bushel, but upon a candlestick, that it may shine to all that are in the house. So let your light shine before men that they may see your good works and glorify your Father who is in heaven.' But He warns the sheep against bad shepherds by saying: 'They have sitten on the chair of Moses, whatsoever they shall say to you do ye, but according to their works do ye not; for they say and do not.'[15] In hearing them, the sheep of Christ hear His voice even through bad teachers, and they do not forsake His unity, because the good which they hear them say is not theirs but His; therefore, the sheep feed in safety, because even under bad shepherds they are nourished in the Lord's pasture. But they do not do the deeds of the bad shepherds, because such works are not His but theirs. On the other hand, those who follow good shepherds not only hear the good things which they say, but also imitate the good deeds which they do. Of such was the Apostle who said: 'Be ye followers of me as I also am of Christ.'[16] That light was enkindled

10 Matt. 3.12.
11 John 10.11,14.
12 Matt. 5.16.
13 Matt. 23.2,3.
14 Matt. 5.14-16.
15 Matt. 23.2,3.
16 1 Cor. 11.1; 4.16.

from the eternal light, the Lord Jesus Christ Himself, and was put upon a candlestick because he gloried in Christ's cross. Thus he said: 'But God forbid that I should glory save in the cross of our Lord Jesus Christ.'[17] And as he did not seek the 'things that were his own, but the things that were Jesus Christ's,'[18] although he exhorted those whom he had begotten by the Gospel[19] to imitate him, he severely upbraided those who made a schism out of the names of Apostles, and rebuked those who said: 'I am of Paul.' 'Was Paul crucified for you?' he said, 'or were you baptized in the name of Paul?'[20]

Hence we understand that good shepherds seek not their own, but the things that are of Jesus Christ, and that, while good sheep imitate the deeds of good shepherds, they do not place their hope in those by whose ministry they have been gathered together, but rather in the Lord by whose Blood they have been redeemed. Thus, when they happen to meet bad shepherds, who preach Christ's doctrine but do their own bad works, they do what these say but they do not do what these do, and they do not forsake the pastures of unity because of the sons of iniquity. There are both good and bad in the Catholic Church, which has spread not in Africa alone, as the Donatist sect has done, but through all nations,[21] as it was promised, and which extends throughout the whole world, as the Apostle says, bringing forth fruit and increasing.[22] Those who are separated from it cannot be good as long as they hold views contrary to it; even if an apparently laudable conduct seems to point out some of them as good, the very division makes them bad, according to the Lord's

17 Gal. 6.14.
18 Phil. 2.21.
19 1 Cor. 4.15.
20 1 Cor. 1.12,13.
21 Gen. 22.18.
22 Col. 1.6.

words: 'He that is not with me is against me, and he that gathereth not with me scattereth.'[23]

Therefore, I urge you, lady deservedly cherished and daughter honored among the members of Christ, to hold faithfully to what the Lord has bestowed on you, and to love Him and His Church with your whole heart,[24] because He has not allowed you to lose the fruit of your virginity or to perish among the lost. For, if you were to go out of this world separated from the unity of Christ's Body, it would profit you nothing to have preserved the integrity of your own body. But God, 'who is rich in mercy,'[25] has dealt with you according to the words of the Gospel. When the guests invited to the supper of the householder made excuses, among other things he said: 'Go out into the highways and hedges, and as many as you shall find, compel them to come in.'[26] Consequently, although you owe a most sincere affection to His good servants through whose agency you were forced to come in, you should place your hope in Him who prepared the banquet, by whom you are also invited to an eternal and blessed life. By confiding your heart to Him, then, as well as your purpose, your holy virginity, your faith, your hope, and your charity,[27] you will not be troubled by the scandals which will abound until the end, but you will be saved by the unshaken strength of your devotion and by your perseverance to the end in the Lord and in His glorious unity. Let me know in your answer how you have felt about my anxiety for you, which I have tried, as best I could, to express in my letter. May the mercy and grace of God guard you.

---

23 Matt. 12.30.
24 Deut. 6.5; Matt. 22.37; Mark 12.30; Luke 10.27.
25 Eph. 2.4.
26 Luke 14.18,23; Matt. 22.3,9.
27 1 Cor. 13.13.

209. *Augustine gives greeting in the Lord to the holy Pope Celestine,*[1] *his saintly lord, revered with all affection (Beginning of 423)*

First of all, I offer you the congratulations due to your merits, since the Lord our God has set you on the chair of Peter, as we have heard, with no dissension among His people. In the next place, I make known to your Holiness the state of affairs among us that you may help us, not only by your prayers for us, but also by your counsel and support. I am writing this to your Blessedness in a state of great affliction, because through a lack of foresight and caution I have brought about a great disaster to certain members of Christ in our neighborhood, though I wanted only to be of service to them.

There is a small settlement named Fussala bordering on the district of Hippo; in ancient times there never was a bishop there, but, along with the adjoining land, it belonged to the diocese[2] of the church at Hippo. That region had few Catholics; the other congregations established there among a large population were subject to the wretched error of the Donatists, with the result that there was not a single Catholic in that particular town. By the mercy of God it came about that all those localities were joined to the unity of the Church; it would take too long to tell you what great labors and perils we endured, such that the priests whom we first appointed there to assemble the flock were robbed, beaten, maimed, blinded, killed. Yet their sufferings were not without effect or fruit, for through them unity was securely accomplished. Now, inasmuch as the aforementioned hamlet is forty miles distant from Hippo, and in governing its people

---

1 Cf. Letter 192.
2 Augustine uses the word *parochia,* which in his day was synonymous with diocese.

and gathering together the remnants, however few, of the wanderers of both sexes, no longer menacing but seeking flight, I saw that I was reaching out to a wider sphere of action than was advisable, and that I was unable to give it sufficient attention, such as the clear light of reason showed that I ought to give it, I arranged to have a bishop ordained and established there.

To accomplish this, I needed a man suitable and well-adapted to that place, and one who was versed in the Punic language. I had in mind a priest properly endowed, and, to provide for his consecration, I wrote to the holy old man[3] who was then primate of Numidia, asking him to make the long journey to us, and I received his acceptance. He had already arrived, and the minds of all were intent on the great ceremony, when, at the last minute, the priest who had seemed suitable to me disappointed me by showing every kind of opposition. As the outcome has proved, I certainly ought to have postponed so critical a matter instead of hurrying it on, but as I did not want the high-ranking and holy old man, after his trouble in coming all the way to us, to have to go back home without completing what he had come so far to do, I proposed a certain young man named Antoninus who was with me at the time, although no request was made for him. We had brought him up in the monastery from early childhood, but beyond the office of lector[4] he had no experience of any clerical ranks or duties. And those poor

---

3 This was probably Silvanus, one of the bishops listed in the address to Letter 176.

4 Second of the minor orders, which precede major orders and priesthood. He had charge of the sacred books. This elevation to the rank of bishop without passing through the intermediate orders was forbidden in the Eastern Church at the Council of Sardica in 343, but continued in the Latin Church until the 9th century. Another irregularity in the consecration is the fact that it was performed by the primate alone, not by three bishops, as prescribed by the Council of Nicaea.

people, not knowing what lay ahead, submitted with entire trust to my nomination of him. To cut a long story short, the deed was done; he began to be their bishop.

What am I to do? I do not want to accuse to your Reverence one whom I fostered and cherished; I do not want to forsake those over whose rescue I travailed with fear and sorrow; how I am to do both I cannot discover. The case has reached such scandalous proportions that those who yielded to me in having him undertake the episcopacy, in the belief that it was to their own interest, have come to me and laid charges against him. Among these charges, the most serious crime, that of revolting immorality, made against him not by those whose bishop he was but by some others, could not be proved at all, and he seemed to be cleared of the most invidious accusations made against him. As a result, he became such an object of pity to us and to others that, whatever allegations were made by the townspeople and the inhabitants of that district, of intolerable tyranny, extortion, and various kinds of oppression and abuse, did not seem to us reason for thinking that he should be deprived of his bishopric because of one of them or of all of them put together, but that he should make restitution for what, upon proof, he had wrongfully taken.

In the end we moderated our sentence so as to save his bishopric, yet not leave his offenses altogether unpunished, since they were of a kind that ought not to be repeated by him hereafter nor offered for the imitation of others. Therefore, we preserved his rank intact to leave room for the young man's amendment, but we diminished his authority as a punishment, that is, we ruled that he should no longer be over those whom he had treated so badly that their justified resentment could not tolerate his being over them at all, and there was danger both for themselves and for him, that their unrestrained anger might break forth into some act of violence. The state of their mind was clearly evident even at the time when the bishops were treating with them about him, although by now the honorable Celer[5]— of whose overbearing official acts against him the bishop had complained—no longer exercises any power in Africa or anywhere else.

But why dwell on this any further? I beg you to second our efforts, most saintly lord and holy Pope, worthy of veneration with all due affection, for your revered piety, and give orders that all the documents addressed to you be read to you. See how he behaved as bishop; how he submitted to our verdict that he be deprived of communion[6] until he had made complete restitution to the people of Fussala; how he afterward, regardless of the verdict, set aside a sum equal to the value of the objects taken, in order that he might be restored to communion; with what wily arguments he induced our holy and venerable primate, a man of great influence, to believe all his story and to recommend him to the venerable Pope Boniface[7] as one entirely blameless. What need is there for me to recall all the rest of the details, when the venerable old man aforesaid will have reported everything to your Holiness?

From those detailed reports, however, in which our verdict on him is comprised, I ought rather to fear that we may seem to have been less severe in our judgment on him than was proper, if I did not know that you are so inclined to mercy as to believe it your duty to spare not only the man

---

5 He became proconsul of Africa in 429. Letters 56 and 57 portray him as a Donatist favorable to Catholic claims; Letter 139 mentions him as opening Donatist churches on his estate. At this time he seems to have been an influential landowner who had held some local office prior to the time of this letter.

6 That is, he was subject to a temporary and partial form of excommunication.

7 Predecessor of Celestine. His death at the end of 422 helps to date this letter.

himself, but us also for sparing him. But what we did through kindness or remissness he is trying to turn into a legal loophole and to make use of it. His cry is: 'Either I ought to sit upon my own episcopal throne or I ought not to be a bishop,' as if he were now sitting on any throne but his own. It was for that reason that those districts in which he was first named bishop were set apart and entrusted to him, that he might not be said to have been transferred illegally to another's see, contrary to the decrees of the Fathers.[8] But, should anyone be such a stickler for either severity or leniency as to inflict no punishment of any kind on men who do not seem to have deserved deprivation of their sees, or, on the other hand, to deprive those who seem to deserve some punishment of the honor of episcopacy?

There are existing precedents in the judgments of the apostolic see itself or its confirmation of the verdicts of others, where men guilty of certain offenses were neither deprived of their episcopal rank nor left altogether unpunished. Not to cite examples too far removed from our times, I will recall some recent ones. Let Priscus,[9] a bishop of the province of Caesarea, utter his protest: 'Either the position of primate ought to be open to me as to others or I ought not to retain my bishopric.' Listen to the protest of Victor,[10] another bishop of the same province, who was left under the same penalty as Priscus was, and was not allowed to receive Communion anywhere, from any bishop, except in his own diocese; listen to him, I say, when he protests: 'I ought either to communicate anywhere or else I ought not even to communicate in my own district.' Hear the protest of Laurentius,[11] a third

---

8 The Council of Nicaea (Canon 15) and later councils forbade this.
9 Bishop of Quiza in 411. Caesarea was part of Mauretania. Augustine's trip there in 418 may have been connected with one or more of these cases. Cf. Letter 190.
10 His see is not known.
11 Bishop of Icosium (modern Algiers).

bishop of the same province, a protest made, in fact, in words identical with those of Antoninus: 'I ought either to sit on the throne to which I was ordained or I ought not to be a bishop.' But who would find fault with those expressions except one who does not observe that none of these offenses should have been left unpunished, yet not all of them deserved the same kind of penalty?

In his letter about Antoninus to his bishop, the blessed Pope Boniface, speaking with the care and precaution of a pastor, used these words: 'If he has faithfully described the sequence of events to me.' So now learn the sequence of events which Antoninus glossed over in his report, as well as the events that happened later, after the letter of that man of blessed memory was read in Africa; come to the assistance of men imploring your help in the mercy of Christ much more earnestly than does he from whose disturbing behavior they long to be delivered. Indeed, threats are being made against them, either by Antoninus himself or by frequent rumors, of legal verdicts and public officials and military attacks that are, so to speak, to enforce the decrees of the apostolic see,[12] and, as a consequence, our poor people, though Catholic Christians, dread worse treatment from a Catholic bishop than they feared under the laws of Catholic emperors when they were heretics. I beg you by the Blood of Christ not to let that happen; I beg it by the memory of the Apostle Peter who warned those in charge of Christian peoples not to lord it over their brethren. I commend to the kindly charity of your Holiness both the Catholic people of Fussala, my children in Christ, and Antoninus, my son in Christ, because I love

---

12 The African bishops sent a request to Celestine that he would not receive appeals from their decisions, nor intervene in excommunications imposed by them, nor send agents to carry out enactments of the Holy See in Africa. Celestine did not attempt to do any of these things, and Antoninus does not seem to have been restored to his see, which was reattached to Hippo until his death, when another bishop was appointed with the appropriate name of Melior.

them both. And I do not blame the people of Fussala for pouring into your ears their justifiable complaint of me that I imposed on them a man of whom I had no experience, or at least one lacking the stability of years, who caused them so much trouble. On the other hand, I do not wish any harm to come to him, because my sincere affection for him is the measure of my opposition to his revolting greed. May your compassion be extended to both: to them, that they may suffer no harm; to him, that he may do none; to them, that they may not hate the Catholic Church if the Catholic bishops and especially the apostolic see itself fail to protect them from a Catholic bishop; to him, that he may not involve himself in such sinfulness as to drive away from Christ those whom he is trying to make his own against their will.

For myself, I must avow to your Blessedness that such fear and grief torture me in that twofold peril that I am thinking of retiring from the administration of my episcopal office and giving myself up to lamentations befitting my fault, if I see the Church of God ravaged by one whose appointment as bishop I imprudently supported, and even—which God forbid!—being destroyed along with the destruction of the ravager. Recalling what the Apostle said: 'If we would judge ourselves we would not be judged'[13] by the Lord, I will judge myself that He 'who shall judge the living and the dead' may spare me. But if you revive the members of Christ who are in that district from their deadly fear and sadness, and console my old age by this merciful justice, He who has established you in that see and who brings us succor through you in this trial will repay you good things for your good deeds, both in the present life and in the life to come.

---

13 1 Cor. 11.31.

210. Augustine and the brethren who are with me send
greeting in the Lord to the beloved and holy
Mother Felicitas,[1] to Brother Rusticus,[2] and to
the Sisters who are with you (c. 423)

'The Lord is good,'[3] and His mercy which extends everywhere comforts us with your love in Him. He shows us most
convincingly how much He loves those who believe and hope in
Him and who love both Him and each other in Him, and
how great a reward He has in store for them in the future
life, by threatening eternal fire in company with the Devil to
the unbelieving, the unhoping, those who are set in an evil
will and who persist in it to the end. In this world, however,
He lavishes good gifts on them 'who maketh his sun to rise
upon the good and bad, and raineth upon the just and the unjust.'[4] This is a short saying intended to reveal many thoughts
to us, for who can count the many benefits and undeserved
gifts which the wicked receive in this life from Him whom they
despise? Among them is this great favor that, by the instances
of alternating trials which, like a good physician, He mingles
with the sweetness of this world, He warns them, if they will
only heed, 'to flee from the wrath to come' and 'whilst they
are in the way,' that is, in this life, 'to be at agreement' with
the word of God which they have made their 'adversary'[5]
by their evil life. What is given to men by the Lord God
that is not a mercy, when even tribulation sent by Him is a
blessing? Prosperity is God's gift when He consoles us; adver-

---

1 Mother Superior of a convent in Hippo founded by Augustine. She
  had succeeded Augustine's own sister in that office, but the members
  of the community made an unseemly disturbance in trying to oust her.
  Augustine wrote this letter to calm the Superior, and Letter 211 to
  recall the Sisters to their duty.
2 Probably the chaplain or director mentioned in Letter 211.
3 Lam. 3.25.
4 Matt. 5.45.
5 Matt. 3.7; 5.25; Luke 3.7.

sity is His gift when He warns us. And if, as I said, He bestows these favors even on the wicked, what is he preparing for those who wait for Him?[6] Be glad that you who are gathered together by His grace are among that number, 'supporting one another in charity, careful to keep the unity of the Spirit in the bond of peace.'[7] For there will be no lack of occasions for you to bear with one another until the Lord has borne you hence when 'death is swallowed up in victory, that God may be all in all.'[8]

Dissension, however, is never to be loved. Sometimes, it is true, it arises from love or is a test of love. It is not easy to find anyone who likes to be reproved. And where is that wise man of whom it is said: 'Rebuke a wise man and he will love thee'?[9] Surely, then, we ought not to refrain from reproving and correcting our brother that he may not heedlessly risk death. It happens regularly and it happens often that a man is cast down for a short time while he is being reproved, that he resists and fights back, but afterwards he reflects in solitude where there is no one but God and himself, and where he does not fear the displeasure of men by being corrected, but does fear the displeasure of God by refusing correction; thereafter, he does not repeat the act which was justly censured, but now loves the brother, whom he sees as the enemy of his sin, as much as he hates the sin itself. On the other hand, if he is one of those of whom it is said: 'Rebuke the fool and he will go on to hate thee,'[10] this strife is not born of love, yet it tries and tests the love of the reprover because it does not return hatred for hatred, while the love which prompts him to reprove remains unmoved even when

---

6 Cf. Ps. 26.14.
7 Eph. 4.2,3.
8 1 Cor. 15.54,28.
9 Prov. 9.8.
10 Prov. 9.8. (Septuagint).

he who is reproved shows his hatred. However, if the one who
reproves tries to return evil for evil to the brother who resents
his reproof, he was not fit to reprove, but was evidently fit to
be reproved himself. Put these rules into practice so that
resentment may either not arise among you or, once aroused,
may be immediately snuffed out by speedy peace. Try harder
to agree among yourselves than to find fault, for, as vinegar
corrodes a vessel if it is left in it too long, so anger corrodes
the heart if it goes over to the next day. Do these things,
then—'and the God of peace shall be with you'[11]—and pray
for me at the same time that I may be ready to carry out the
good advice I give.

211. Letter of Aurelius Augustine to the consecrated virgins[1] (c. 423)

As severity is ready to punish the sins which it discovers,
so charity does not wish to discover anything to punish. That
was the reason which kept me from coming to you when
you were expecting my presence, which would not have been
a joy added to your peace, but an increase of your strife.
For how could I have overlooked your quarrel or left it
unpunished if it had burst out in my presence as violently as
it did in my absence; when it was not visible to my eyes, yet

---

11 Phil. 4.9.

---

1 There is no title of address in the text. One manuscript furnishes this
one. The virgins addressed are probably those of Letter 210. This
letter is commonly regarded as the source of the Augustinian Rule,
the first actual monastic legislation in Western Europe. It was early
adapted to communities of men, canons regular, knights of the
military orders, preaching friars, hospital brothers and sisters of
non-contemplative religious Orders. It is far from complete and needs
to be supplemented from other ascetical works of Augustine, such as
De opere monachorum and *De sancta virginitate*.

assailed my ears with your clamor? Perhaps your rebellion might have been even worse in my presence which I was obliged to withhold from you, since you were demanding something that was not good for you, and that would have formed a most dangerous precedent against sound discipline; thus, I should not have found you such as I wished and you would have found me such as you did not wish.

When the Apostle writes to the Corinthians, he says: 'I call God to witness upon my soul that to spare you I came not any more to Corinth; not because we exercise dominion over your faith but we are helpers of your joy.'[2] I also spared myself lest 'I have sorrow upon sorrow,'[3] and rather than show my face among you I chose to pour out my heart to God for you and to plead the cause of your great peril, not in words before you, but in tears before God, that He may not turn to sorrow the joy I am wont to feel on your account. Even in the midst of the great scandals which abound everywhere in this world I oftentimes comfort myself with the thought of your numerous community, your chaste love, your holy conversation, and the grace of God which has been given more generously to you that you might not only despise carnal marriage, but might also choose the fellowship of dwelling together in a house in unity,[4] that you may have one soul and one heart[5] toward God.

When I think upon these good things among you, these gifts of God, my heart is accustomed to find some kind of rest amid the many storms arising from other evils by which it is shaken. 'You did run well; who hath bewitched you? This persuasion is not from God who hath called you. A little leaven'[6]—I hate to repeat the rest; this, rather, I desire and

---

2 2 Cor. 1.23.
3 2 Cor. 2.3; Phil. 2.27.
4 Ps. 132.1.
5 Acts 4.32.
6 Gal. 5.7-9; 3.1; 1 Cor. 5.6.

pray for and urge that the same leaven may be changed for the better that the whole lump may not be changed for the worse, as had almost happened. If, then, you have put forth new growth of sound wisdom, 'Pray that ye enter not into temptation,'[7] that you enter not again into 'contentions, envying, animosities, dissensions, detractions, seditions, whisperings.'[8] For we have not planted and watered[9] the Lord's garden in you only to reap these thorns[10] from you. But if your weakness still stirs up a storm, pray that you may be delivered from temptation.[11] Those among you who trouble you, whoever they may be, will incur judgment unless they amend their lives.

Think what a misfortune it is that in the midst of our rejoicing over those born of God in unity[12] we should have to bewail internal schism in the monastery. Stand firm in your good purpose and you will not want to change your Superior, who has persevered in that monastery for so many years, during which you have increased in numbers and in age, and who has borne you as a mother—not in her womb, but in her heart. All of you at your entrance found her there, either serving under the holy Superior, my sister, or winning approval as actual Superior herself when she received you. Under her you have been trained, under her you have received the veil, under her your numbers have multiplied, yet you make all this disturbance to force us to change her for you—when you ought to grieve if we wanted to change her for you. She is the one you have known, she is the one to whom you came, she is the one you have had for so many

---

7 Matt. 7.41; Mark 14.38; Luke 22.46.
8 2 Cor. 12.20.
9 1 Cor. 3.6-8.
10 Jer. 12.13.
11 Ps. 17.30.
12 An evident reference to the recent wholesale conversion of Donatists; in fact, the Maurist editors conjecture the reading *Donatistas* for *Deo natis* as found in the manuscript.

years of your increase. You have not received any new
Superior except your spiritual director, and if it is because
of him that you are seeking a change, through envy for him
that you have thus rebelled against your Mother, why have
you not rather demanded that he should be changed for you?
If you shrink from doing this, for I know what respect and
affection you have for him in Christ, why should you not
shrink even more from attacking her? For the beginnings of
your director's term of authority have been thrown into such
disorder that he should be the one to desert you sooner than
be subject to the invidious criticism of having it said that you
would not have asked for another Superior if you had not
begun to have him for spiritual director. May God, then,
calm and pacify your minds; may the work of the Devil make
no headway among you, but may 'the peace of Christ rule in
you hearts.'[13] Do not rush to destruction in your acute regret,
either because you are vexed at not having the accomplishment of what you want, or because you are ashamed of
wanting what you ought not; rather, by repenting renew your
courage, and let it not be the repentance of the traitor Judas,[14]
but the tears of the shepherd Peter.[15]

These are the rules which we prescribe for the observance
of those of you who have been admitted to the monastery. In
the first place, as you are gathered into one community, see
that you dwell together in unity in the house and that you
have 'one heart and one soul' toward God; that you do not
call anything your own, but that you have all things in
common. Let your Superior distribute food and clothing to
each one of you, not equally to all, because you are not all
of the same bodily strength, but to each one according to her
need. It is thus that you read in the Acts of the Apostles that

13 Cf. Col. 3.15.
14 Matt. 27.3-5.
15 Matt. 26.75; Mark 14.72; Luke 22.62.

'all things were common unto them, and distribution was made to everyone according as he had need.'[16] Let those who had something in the world before they entered the monastery be entirely willing for it to become common property, but let those who had nothing not seek in the monastery for what they could not have had outside. However, if they are sickly, let them receive what is needful, even if their poverty could not procure them those necessities when they were outside, but they are not to think themselves fortunate merely because they now have food and raiment such as they could not have provided outside.

Let them not go about with their heads in the air because they associate with those whom they would not have dared to approach outside, but let them lift up their hearts,[17] not seeking earthly goods; otherwise, monasteries might begin to be useful to the rich but not to the poor, if in them the rich are humbled but the poor puffed up. Again, those who seemed to be something in the world should not look down with scorn on their Sisters who have come to that holy community from poor circumstances, they should strive to take greater pride in the company of their poor Sisters than in the important position of their wealthy parents. Let them not have a high opinion of themselves if they have made some contribution from their resources to the common life, lest they become more proud of their wealth because they are sharing it with the monastery than they would be if they were enjoying it in the world. Every other kind of wrong-doing operates to further evil deeds, but pride hides itself even in good deeds to spoil them. What good does it do to distribute one's goods by giving them to the poor and to become poor oneself, if the wretched soul becomes prouder by despising wealth than it had been by possessing it? Live then, all of

16 Acts 4.32,35.
17 Preface of the Mass.

you, in unity and harmony; honor God in each other, for you have become His temples.[18]

Be instant in prayer[19] at the hours and times appointed. Let no one do anything in the oratory but that for which it was made and from which it takes its name, so that if some of the Sisters have time and wish to pray even outside the appointed hours, those who wish to do something else there may not be a hindrance to them. When you pray to God in psalms and hymns, meditate in your heart on what you utter with your voice, and do not sing anything that is not noted to be sung; what is not noted to be sung is not to be sung.

Subdue your flesh by fasting and abstinence from food and drink as far as your health allows. When a Sister is not able to fast, she should not for that reason take any food outside the time of meals, unless she is sick. From the time when you come to the table until you rise from it, listen without noise or argument to what is read according to custom; let it not be only your mouth that takes food, but let your ears also drink in the word of God.

If those who are weak in health as a result of their former mode of living are treated differently in the matter of food, this ought not to be irksome or to seem unfair to others whom another kind of life has made more robust. They are not to think the former more fortunate because they have food which the latter do not enjoy, but they are rather to congratulate themselves on being in good health as the others are not. And if those who have come to the monastery from a more luxurious manner of life are given something in the way of food, clothing, bedding and covering, which is not given to the others who are stronger and therefore more fortunate, these latter to whom it is not given should reflect how great a step the former have taken in coming down from

18 1 Cor. 3.16; 2 Cor. 6.16.
19 Col. 4.2.

their worldly life to this one, although they have not been able to attain to the asceticism of those who are stronger in body. And they should not be troubled at seeing these others receive more than they do, not as a mark of honor but as a form of concession; otherwise there might arise in the monastery that hateful reversal whereby, as far as it can be done, the rich become toilers and the poor enjoy luxury. Certainly, in the case of the sick, as they must of necessity take less food in order not to grow worse, so, after the illness they must be treated in a manner to speed their recovery, even if they came from the lowest state of poverty in the world, just as if their recent illness were to confer on them what the rich have because of their former state. But when they have recovered their former strength, let them return to their own more fortunate mode of life, which is more fitting for the handmaids of God in proportion as it has fewer wants, and let them not want to retain, when they are well, the dispensations which necessity required when they were ill. Let those who have been more courageous in bearing austerity esteem themselves the richer, for it is better to need less than to have more.

Let your garb be inconspicuous; do not aim at winning favor by your garments, but by your conduct. Do not wear such thin head-covering that your hairnets show underneath. Do not let any part of your hair be uncovered[20] or go out of doors with it either flying carelessly or arranged fastidiously. When you go abroad, walk together; when you have arrived at the place to which you were going, stop together. In walking, in standing, in your costume, in all your movements, let there be nothing that could rouse passion in anyone, but let all accord with your sacred character. If your eyes glance at anyone, let them rest upon no one, for you are not

---

20 According to St. Jerome (*Ep.* 147.5) it was the custom in the East for consecrated virgins to cut their hair, but in the West this custom had not yet been adopted.

forbidden to look at men when you go out, but to desire them or to wish to be desired by them. It is not by touch alone, but also by feeling and sight, that a woman desires and is desired. Do not claim to have chaste minds if you have unchaste eyes, because the unchaste eye is the messenger of the unchaste heart; and when unchaste hearts reveal themselves to each other by a mutual glance, even though the tongue is silent, and when they take pleasure in each other's passion according to the lust of the flesh, chastity flees from the character though the body remain untouched by impure violation. The virgin who fastens her glance upon a man and loves to have his fastened on her must not think she is unseen by others. When she does so she is indeed seen, and by those of whom she is not thinking. But suppose she does escape notice and is observed by no human being, what will she do about that Observer from above from whose notice nothing can escape?[21] Or are we to think that He does not see because His seeing is accomplished with equal patience and wisdom? Therefore, let the holy woman fear to displease Him so as to avoid the desire of wrongfully pleasing a man; let her reflect that He sees everything, and thus she will avoid the desire of gazing sinfully upon a man. In this matter fear of Him is recommended to us by the passage: 'One that fixeth the eye is an abomination to the Lord.'[22] So, then, when you are together in church or in any place where men are present, keep mutual guard over your chastity, for God who dwells in you[23] guards you in that way even from yourselves.

If you notice in any of your number this roving glance of which I speak, warn her at once that beginnings may go no further, but may be remedied at once. But if, after the

---

21 Prov. 24.12.
22 Prov. 27.20 (Septuagint).
23 1 Cor. 3.16; 2 Cor. 6.16.

warning, you see her doing the same thing again on any other day, let whoever has discovered her report her as one wounded and in need of treatment; but let her first be pointed out to a second or a third that she may be convicted out of the mouth of two or three witnesses[24] and may be disciplined with proper severity. Do not consider yourselves mean when you report thus, for, indeed, you are not without guilt if through your silence you allow your Sisters to perish when you are able to correct them by reporting them. If your Sister through fear of the knife were trying to hide a sore which she had on her body, would not silence on your part be cruelty and notification kindness? How much greater, then, is your obligation to point out one in whose heart a deadly infection may lurk! But before she is pointed out to the others through whom she is to be convicted if she denies her guilt, she ought to be named to the Superior, so that by a secret correction she may escape being made known to others. If, however, she denies her guilt, her lie is to be confronted with others, so that in the presence of all she may be not merely charged by one, but convicted by two or three witnesses. When convicted, she is to be subjected to some corrective discipline at the discretion of the Superior or the spiritual director. If she refuses to submit and does not leave of her own accord, she is to be expelled from your community. This is not an act of cruelty, but of kindness—to prevent her from destroying many companions by her deadly contagion. What I have said about custody of the eyes is to be observed, with love for the person and hatred for the sin, in discovering, preventing, reporting, convicting and punishing other offenses. But if any Sister is so far gone in sin that she is secretly receiving letters or keepsakes of any kind from a man, she is to be spared and prayed for if she confesses it voluntarily, but if she is caught and her guilt is proved, she is to receive a more

---

24 Deut. 19.15; Matt. 18.16; 2 Cor. 13.1.

serious punishment at the discretion of the Superior or the
spiritual director or even the bishop.

Have your clothing kept under the care of one or two or as
many as may be needed to shake out the garments in order
to preserve them from moths; and just as you receive food
from one storeroom so you must be clothed from one wardrobe. Whenever something is offered you to wear in accord
with the season, do not be concerned, if that is possible,
whether each one of you receives back what she had given
up, or something else which another had worn, so long as no
one is refused what she needs. If strife and murmurings arise
among you from this source, when one complains that she
has received something worse than she had previously worn,
and thinks she is slighted in being dressed as another of her
Sisters was, let this prove how far you are from that inward
'holy attire'[25] of the heart when you quarrel about the attire
of the body. However, if your weakness is indulged so far
that you receive back the dress which you had put off, let
what you take off still be kept in one place under community
care. Thus, no one will work at anything for her own use,
whether it be clothing or bedding or underclothing or covering
or head-dress, but let all your work be done for the common
good, with greater zeal and more constant eagerness than if
you were making things for your own use. For the charity of
which it is written that 'she seeketh not her own'[26] is understood in the sense of preferring the general good to personal
good. And so, the more care you take to promote the general
good rather than your own, the more progress in perfection
you will know that you have made, so that in all things of
which passing necessity makes use the 'charity which en-
dureth'[27] may superabound. It follows, then, that whatever

25 Titus 2.3.
26 1 Cor. 13.5.
27 Eph. 3.19; 1 Cor. 13.8.

any man or woman bestows upon the inmates of the monastery, either to daughters or to persons bound to them by any
other tie of kinship, whether it be clothing or anything else
rated among necessities, it is not to be received in secret,
but is to be left to the disposal of the Superior to put it in
the common stock or to give it to anyone who needs it. If
anyone conceals what has been given her, let her be judged
guilty of theft.

Let your clothes be washed, either by yourselves or by
laundresses, at the discretion of the Superior, so that excessive
craving for clean clothing may not sully your soul with inward
filth. The washing of the body, also, and the use of baths is
not to be too frequent, but may be allowed at the usual
interval of time, that is, once a month. In the case of illness,
however, where there is urgent need of bathing the body, let
it not be postponed too long, but let it be done without
objection for medical reasons. If the patient herself objects,
she must do what health requires to be done at the bidding
of the Superior. If she wishes it and it is not good for her,
there should be no yielding to her caprice, for there are times
when something agreeable is believed to be beneficial whereas
it is hurtful. Finally, if a handmaid of God has a hidden pain
in her body and tells what ails her, she should be believed
without reserve, but when it is not certain whether something
pleasant would be good for her, a doctor should be consulted.
If they go to the baths or wherever they have to go, let there
be not less than three. The one who is under the necessity of
going somewhere shall not go with the companions of her
choice, but with those whom the Superior shall ordain. The
care of the sick, whether they are convalescent or suffering
from some weakness not accompanied by fever, should be
entrusted to someone who may procure from the storeroom
what she sees needful for each. Moreover, those who have

charge of the storeroom or of the wardrobe or of the library[28] should serve their Sisters without grumbling. Books are to be applied for at a stated hour each day; those who apply outside that time are not to receive them. But in the case of clothing and shoes, when required for someone in need, those who have charge of them should not delay to give what is asked.

You should either have no quarrels or put an end to them as speedily as possible, lest anger grow into hatred, turn a mote into a beam,[29] and make the soul a murderer. The saying of Scripture, 'Whoever hateth his brother is a murderer,'[30] does not apply to men alone; the female sex, too, has received this teaching as well as the male sex, which God created first. Whoever has injured another, either by reviling her or taunting her or accusing her of wrong-doing, should remember to make amends as quickly as possible, so as to heal the hurt she has caused, and the injured Sister must forgive without reserve. If the injury has been mutual, they will be obliged to make mutual amends because of your prayers, which must be more holy in proportion to their frequency. The Sister who is often tempted to anger but quickly begs pardon of the one she knows she has injured is better than the one who is slower to anger, but less easily moved to ask pardon. She who refuses to forgive her Sister should not hope to feel the effect of prayer, but the one who is never willing to ask pardon or who does not ask it sincerely has no place in the monastery even if she is not actually expelled. Refrain, therefore, from harsh words; if any slip from your mouth, do not be ashamed to utter healing words from the same mouth that caused the wounds. However,

---

28 It was not unusual for convents, as well as monasteries and churches, to have a supply of books.
29 Matt. 7.3-5; Luke 6.41-42.
30 1 John 3.15.

when the duty of discipline obliges you to speak sharply in order to restrain the younger members, you have no obligation to ask their pardon even if you feel that you have gone too far in your words; otherwise, by a too great regard for humility toward those who ought to be subject to you, you might undermine the authority needed to control them. You should, however, ask pardon of the Lord of all who knows how great is your kindness and love even for those whom you rebuke, perhaps with undue severity. The love between you, however, ought not to be earthly but spiritual, for the things which shameless women do even to other women in low jokes and games are to be avoided not only by widows and chaste handmaids of Christ, living under a holy rule of life, but also entirely by married women and maidens destined for marriage.

Let your Superior be obeyed as a mother, with due respect, lest God be offended in her person; and even more readily should you obey the priest who has charge of you all. It will be the particular responsibility of the Superior to see to the observance of all these regulations; and if anything is not observed she is not to neglect or overlook the lapse, but to take pains to amend and correct it. In matters that exceed her authority she is to refer to the priest who watches over you. Let her esteem herself happy not in having power to rule, but in having charity to serve.[31] Let her be set over you in honor before men; before God let her be beneath your feet. Toward all let her show herself an example of good works.[32] Let her rebuke the unquiet, comfort the feeble-minded, support the weak, be patient toward all;[33] let her maintain her authority with good will, but impose it with fear. And, however necessary both may be, let her seek to be loved by

31 Dan. 11.4; Gal. 5.13.
32 Titus 2.7.
33 1 Thess. 5.14.

you rather than feared, always bearing in mind that she will have to give an account of you to God. Thus, by your ready obedience you will show consideration not only for yourselves but also for her, because, as between you, the one who is in the higher position runs the greater risk.

May the Lord grant you to observe all these regulations with love, as souls whose affections are set on spiritual beauty, whose good conduct is fragrant with the good odor of Christ,[34] not as bondswomen under the law, but as free women established under grace.[35] Now, in order that you may look at yourselves in this book as in a mirror, and that you may not omit anything through forgetfulness, let it be read to you once a week, and when you find yourselves practising what is written, give thanks to the Lord, the giver of all good gifts; but, when any one of you sees that she falls short in any point, let her feel sorrow for the past and take precautions for the future, praying that her trespass may be forgiven and that she may not be led into temptation.[36]

212. Augustine gives greeting in the Lord to Quintilian,[1] his saintly lord, deservedly revered brother, and fellow bishop (c. 425)

I commend to your Reverence in Christ the honorable servants of God, chosen members of Christ, Galla, a widow living under a religious rule, and her daughter, Simpliciola, a consecrated virgin, inferior to her mother in age but superior

---

34 2 Cor. 2.15.
35 Rom. 6.14,15.
36 Matt. 6.12,13; Luke 11.4.

1 Bishop of the diocese, probably in Africa, but not otherwise identified, to which the two pilgrims belonged.

to her in holiness, whom I have nourished with the word of
God as best I could. By this letter, as by my own hand, I
entrust them to you to be consoled and helped in every way,
according as their interest or necessity requires. I have no
doubt that your Holiness would do this without my recom-
mendation. If we are bound, for the sake of the heavenly
Jerusalem, of which we are all citizens and in which they
aspire to a place of higher sanctity, to show them the love not
only of fellow citizens but also of brothers, how much more
are you bound to it who share with them an earthly fatherland
in which these ladies show their contempt of worldly nobility
for the love of Christ! I ask you to be so kind as to receive
through them the courtesy of my greeting with the same
charity with which I send it. They are carrying with them
some relics of the most blessed and glorious martyr Stephen,
and your Holiness knows how fitting it is for you to honor
them as we have done.[2]

213. Here begins the record of what the blessed bishop Augustine did when he chose the priest Eraclius as his successor[1] (Excerpt from church records, September 26, 426)

On the 26th day of September, in the 12th consulship of
the most glorious Theodosius and the 2nd of Valentinian
Augustus, after Bishop Augustine had seated himself on his
throne in the Basilica of Peace, attended by his brother bishops,

---

2 In *City of God* 22.8 St. Augustine lists a number of miracles performed
at the shrine of St. Stephen at Hippo Regius, which had been con-
structed two years before the book was written. Other districts in
Africa, as Calama and Utica, had similar shrines and claimed similar
miracles.

---

1 Title supplied from an alternative manuscript reading.

Religianus and Martinianus, in the presence of Saturninus, Leporius, Barnabas, Fortunatianus, Rusticus, Lazarus, and Eraclius, his priests, as well as of the accompanying clerics and a large crowd of people, Bishop Augustine spoke thus: 'Yesterday I made a promise to your Charity because I wished you to be here in large numbers; I see that you are here in large numbers, so we must now forego all delay and proceed to business, for if I were to speak of anything else you would not listen because your attention is on the proceedings. In this life we are all mortal men and the last day of this life is always uncertain for every man. In infancy our hopes are fixed on childhood, in childhood we look to adolescence, in adolescence we look forward to manhood, in manhood to middle age, and in middle age to old age. Whether this will be our lot we do not know, but it is what we hope for. Old age, however, has no other period to expect. How long old age itself will last is hidden from man, but it is certain that there is no other age to follow old age. God willed that I should come to this city in the vigor of manhood, but I have now passed through middle age and have reached old age. I know that after the decease of bishops churches are regularly thrown into confusion by ambitious or restless men, a fact which I have often observed and grieved over, and I consider it my duty, as far as it depends on me, to take measures that it may not happen to this city. As your Charity knows, I went recently to the church at Milevis; the brothers and especially the servants of God who are there begged me to come because there were fears of some disturbance there after the death of my brother and fellow bishop, Severus[2] of blessed memory. I went and God helped us in His mercy, according to His will; they received the bishop[3] whom their

---

2 One of Augustine's dearest friends; cf. Letters 31, 38, 62, 63, 84, and 110.
3 That is, they ratified this choice in the election at which Augustine presided.

late bishop had designated before his death. When this had
been made known to them, they readily bowed to the will
of their late bishop. There was, however, something missing
which caused regret to some; namely, that brother Severus
had thought it would suffice to name his successor to the
clergy, and for that reason had not mentioned it to the people.
There was, in consequence, some regret on the part of several.
But why say more? It pleased God to banish sadness, joy
returned, the bishop whom their late bishop had designated
was ordained. Therefore, that no one may complain of me,
I make known to all of you my choice which I believe is the
choice of God: I want the priest Eraclius for my successor.'
The people raised a shout: 'Thanks be to God! Praise to
Christ!'—this was said twenty-three times; 'Hear us, O
Christ! Long life to Augustine!'—this was said sixteen times;
'You are our father, you our bishop!'—this was said eight
times.

When silence was restored, Bishop Augustine said: 'I have
no need to speak in his praise; I am silent about his wisdom,
I yield to his modesty; it is enough that you know him, and
I say that I wish what I know is your wish; if I had not
known it before, I should have proof of it today. Therefore,
I wish this, I ask it of the Lord our God with prayers that
are ardent even in the chill of age, and I exhort, advise, and
entreat that you join with me in praying that, while the
minds of all are transformed and welded together in the peace
of Christ, God may confirm what He has wrought in us.[4]
May He who sent this man to me keep him, may He keep
him safe, may He keep him blameless, so that as he is my
joy in life he may take my place at my death. What we are
saying is being taken down, as you see, by the stenographers

---

4 Ps. 67.29. These words form part of the Offertory of the Mass for
  Pentecost and are used in the sacrament of confirmation and in the
  consecration of churches and altars.

of the Church; what you say is being taken down. Neither my words nor your acclaim fall useless to the ground. To speak more openly, we are now making Church history, for I wish this act to be ratified, as far as it rests with men.' A shout was raised by the people: 'Thanks be to God! Praise to Christ!'—said thirty-six times; 'Hear us, O Christ! Long life to Augustine!'—said thirteen times; 'You are our father, you our bishop!'—said eight times; 'It is right and just!'[5]—said twenty times; 'He is well-deserving, he is truly worthy!'—said five times; 'It is right and just!'—said six times.

When silence was restored, Bishop Augustine said: 'Therefore, as I was saying, I wish the ratification of my choice and your choice, as far as it rests with men, to be recorded in the annals of the Church; but as to what belongs to the hidden will of almighty God, let us pray, as I said, that He may confirm what He works in us.' A shout was raised by the people: 'We give thanks for your decision!'—said sixteen times; 'May it be so, may it be so!'—said twelve times; 'You are our father, Bishop Eraclius!'—said six times.

When silence was restored, Bishop Augustine said: 'I know what you also know, but I do not want what happened to me to happen to him. Many of you know what happened; the only ones who do not know are those who were either not yet born or had not yet attained the age of knowledge. While my father and bishop, the elder Valerius of blessed memory, was still alive, I was ordained bishop and I sat with him; something which I did not know had been forbidden by the Council of Nicaea,[6] nor did he know it. Therefore, I do not wish my son to be blamed for what was blamed in me.' A shout was raised by the people: 'Thanks be to God, praise to Christ!'—said thirteen times.

5 From the Preface of the Mass.
6 Church law now allows an archbishop to have one or more coadjutor bishops.

When silence was restored, Bishop Augustine said: 'He will be a priest as he is, and when God wills he will be a bishop. But now at least I shall do, with the help of God's mercy, what up to now I have not done. You know what I wanted to do a few years ago, and you did not let me. It was agreed between you and me that no one should disturb me for five days, so that I might devote myself to the study of the Scriptures which my brothers and fathers, my fellow bishops, were pleased to lay upon me at the two Councils of Numidia and Carthage.[7] It was entered in the acts, it was voted, you acclaimed it, your vote and your acclaim were read out to you. It was kept in my regard for a short time, then it was rudely broken, and I am not allowed time for the work I wish to do. Both morning and afternoon I am enmeshed in men's affairs. I beg you and I enjoin you by Christ to allow me to lay some of the burden of my duties on this young man, that is, the priest Eraclius, whom I designate today in the name of Christ to succeed me as bishop.' A shout was raised by the people: 'We give thanks for your decision!'—said twenty-six times.

When silence was restored, Bishop Augustine said: 'I give thanks before the Lord our God to your charity and kindness; nay I give thanks for it. Therefore, my brethren, whatever is now referred to me, let it be referred to him. When my advice is needed I will not refuse it. God forbid that I should withdraw my help. However, what has been referred to me up to now, let it be referred to him. Let him either consult me if he does not discover what he ought to do or call on the help of one whom he knows as a father, so that you may suffer no loss and, if God gives me even a little time, that I may at length busy myself with the holy Scriptures, and, as far as He permits and grants it, that I may not spend the

7 In 416.

little remnant of my life in idleness or give myself over to laziness. This will be advantageous to Eraclius, and through him to you. Let no one, then, begrudge me my leisure, because my leisure implies great labor.[8] I see that I have paid my debt in full by transacting with you the matter for which I invited you to be here. I ask this one last favor: that those of you who are able would please sign these official records. I need your assent to this, show me some agreement by your acclaim.' A shout was raised by the people: 'So be it, so be it!'—said twenty-five times; 'It is right and just!'—said twenty-eight times; 'So be it, so be it!'—said fourteen times; 'Long worthy, long deserving!'—said twenty-five times; 'We give thanks for your decision!'—said thirteen times; 'Hear us, O Christ! Protect Eraclius!'—said eighteen times.

When silence was restored, Bishop Augustine said: 'It is well that we are able to transact the affairs of God about the time of His Sacrifice.[9] In that hour of our prayer I especially recommend your Charity to lay aside all your interests and occupations and pour forth prayer to the Lord for this church, for me and for the priest Eraclius.'

214. Augustine gives greeting in the Lord to Valentine,[1] his well-beloved lord and brother, worthy of honor among the members of Christ, and to the brethren who are with you (c. Easter, 426 or 427)

Two young men, Cresconius and Felix, have come to us, declaring that they are members of your community, and

---

8 This is one of Augustine's neatest puns: *otium,* 'leisure'; *negotium,* 'business.'
9 The Mass.

1 Abbot of the monastery of Adrumetum, capital of Byzacenum (modern Sousse) .

bringing us word that your monastery is somewhat disturbed by a difference of opinion, because some among you extol grace so much that they deny man's free will, and, what is more serious, they say that in the Day of Judgment God will not render to every man according to his works.[2] However, they have also made known that many of you do not hold this opinion, but confess that our free will is aided by the grace of God to know and do what is right, so that, when the Lord shall come to render to every man according to his works, He may find our works good, 'which God hath prepared that we should walk in them.'[3] Those who think this think correctly.

I beseech you, therefore, brethren, as the Apostle besought the Corinthians 'by the name of our Lord Jesus Christ, that you all speak the same thing, and that there be no schisms among you.'[4] In the first place, it is written in the Gospel of the Apostle John that the Lord Jesus did not come 'to judge the world, but that the world might be saved by him';[5] secondly, as the Apostle Paul writes: 'God shall judge the world,'[6] when 'He shall come,' as the whole Church professes in the Creed,[7] 'to judge the living and the dead.' If, then, there is no grace of God, how does He save the world? And if there is no free will, how does He judge the world? Therefore, the aforementioned treatise or letter of mine,[8] which the aforementioned brothers have brought with them to us, you are to understand according to this belief: that you

---

2 Matt. 16.27; Rom. 2.6; Apoc. 22.12.
3 Eph. 2.10.
4 1 Cor. 1.10.
5 John 3.17; 12.47.
6 Rom. 3.6.
7 The Nicene Creed, recited at Mass after the Gospel.
8 Letter 194, on grace and free will, addressed to Sixtus. Florus and Felix, monks at Adrumetum, had read and copied it on a visit to Uzala, and on their return home had read it to the brothers of their community.

neither deny the grace of God nor so uphold free will as to sever it from the grace of God, as if we were able in any way to think or do anything pleasing to God—and that we are utterly unable to do.[9]

Consequently, you must know that the above-mentioned letter was written to Sixtus, a priest of the Church at Rome, against the Pelagians, some new heretics, who say that the grace of God is given according to our merits, and that he who glories should glory not in the Lord but in himself, that is, in man, not in the Lord. This the Apostle forbids when he says: 'Let no man glory in man,'[10] and in another passage where he says: 'He that glorieth let him glory in the Lord.'[11] But those heretics, thinking that they are made just by their own efforts, as if it were not God but themselves that gave it to them, certainly do not glory in the Lord, but in themselves. To such men the Apostle says: 'For who distinguisheth thee?'[12] And he says this to show that what distinguishes a man from that clay of perdition which originated in Adam, so as to make of him a vessel unto honor not unto dishonor,[13] is God alone. But since carnal man, puffed up with vanity, on hearing the question: 'Who distinguisheth thee?' might be able to answer in words or in thought and to say: 'My faith distinguishes me, my prayer distinguishes me, my justice distinguishes me,' the Apostle anticipates his thought and says: 'What hast thou that thou hast not received, and if thou hast received it why dost thou glory as if thou hadst not received it?'[14] For those glory as if they had not received it who imagine that they are justified by their own efforts, and thus they glory in themselves, not in the Lord.

---

9 Cf. John 15.5.
10 1 Cor. 3.21.
11 1 Cor. 1.31.
12 1 Cor. 4.7.
13 Rom. 9.21; 2 Tim. 2.20.
14 1 Cor. 4.7.

That is why, in this letter which has reached you, I am the one[15] who have proved by the testimony of the holy Scriptures, which you can examine therein, that our good works, our holy prayers, and our upright faith could not have existed in us at all if we had not received them from Him of whom the Apostle James says: 'Every best gift and every perfect gift is from above, coming down from the Father of lights.'[16] This prevents anyone from saying that the grace of God is given him as a reward for his works, a reward for his prayers, or a reward for his faith, or from imagining that what the heretics say is true: that the grace of God is bestowed according to our merits. This is absolutely untrue, not in the sense that there is no requital, either good for the virtuous or evil for the wicked—otherwise, how will God judge the world?—but that it is the mercy and grace of God that converts a man, as the psalm says: 'My God, his mercy shall prevent me.'[17] Thus the wicked man is to be justified, that is, from wicked he is to become just and begin to have good merit which the Lord will crown when the world shall be judged.

There are many writings which I wished to send you so that by reading them you could be more accurately and fully informed about this whole case which has been defined in the councils of bishops against these same Pelagian heretics, but the brothers who had come to us from your ranks were in haste. We are sending this letter through them, not as an answer to any of yours, for they brought us no letters from your Charity. However, we received them, as their frankness was a clear enough sign that they could not have made up any of this. The reason for their haste was to keep Easter

---

15 The emphatic use of the pronoun was probably intended to refute the rumor current among the monks that Florus had written the tract himself.
16 James 1.17.
17 Ps. 58.11.

with you, so that so holy a day, by the Lord's help, may find you at peace rather than in strife.

However, it will be better for you to do what I urgently request, namely, that you make no objection to sending me the brother by whom they say they were upset, for either he misunderstands my treatise or perhaps he is himself misunderstood when he attempts to explain and unravel a question so very difficult and intelligible to few. It is this same question of the grace of God which has made unintelligent men imagine that the Apostle Paul says: 'Let us do evil that good may come.'[18] Therefore, the Apostle Peter in his second Epistle says: 'Wherefore, dearly beloved, seeing that you look for these things, be diligent that ye may be found undefiled and unspotted to him in peace, and account the longsuffering of our Lord salvation: as also our most dear brother Paul, according to the wisdom given him, hath written to you. As also in all his epistles, speaking in them of these things, in which are certain things hard to be understood, which the unlearned and unstable wrest, as they do also the other scriptures, to their own destruction.'[19]

Take care, then, to avoid what the great Apostle sets forth so fearfully, and when you feel that you do not understand, make an immediate act of faith in what is divinely revealed, that there is both free will in man and grace from God; and pray that what you religiously believe you may also wisely understand. Indeed, it is for this very reason that we have free will that we may wisely understand, for, unless our understanding and wisdom were regulated by free will, we should not be commanded in the words of Scripture: 'Understand, ye senseless among the people: and you fools be wise at last.'[20] The very fact, then, that we are instructed and

18 Rom. 3.8; a quotation wrested from its context.
19 1 Peter 3.14-16.
20 Ps. 93.8.

commanded to understand and be wise is proof of a demand
on our obedience, which cannot exist without free will. But,
if it were possible for this to be accomplished by free will
without the grace of God, namely, that we should understand
and be wise, we should not have to say to God: 'Give me
understanding that I may know thy commandments';[21] nor
would it be written in the Gospel: 'Then he opened their
understanding that they might understand the scriptures';[22]
nor would the Apostle James have said: 'But if any of you
want wisdom let him ask of God who giveth to all men
abundantly and upbraideth not: and it shall be given him.'[23]
But the Lord is able to grant both to you and to us to rejoice
in the speedy tidings of your peace and religious harmony.
I greet you not only in my own name but also in that of the
brothers who are with me, and I ask you to pray for me
wholeheartedly and constantly. The Lord be with you. Amen.

215. Augustine gives greeting in the Lord to Valentine, his well-beloved lord and brother, worthy of honor among the members of Christ, and to the brethren who are with you (426 or 427, after Easter)

Your Charity knows that Cresconius, Felix, and another
Felix, servants of God, who came to us from your community,
spent Easter with us. We kept them somewhat longer so that
they might return to you better equipped to oppose the new
Pelagian heretics. Their error entraps anyone who believes
that the grace of God, through which alone man is saved by
our Lord Jesus Christ, is given according to human merits.
But, besides that, it is no less an error to think that, when

---

21 Ps. 118.125.
22 Luke 24.45.
23 James 1.5.

the Lord shall come to judgment, man, who throughout life had the power of choice in the use of his free will, will not be judged according to his deeds. Little children alone who have performed no deeds of their own, either good or bad, will be condemned solely because of original sin, unless the grace of the Saviour has freed them from it through 'the laver of regeneration.'[1] All others, who have used their free will to add their own sins to original sin, will be judged not only on the score of original sin, but also for the deliberate acts of their own will, unless they are delivered from the power of darkness and translated to the kingdom of Christ[2] by the grace of God. The good, it is true, will win their reward according to the meritorious acts of their good will, but this very good will has been an effect of the grace of God. Thus we have the fulfillment of what is written: 'Wrath and indignation and anguish upon every soul of man that worketh evil; of the Jew first and also of the Greek; but glory and honor and peace to every one that worketh good, to the Jew first and also the Greek.'[3]

There is no need for me to discuss this very difficult question, that is, of the will and grace, at greater length in this letter, since I had already given the brothers another letter when they were planning an early return. I have also written a book[5] for you, and if you will read it carefully and apply yourselves vigorously to understand it, I think there will be no further difference among you on this matter. They are also taking with them some other documents which we thought well to address to you, so that you may know how the Catholic Church, by the mercy of God, has repudiated

---

1 1 Titus 3.5.
2 Col. 1.13.
3 Rom. 2.8-10.
4 Letter 214.
5 *De gratia et libero arbitrio.*

the poison of the Pelagian heresy. There is an account of
the provincial Council of Carthage, written to Pope Innocent,
and one of the Council of Numidia; and another, somewhat
more detailed, written by five bishops, as well as the answer
he wrote to these three;[6] likewise, the report to Pope Zozimus
of the Council of Africa, and his answer which was sent to
all the bishops of the world;[7] also, a brief report of what we
decided against this error at the recent plenary Council of
Africa;[8] and a copy of the above-mentioned book of mine,
which I have just written for you. All these we read to them
in person and by them we are sending them to you.

We have also read to them the blessed martyr Cyprian's
work on the Lord's Prayer, and we showed them how he
teaches that everything we need for the guidance of our
conduct and for right living is to be asked from our Father
who is in heaven, lest we rely on our own free will and fall
from divine grace. Moreover, we pointed out how the same
glorious martyr urged our duty of praying even for our
enemies who do not yet believe in Christ, which would
assuredly be useless if the Church did not believe that even
the wicked and unbelieving wills of men can be turned to
good by the grace of God. We did not send this book of St.
Cyprian, because they said you had it at home. I also read
with them my letter to Sixtus, priest of the Church at Rome,[9]
which they brought here with them, and showed that it had
been written against those who say that the grace of God is
given according to our merits, that is, against the same
Pelagians.

As strongly as we could, we urged on them, as on your

---

6 Letters 175, 176, 177, 181, 182, and 183.
7 Cf. Letter 190.
8 Held at Carthage on May 1, 418, presided over by Aurelius, attended
   by 203 bishops from all the African provinces and even from Spain.
9 Letter 194.

and our brothers, to persevere in the Catholic faith, which neither denies free will whether for a bad life or a good one, nor allows it so much effect that it can do anything without the grace of God, whether to convert the soul from evil to good, or to persevere and advance in good, or to attain eternal good, where there is no more fear of falling away. To you, also, dearly beloved, I send in this letter the exhortation which the Apostle addresses to us all: 'Not to be more wise than it behooveth to be wise, but to be wise unto sobriety, and according as God hath divided to every one the measure of faith.'[10]

Attend to what the Holy Spirit advises us through Solomon: 'Make straight the paths for thy feet, and direct all thy ways; decline not to the right hand nor to the left. Turn away thy foot from the evil way. Fod God knoweth the ways that are on the right hand; but those are perverse that are on the left. But he will make thy course straight; he will bring forward thy ways in peace.'[11] In these words of holy Scripture consider, brothers, that if there were no free will it would not say: 'Make straight the paths for thy feet, and direct all thy ways; decline not to the right hand nor to the left.' Yet, if this were possible without the grace of God, it would not say afterwards: 'He will make thy course straight, he will bring forward thy ways in peace.'

Do not, then, decline to the right, although the ways on the right are praised while those on the left are disparaged. That is why these words are added: 'Turn away thy foot from the evil way,' that is, from the left, which is made clear by what follows: 'For God knoweth the ways that are on the right hand, but those are perverse that are on the left.' Therefore, we ought to walk in the ways that God knows,

10 Rom. 12.3.
11 Prov. 4.26.

of which we read in the psalm: 'The Lord knoweth the way
of the just and the way of the wicked shall perish.'[12] This
way the Lord does not know because it is on the left, as He
will say to those who are set on His left: 'I know you not.'[13]
But how is it that He does not know them when He surely
knows all things, man's good as well as his evil? What does
He mean by 'I know you not' except 'You are not such as I
made you'? When it is said of the Lord Jesus Christ Himself
that 'He knew no sin,' what does it mean but that 'He did
no sin'?[14] How, then, are we to understand the words: 'The
Lord knoweth the ways that are on the right hand,' except
that He Himself made the ways on the right hand, that is,
the ways of the just, which are certainly the good works
'which God hath prepared,' as the Apostle says, 'that we
should walk in them'?[15] Surely, He does not know the perverse
ways on the left, that is, the ways of the wicked, because He
Himself did not make them for man, but man made them
for himself. That is why He says: 'I have hated the perverse
ways of the wicked;'[16] these are the ways on the left hand.

The objection is made to us: Why, then, does He say:
'Decline not to the right hand nor the left,' when it seems as
if He should rather have said: 'Hold to the right and decline
not to the left,' if the ways on the right are good? Why else,
we think, except that the ways which are on the right are so
far good that it is not good to decline to the right? Doubtless
we are to understand that he declines to the right who wishes
to attribute his own good works, which symbolize the ways
on the right, to himself instead of to God. Therefore, when he
said: 'God knoweth the ways that are on the right hand, but
those are perverse that are on the left,' he continues as if

12 Ps. 1.6.
13 Matt. 25.12; Luke 13.27.
14 2 Cor. 5.21; 1 Peter 2.22.
15 Eph. 2.10.
16 Cf. Ps. 118.104.

someone had said to him: 'Why, then, do you not wish us to decline to the right?' and adds at once: 'But he will make thy course straight; he will bring forward all thy ways in peace.' It is in this sense that you must understand what is commanded you: 'Make straight the paths for thy feet, and direct all thy ways,' that you may know when you do this that the Lord God grants you to do it, and you will not decline to the right hand, although you walk in the ways to the right, not trusting in your own strength; and He will be your strength who 'will make all thy course straight and will bring forward all thy ways in peace.'

Therefore, dearly beloved, whoever says 'My own will is sufficient for the performance of good works' declines to the right. On the other hand, those who think the good life is to be abandoned when they have the grace of God, so described that it is believed and understood as making man's bad will into a good will, and also preserving the wills it has thus made; who therefore says: 'Let us do evil that good may come of it,' these decline to the left. So, then, I have said to you: 'Decline not to the right nor to the left, that is, do not defend free will so as to attribute your good works to it without the grace of God; and do not defend grace so as to love evil works because you rely on it. May the same grace of God keep this far from you! As if he were expressing to himself the words of such objectors, the Apostle says: 'What shall we say, then? shall we continue in sin that grace may abound?' And he answers these words of erring men who fail to understand the grace of God by saying, as he ought: 'God forbid! For we that are dead to sin, how shall we live any longer therein?'[17] Nothing shorter or better could be said. For, what more useful gift does the grace of God confer on us than to make us die to sin? Anyone who would wish to live in sin because of the grace through which we die to

17 Rom. 6.1,2.

sin would thereby be proved ungrateful to this very grace. But may God, who 'is rich in mercy,'[18] grant you both to be soundly wise and to continue to progress to the end in your good resolution. Be constant and watchful in prayer in brotherly peace, and ask this for yourselves, for us, for all who love you and who hate you. May you live in God.

If I deserve a favor from you, let brother Florus[19] come to me.

216. *Valentine, servant of your Holiness, and the whole community which joins me in placing our hope in your prayers, give greeting in the Lord to our truly holy lord and blessed prelate, Augustine, worthy to be esteemed above all and cherished with pious joy (426 or 427)*

We received the revered writings and the book from your Holiness with such heartfelt awe that we imitated blessed Elias when he stood at the entrance to the cave and veiled his face as the glory of the Lord passed by.[1] So we, too, being abashed, covered our eyes because we blushed at the judgment made of us on account of the uncouthness of our brothers, and we shrank from sending greetings to your Beatitude at the time of their irregular journey, because there 'is a time to speak and a time to keep silence,'[2] lest, if we sent a letter by doubters and waverers in the truth we should seem to doubt with the doubters about the words of your wisdom which is like 'the wisdom of an angel of God.'[3] We had no

---

18 Eph. 2.4.
19 Cf. Letter 214, notes 8 and 15.

---

1 3 Kings 19.13.
2 Eccle. 3.7.
3 2 Kings 14.20.

need to put questions to your Blessedness and your wisdom is known to us by the Lord's grace. For we were filled with such lively joy when the book of your most sweet Holiness appeared that we were like the Apostles who did not dare to ask the Lord who He was when He dined with them after the Resurrection—for they knew that it was Jesus.[4] We also neither wished nor dared to ask whether the book[5] was the work of your Holiness, for the faithful grace, which is there so nobly praised, proves to us by the most spirited language that it is yours, my lord and holy prelate.

But allow us, my lord and blessed prelate, to set forth the sequence of that disturbance. Our dear brother Florus, the servant of your Paternity, went to Uzala, his native town, at the bidding of charity, and as a blessing to our monastery he brought us from among your works this same book, which one of the brothers Felix generously dictated to him during his stay in his native town—he is distinguished as having come to your Holiness later, after his companions. He arrived at the monastery with the same book after Florus had left the town of Uzala and started for Carthage. Without showing me the book, they began to read it to untutored brethren. It troubled the hearts of some who did not understand that when the Lord said: 'Whoever does not eat the flesh of the Son of man and drink his blood shall not have life in him,'[6] the fault was not in the Lord's words but in the hardness of sinful hearts that those who misunderstood went away.

The above-mentioned brothers who upset everything began to trouble the minds of the innocent while my insignificance was still in ignorance of it; in fact, I was so unaware of this protesting group that, if brother Florus, who knew about their outbreak, had not retraced his steps from Carthage and

4 John 21.12.
5 Letter 194.
6 Cf. John 6.54,67.

taken pains to inform me,[7] there was likely to be a secret and almost slavelike quarrel among them about this misunderstood truth. As a way of quelling these shocking doubts, I proposed sending to father Evodius and asking him to write us something more definite about this blessed[8] book for the sake of the uninstructed. They were no more willing to receive this with patience, but took a step so contrary to my wish that brother Florus was almost deranged by their fury, for they raged against him for having, as they thought, wounded them with this book in which those affected could not discover a remedy. Therefore, we appealed to the holy priest Sabinus, as to a higher authority, and his Holiness read the book with clear explanations. But not even thus was their wounded soul healed. Because of our true affection for them, we gave them money for a journey, lest we add to their wounds which could be healed only by the grace of that same book in which your holy presence shines forth. After they had set out, quiet and peace spread joyfully among all the brothers in the Lord. That strife arose from the enmity of five brothers or more.

But because, in the meantime, lord Pope, joy has come out of sadness, we do not regret too much that we have deserved to be enlightened through inexperienced and inquisitive men by the sweet warnings of your Holiness. The doubt of the blessed Apostle Thomas, probing the openings of the nails,[9] has effected a strengthening of faith in the whole Church. Therefore, lord Pope, we have received, together with grace, the remedy of your loving and curative letter, and we have struck our breast[10] that thus there may be healing for our conscience, which grace heals and quickens through our free

---

7 Goldbacher indicates a lacuna here, but the sense is complete, and grammar is not violated by allowing an indicative verb to stand in the apodosis of a contrary to fact condition.

8 He uses the word *sacrosancto* in a vexed tone.

9 John 20.25.

10 A sign of sorrow.

will, given by His mercy, at least at this time, while we still sing His mercy during our stay here. For, when we begin to sing justice to the Lord[11] we shall bear away a reward for our work, because the Lord is merciful and just, compassionate and upright,[12] and because, as your Holiness teaches us: 'We must all be manifested before the judgment seat of Christ, that every one of us may receive the proper things of the body, according as he has done, whether it be good or evil';[13] because the Lord shall come as a burning furnace and shall burn the wicked like stubble;[14] and to those who fear the name of the Lord the Sun of justice shall arise, when the wicked shall be punished with the judgment of justice.[15] This just man, whose friend you are, lord Pope, cries out, trembles, and says suppliantly: 'Lord, enter not into judgment with thy servant.'[16] If grace were a reward of merit, the just man would not fear the secret place of the judgment of majesty.[17] This is the faith of your servant Florus, father, and it is not as those other brothers have said. They heard him say in their presence that the gift of piety is not given according to our merits, but by the grace of the Redeemer. Who doubts that on that day grace will be far away when justice begins to show its wrath? Following your teaching, father, this is what we proclaim, this is what we sing—not in certainty, but in fear: 'O Lord rebuke me not in thy indignation nor chastise me in thy wrath'.[18] This is what we say: 'Instruct us, O Lord, and teach us out of thy law, that thou mayst give us rest from the evil days.'[19] This is

---

11 Ps. 100.1.
12 Ps. 111.4.
13 2 Cor. 5.10.
14 Isa. 40.10.
15 Cf. Mal. 4.1-3.
16 Ps. 142.2.
17 Prov. 11.31; 1 Peter 4.18.
18 Ps. 6.2.
19 Cf. Ps. 93.12,13.

what we believe, on your teaching, revered father, that the Lord examines the just and the wicked; that He assigns and allots to the good and bad, placed on His right or left hand,[20] works of piety to be rewarded or obstinacy in evil to be punished. Where will grace be when good or bad works are checked off according to each one's character?

But why is there no fear of uttering an indirect lie? We do not deny that free will is healed by the grace of God, but we believe that we make progress through the daily grace of God, and we trust in its help. And men say: 'It is in my own power to do good.' If only men did do good! O empty boasting of wretchedness! Every day they disclaim sin and in their boasting they attribute to themselves unaided free will, not scrutinizing their conscience which cannot be healed but by grace, so as to say: 'Be merciful to me, heal my soul, for I have sinned against thee.'[21] What would those do who boast of their own free will—which is not denied so long as it is helped by the grace of God—if death had now been swallowed up in victory, if our mortal were putting on immortality and our corruptible were putting on incorruption?[22] Behold, their wounds fester and they seek a remedy in pride. They do not say with the just man: 'Unless the Lord had been my helper, my soul had almost dwelt in hell.'[23] They do not say with the saint: 'Except the Lord keep the city, he watcheth in vain that keepeth it.'[24]

But pray, most loving father, that we may now have no other object than to expiate our sin with tears and to extol the grace of God. Pray, lord father, that the pit may not shut her mouth upon us,[25] that we may be saved from them

20 Matt. 25.31-46.
21 Ps. 40.5.
22 Cf. 1 Cor. 15.54,53.
23 Ps. 93.17.
24 Ps. 126.1.
25 Ps. 68.16.

that go down into the pit,[26] that our soul may not be taken away with the wicked[27] because of our pride, but may be healed by the grace of the Lord. Therefore, as you have directed, lord Pope, our brother Florus, the servant of your Holiness, has set out with all eagerness; his fatigue, instead of staying him, is urging him on that his heart may draw near to its illuminating instruction. We humbly recommend him to your Holiness, and we also entreat that in your prayers you mercifully commend to the Lord the reconciliation of our inexperienced brothers. Pray, lord and most sweet father, that the whole storm of controversy stirred up from outside may be quelled so that the ship of our religious life, loaded with peaceful sea-going soldiers, as long as it sails over this great, unbounded sea may anchor without fear within the shelter of a most sure harbor, and may receive in that harbor, within which no further voyage has to be feared in life, a suitable price for its pleasing merchandise. We trust that we shall win this with the help of your Holiness, through the grace which is in Christ Jesus, our Lord. We beg you to be so kind as to greet in our name all the sons of your apostolate, our lords, the clerics and saints serving in the religious life of your community, that they may all deign, together with your Beatitude, to pray for us. May the co-equal Trinity of the Lord our God preserve for us in His Church your holy apostolate which He has chosen by His grace; may He make you mindful of us, my lord, and grant you the crown which we wish for you in His great Church. If brother Florus, the servant of your Holiness, makes any suggestion, we beg you to receive him in accordance with the monastic rule, and deign to instruct us weak members in all these matters.

---

26 Ps. 29.4.
27 Ps. 25.9.

216A. Augustine gives greeting in the Lord to Valentine, his well-beloved lord and brother worthy to be cherished in the heart of Christ (426 or 427)[1]

I give sincere thanks to your Charity for having sent brother Florus[2] in response to my desire, and I give even more heartfelt thanks to our God because I have found him just as I had hoped he would be. It may seem, perhaps, that he has been rather slow in returning to you, but his stay with me was shorter than I could have wished. As a matter of fact, while he was here I had a wretched illness for so many days that I could not enjoy his company, my cherished lord and brother worthy to be embraced in the heart of Christ. So I ask you a second time to be so kind as to send him back that he may stay with us awhile, to satisfy not only my longing but his as well. For I think this will be profitable both for him and for us, and that the more ample instruction we shall be able to give him, with the Lord's help, will also be beneficial to the brethren. May you always be pleasing to God.

---

1 This letter, called 'a little letter to Valentine about brother Florus,' was published in *Revue Bénédictine,* 18, pp. 241-256, by Dom Germain Morin. It was found in a ninth-century manuscript in the Royal Library of Munich, having come from the Church of St. Martin at Mainz. Besides this letter, the codex contains two letters to the Abbot of Hadrumetum, one from a priest named Januarianus and one from Evodius, as well as copies of the *Retractations,* of Letter 187 to Dardanus (*On the Presence of God*), of the books *De gratia et libero arbitrio* and *De correptione et gratia.* According to Dom Morin: 'This little letter in which the charity, humility and zeal of Augustine shine forth, was intended to be sent with the treatise *De correptione et gratia* as Letter 215 was sent with his *De gratia et libero arbitrio.*'

2 The monk mentioned in Letter 215 who copied out Letter 194 and thereby set his community in an uproar. From this letter we see that Augustine's modest request at the end of Letter 215 was granted by Valentine and that Florus turned out to be a person of irreproachable orthodoxy on the subject of grace and free will. It is not known whether the second visit asked for in this letter took place.

217. Augustine, bishop, servant of Christ and through Him servant of His servants, gives greeting in Him to his brother Vitalis[1] (426 or 427)

Having received bad news about you, I have asked God, and, until I receive good news, I keep on asking Him that you may not scorn my letter but may read it for your own profit. If He hears this prayer of mine for you, He will also give me reason for offering thanks for you. If I win my request, you undoubtedly agree with this beginning of my letter. What I ask for you is that you may have the right faith. If you are not displeased that we make this prayer for those dear to us, if you acknowledge that this is a Christian prayer, if you recall that you either make similar pleas for those dear to you, or recognize that you ought so to pray, how can you say—as I hear you do say—that when we have a right belief in God and adherence to the Gospel, it is not a gift of God, but something we have of ourselves, that is, through our own wills, something which He has not effected in us? And when you hear someone objecting to this: What, then, does the Apostle mean by saying: 'God worketh in us to will'?[2] you answer that God works in us to will through His law, through His Scriptures, which we either read or hear, but to adhere to them or not to adhere to them is so far our own work that it is accomplished if we will it, but if we do not will it we make the work of God in us of no avail. Doubtless, He works, you say, to make us will as far as it rests with Him and inasmuch as His words are known to us, but if we refuse to agree to them we make His work ineffective in us. If you say this, you surely contradict our prayers.

Say openly, then, that we ought not to pray that those to

1 A layman spoken of as 'a learned man in the Church at Carthage."
2 Phil. 2.13.

whom we preach the Gospel may believe, but we ought only to preach to them. Use your arguments against the prayers of the Church, and, when you hear the priest of God at the altar of God exhorting the people of God to pray for unbelievers that God may convert them to the faith, and for catechumens that He may breathe into them a desire of regeneration, and for the faithful that they may persevere in His service as they have begun,[3] mock at these pious words and say that you do not do what he asks, that is, you do not pray to God for unbelievers that He may make them believers, because this does not come through the bounty of His divine mercy, but through the action of the human will. Learned man that you are in the Church at Carthage, condemn even the book of blessed Cyprian on the Lord's Prayer, in which the holy Doctor explains that these things are to be asked for from God the Father, while you say that they come to man from man, that is, from himself.

But if you think that what I have said of the prayers of the Church and of the martyr Cyprian is insignificant, dare something greater; find fault with the Apostle Paul because he said: 'We pray God that you may do no evil.'[4] You are not likely to say that he who does not believe in Christ or who abandons the faith of Christ does no evil. Therefore, he who says 'that you may do no evil' does not wish evil to be done and is not satisfied with preaching, but confesses that he asks God that evil may not be done, knowing that the will of man is corrected and directed by Him so as not to do it. For, 'by the Lord shall the steps of a man be directed and he shall like well his way.'[5] The Psalmist did not say: 'And he shall learn his way,' or 'hold to it,' or 'walk upon it,' or anything

---

3 These prayers for all classes of men which formed a large part of the early liturgy of the Church, now survive in the Latin rite in the Collects of Good Friday, and in some Oriental rites, at daily Mass.
4 2 Cor. 13.7.
5 Ps. 36.23.

of that sort which could make it possible for you to say that it was indeed given by the Lord but given to a man who already willed it. Thus man, by his act of will, would forestall this same benefit of God by which He directs the steps of a man that he may learn and hold to and walk upon His way, and would merit this gift of God by his antecedent will. But he said: 'By the Lord shall the steps of a man be directed and he shall like well his way,' to make us understand that the good will itself by which we begin to will to believe—and what is the way of God but an upright faith?—is a gift from Him who first directs our steps to the end that we may will. For the Scripture does not say: 'By the Lord are the steps of a man directed because he had liked well the way,' but it says: 'they are directed and he shall like well.' Therefore, they are not directed because he liked well, but he will like it well because they are directed.

Here, perhaps, you will repeat that this is done by the Lord during the reading or hearing of His teaching if man yields the consent of his will to the truth which he reads or hears. For you say: 'if the teaching of God were not known to him, his ways would not be directed, nor would he like well the way of God on which he was directed.' According to this, you think that the steps of man are directed by the Lord to the choosing of the way of the Lord, because without the teaching of God truth cannot be made known to him, and to truth alone does his will yield assent. 'If he yields the assent,' you say, 'which is already established in his free will, surely it is correct to say that his steps are directed by the Lord that he may like well His way whose teaching he follows by an antecedent impulse and a subsequent consent. If he wills, he acts by an innate liberty; if he does not will, he does not act because he will receive reward or punishment for what he has done.' This is that doctrine of the Pelagians, unfortunately widespread, but justly repudiated and condemned by Pelagius himself at the time when he feared condemnation by the verdict of the Eastern bishops; a doctrine which makes them say that the grace of God is not granted for separate acts, but is innate in free will or in the law and teaching of God. Thus, brother, we shall be so dull of heart[6] as to hold that Pelagian doctrine about the grace of God—nay, rather, against the grace of God—which Pelagius himself condemned, with an insincere heart, it is true, but out of fear of Catholic judges!

'And how,' you will say, 'are we to answer?' What easier or plainer way can you think of than by accepting what we said above about prayer to God so strongly that no onset of forgetfulness can steal it from us, no subtlety of argument wrest it from us? If, then, in these quotations: 'By the Lord are the steps of a man directed and he shall like well his ways,' and 'The will is prepared by the Lord,'[7] and 'It is God who worketh in you both to will and to accomplish,'[8] and in many other like passages, the true grace of God is presented to us, that is, that when it is given it gives merit because it goes before the good will of men and does not find it in any heart but produces it—then, if God so prepared and so worked upon the will of man that He only offered His law and His teaching to the free will, but did not act upon his inner consciousness by that high and secret call so as to make him yield assent to the same law and teaching, undoubtedly it would be enough to read it or to understand it when read, or even to explain and preach it, but there would be no need to pray that God would convert the hearts of unbelievers to His faith and to endow those converted with the abundance of His grace that they may persevere and advance. If you do not refuse to admit that these same favors

---

6 Ps. 4.3.
7 Prov. 8.35 (Septuagint).
8 Phil. 2.13.

are to be asked of the Lord, what else can you do, brother Vitalis, but admit that they are given by Him from whom you agree they are to be asked? But, if you refuse to admit that we ought to ask them, you speak against His very teaching, because in it we learn that we should ask these things of Him.

You know the Lord's Prayer, and I do not doubt that you say: 'Our Father who art in heaven,'[9] and the rest. Read its interpreter, blessed Cyprian;[10] note carefully and understand submissively how he explains what is there said: 'Thy will be done on earth as it is in heaven.' Certainly he will teach you to pray for the unbelieving enemies of the Church according to the commandment of the Lord, who said: 'Pray for your enemies,'[11] and to pray that the will of God may be done in those who because of their unbelief bear the image of the earthly man and are therefore rightly named from the earth, as it is in those who are now believers and who bear the image of the heavenly man and are therefore worthy of the name of heaven.[12] Undoubtedly, those for whom the Lord commanded us to pray as enemies, and of whom the glorious martyr explained that when we say in the prayer: 'Thy will be done on earth as it is in heaven,' we ask for them the faith which believers have; those, I say, who are the enemies of Christian piety either refuse absolutely to hear the law of God and the doctrine by which the faith of Christ is preached, or they listen to it or even read it in order to mock at it and show their hatred of it and blaspheme it by every possible contradiction. Therefore, the prayers which we pour forth to God for them, that they may consent to believe what they oppose, are offered vainly and perfunctorily rather than

9 Matt. 6.9,10.
10 *De Dominica oratione* 14-17.
11 Matt. 5.44; Luke 6.28.
12 1 Cor. 15.47-49

sincerely, if it is not a function of His grace to convert to His faith the wills of men opposed to His faith. Likewise, the hearty thanks which we joyfully give to God when some of them do believe are similarly vain and perfunctory rather than sincere if He does not effect this in them.

Let us not deceive men, for we cannot deceive God. In a word, we do not pray to God, but we pretend to pray, if we do not believe that He does what we pray for; just as we do not thank God, but pretend to thank Him, if we do not think He does that for which we thank Him. If there are deceitful lips[13] in some of the speeches of men, at least let there be none in our prayers. God forbid that with our mouths and voices we should ask God to do what in our hearts we deny that He does; and, what is worse, that we should not refrain from using our arguments to mislead others; and, by attempting to defend free will, that we should lose the help of prayer and be unable to render true thanks because we do not acknowledge true grace.

If we truly desire to defend free will, let us not assail the source of its freedom. For he who assails grace by which our will is set free to turn from evil and to do good is himself the one who wishes his will to remain a captive. Answer me, please: How can the Apostle say: 'Giving thanks to the Father who hath made us worthy to be partakers of the lot of the saints in light; who hath delivered us from the power of darkness and hath translated us into the kingdom of the Son of his love,'[14] if it is our own will that has delivered itself and not He that has delivered our will? Therefore, it is deceitful of us to give thanks to the Father as if He were doing what He does not do, and the Apostle was wrong in saying that 'He hath made us worthy to be partakers of the lot of the saints in light' and that 'He hath delivered us from

---

13 Ps. 11.3,4; 16.1; 30.19.
14 Col. 1.12,13.

the power of darkness and hath translated us into the kingdom of the Son of his love.' Answer: How did we have a will free to turn from evil and do good when it was under the power of darkness? If, as the Apostle says, God delivered us from it, then He surely made the will free. But, if He effected this great good in us through the mere preaching of His doctrine, what shall we say of those whom He has not yet delivered from that power of darkness? Is it enough for the divine doctrine to be preached to them, or should we also pray for them that they may be divinely delivered from the power of darkness? If you say that preaching is enough, you go counter to the command of the Lord and the prayers of the Church; if, however, you admit that prayer should be made for them, you thereby admit that this prayer should be made that they may assent to the same doctrine after their will has been delivered from the power of darkness. Thus, on the one hand, the grace of God is not denied, but is shown to be truly active without any antecedent human merits; on the other, free will is so defended that it is grounded in humility and not dashed to destruction by pride, and that he who glories should glory not in man or in anything else or even in himself, but in the Lord.[15]

As for the power of darkness, what is it but the power of the Devil and his angels, who, after being angels of light, did not use their free will to stand in the truth but by falling from it became darkness?[16] I am not teaching you this; I am advising you to call to mind what you know. So, the human race became subject to this power of darkness by the fall of the first man who was induced by that power to commit sin, and in him we have all fallen.[17] Hence, little children also are delivered from this power of darkness when they are

---

15 1 Cor. 1.31; 2 Cor. 10.17.
16 Matt. 25.41; 2 Cor. 11.14; John 8.44.
17 Gen. 3.1-6; 1 Tim. 2.14; Rom. 5.12.

regenerated in Christ. But there is no evidence in them of free will until their age reaches the years of reason; their will then assents to the doctrine of salvation in which they have been brought up and they end their life in the same faith, if they have been chosen from before the foundation of the world that 'they may be holy and unspotted in his sight in charity, predestinated unto the adoption of children.'[18]

But this power of darkness, that is, the Devil who is called 'the prince of the power of the air, . . . worketh on the children of unbelief,'[19] this prince, the ruler of darkness,[20] that is, the Devil, rules the children of unbelief according to his will, which is not free to do good, but is hardened to the utmost malice as a punishment for his crime. Hence, no one of sane faith believes or says that those apostate angels are ever converted to their original goodness by any change in their will. What, then, does this power effect in the children of unbelief but his own evil works; first and foremost, that very unbelief and infidelity by which they are enemies of the faith through which he knows they can be cleansed, can become perfectly free to reign forever—something he violently envies them? Therefore, he selects some of them through whom he aims to carry his deception further and allows them to perform good deeds for which they are praised among certain peoples; and chief among these were some of the Roman race who lived illustrious and famous lives. But since, as the most truthful Scripture says: 'All that is not of faith is sin'[21] and 'without faith it is surely impossible to please God,'[22] this prince works at nothing so much as to prevent men from

18 Cf. Eph. 1.4,5.
19 Eph. 2.2.
20 Eph. 6.12.
21 Rom. 14.23.
22 Heb. 11.6.

believing in God and coming by faith to the Mediator by whom his works are brought low.

Now, that Mediator enters 'into the house of the strong,'[23] that is, into this world of men, bound under the power of the Devil, as far as it rests with him; of him it also is written that 'he has the empire of death.'[24] He enters into the house of the strong, that is, of one holding the human race in thrall, and He first binds him, that is, He restrains and confines the exercise of his power by stronger bonds, and so He rifles his goods,[25] takes whatever He has predetermined to take from him, freeing men's will from his power, so that with free will they may believe in Him, once the inhibiting power is removed. Manifestly, this is the power of grace, not of nature. It is the work, I say, of grace, which the second Adam has brought us; not of nature, which the first Adam had totally ruined in himself. It is the work of grace, taking away sin and reviving the dead sinner; not the work of the law, pointing out the sin, but not restoring to life from sin. That greater teacher of grace said: 'I did not know sin but by the law'[26] and 'if there had been a law given which could give life, verily justice should have been by the law.'[27] This is the work of grace, and those who receive it become favorable to the saving doctrine of holy Scripture even though they were hostile to it; it is not the work of this same doctrine which they may read and hear, but lacking the grace of God they are made more hostile to it.

Therefore, the grace of God is not found in the nature of free will, or in the law, or in doctrine, as the Pelagian

---

23 Matt. 12.29.
24 Heb. 2.14.
25 Matt. 12.29.
26 St. Paul.
27 Rom. 7.7.
28 Gal. 3.21.

aberration falsely claims, but it is given to separate acts of
the will, of which it is written: 'God sets aside a free rain
for his inheritance.'[29] The reasons for this are that we lost
the freedom of our will to love God by the magnitude of the
first sin, and also that the law of God and doctrine, although
holy and just and good, bring death[30] if the Spirit does not
quicken us;[31] hence it follows that the law is kept by obeying,
not by hearing it; by loving, not by reading it. So, then, that
we should believe in God and live virtuously, 'it is not of
him that willeth, nor of him that runneth, but of God that
showeth mercy,'[32] not because we ought not to will and to
run, but because He works in us to will and to run.[33] Hence,
the Lord Jesus Himself, distinguishing believers from unbelievers, that is, vessels of mercy from vessels of wrath,[34]
said: 'No man cometh to me unless it be given him by my
Father,' and His reason for saying it was that His disciples
had been scandalized at His doctrine and afterward ceased
to follow Him.[35] Therefore, we do not say that grace is
doctrine, but we acknowledge that grace makes doctrine
beneficial to us, and if grace is lacking we see that doctrine
is a stumbling block.

Thus, when God, in His predestination, foresaw all His
future works, He so disposed them that He converts certain
unbelievers to His faith by hearing the prayers of believers on
their behalf. Thereby He refutes, and if He is merciful to
them He corrects, those who think that the grace of God is
the nature of free will with which we are born, or that the
grace of God is doctrine which, however useful, is preached

---

29 Cf. Ps. 67.10.
30 Cf. Rom. 7.11,12.
31 2 Cor. 3.6; John 6.64.
32 Rom. 9.16.
33 Phil. 2.13.
34 Rom. 9.22,23.
35 John 6.66, 61-62, 67.

by word and writing. Yet, we do not make this prayer for unbelievers that their nature may be created, that is, that they may be men, or that doctrine should be preached to them, which they hear to their own loss if they do not believe—and often we do pray for those who refuse to believe after reading or hearing—but we pray that their will may be reformed, that they may assent to doctrine, that their nature may be healed.

What is more, the faithful even pray for themselves that they may persevere in the course which they have begun. Indeed, it is useful for all, or nearly all, for the sake of wholesome humility, that they cannot know what they are going to be. On this point we have the words: 'He that thinketh himself to stand, let him take heed lest he fall.'[36] This fear is useful to us lest, after being regenerated and having begun to live piously, we should 'mind high things,'[37] as if sure of ourselves, and therefore by the permission or provision or decree of God there is a mingling of some who will not persevere with those who will, that when the former fall we may be terrified 'with fear and trembling,'[38] and may advance on the way of justice until we pass from this life, which is a 'warfare upon earth,'[39] to that other where there is no pride to be suppressed or struggle to be carried on against its incitements and temptations.

Let each one search into this matter as he can, that is, why some who are not going to persevere in the faith and in Christian holiness nevertheless receive this grace for a time and are suffered to live here until they fall, when they could be hurried out of this life, 'lest wickedness should alter their understanding,'[40] as it says in the Book of Wisdom about the

---

36 1 Cor. 10-12.
37 Rom. 11.20; 12.16.
38 2 Cor. 7.15; Eph. 6.5; Phil. 2.12.
39 Job 7.1.
40 Wisd. 4.11.

saint who dies an untimely death. If anyone finds a probable
answer, different from the one I have given, which does not
vary from the right rule of faith, let him hold it and I will
hold it with him, if it is clear to me. Meanwhile, 'whereunto
we are come, let us walk in the same,' until God reveals it to
us if we are otherwise minded,[41] as we are advised in the
Apostle's letters. But we have come to these truths which we
know belong most firmly to the true and Catholic faith, in
which we must walk, by the help and mercy of Him to whom
we say: 'Conduct me, O Lord, in thy way and I will walk
in thy truth,'[42] so that we may not depart from them.

Since, therefore, by the favor of Christ, we are Catholic
Christians:

We know that children not yet born have done nothing
either good or evil in their own life,[43] nor have they any
merits of any previous life, which no individual can have as
his own; that they come into the miseries of this life; that
their carnal birth according to Adam involves them at the
instant of nativity in the contagion of the primal death; that
they are not delivered from the penalty of eternal death,
which a just verdict passing from one lays upon all,[44] unless
they are born again in Christ through grace.

We know that the grace of God is given neither to children
nor to adults according to their merits.

We know that in adults it is given for separate acts.

We know that it is not given to all men, and, where it is
given, not only is it not given as a reward for good deeds,
but it is not even given as a reward for good will in those to
whom it is given, as is plainly evident in the case of children.

We know that, when it is not given, it is withheld by a
just judgment of God.

---

41 Phil. 3.16;15; 2 John 1.6.
42 Ps. 85.11.
43 Rom. 9.11.
44 Rom. 5.12.

We know that 'we shall all stand before the judgment seat of Christ, that every one may receive the proper things of the body, according as he hath done whether it be good or evil,'[45] not according to what he would have done if he had lived longer.

We know that even children will receive either good or evil according to what they have done in the body. For they have done it, not by themselves but through those who answer for them when they are said to renounce the Devil and to believe in God. For this reason they are counted in the number of the faithful, as being referred to in the statement of the Lord when He said: 'He that believeth and is baptized shall be saved.' Therefore, those who do not receive this sacrament are subject to what follows: 'But he that believeth not shall be condemned.'[46] Consequently, even those, as I said, who die at that tender age are judged according to what they have done in the body, that is, in the time they have been in the body, when they believed or did not believe through the mouths and hearts of those who carried them, when they were baptized or were not baptized, when they ate the flesh of Christ or did not eat it, when they drank His Blood or did not drink it—according to these things which they have done in the body, not according to what they would have done if they had lived longer in this world.

We know that the dead who die in the Lord are blessed,[47] and they have no concern with what they would have done if they had lived a longer time.

We know that those who believe in the Lord from their own heart do this of their own will and free choice.

We know that we who now believe act with an upright faith when we pray to God for those who refuse to believe, that they may will to do so.

---

45 Rom. 14.10; 2 Cor. 5.10.
46 Mark 16.16.
47 Apoc. 14.13.

We know that when some of these do believe we are accustomed, and we ought, to thank God uprightly and sincerely for this as a blessing from Him.

You recognize, I think, that among these things which I said we know I have not intended to enumerate everything which belongs to the Catholic faith but only those points which have to do with this question of the grace of God: whether this grace precedes or follows the will of man. That is, I wanted to explain more fully whether it is given to us because we will or whether God effects through it that we should will. If, then, you also, my brother, hold with us that those twelve statements of what I said we know belong to the correct Catholic faith, I give thanks to God, which certainly I could not truthfully do unless your holding them were a result of the grace of God; and if you do hold them, there is not a single difference left between us on this matter.

To run over these twelve with a brief explanation, how can grace follow the merit of the human will when it is given even to infants who cannot yet will or not will? How can the merits of the will even in adults be said to precede grace, if grace, in order to be truly grace, is not given according to our merits? Pelagius himself had such fear of this statement that he did not hesitate to condemn those who say that the grace of God is given according to our merits, lest he should be condemned by Catholic judges. How can the grace of God be identified with the nature of free will or with the law and doctrine when Pelagius himself repudiated that statement, thereby admitting without question that the grace of God is given to separate acts, especially in those who enjoy the use of free will?

How is it possible to say that all men would have received it if those to whom it is not given did not reject it of their own will, since 'God will have all men to be saved,'[48] when

48 1 Tim. 2.4.

there are many children to whom it is not given and many die without it, although they have no will opposed to it? Sometimes, even, their parents are in great desire and haste, with the ministers willing and ready, but as God does not will it, it is not given to them, and they die suddenly before it is given, although all haste was made for them to receive it? From this it is clear that those who resist this clear truth do not in the least understand the meaning of the saying that 'God will have all men to be saved,' when so many are not saved, not because they do not will it, but because God does not, which is evident without any shadow of doubt in the case of children. But, just as that saying: 'In Christ all shall be made alive'[49] although so many are punished with eternal death—means that all who receive eternal life receive it only in Christ, so also the saying, 'God will have all men to be saved'—although He wills that so many should not be saved—means surely that all who are saved would not be so without His will, and if there is any other possible way of understanding those words of the Apostle, it cannot contradict this most evident truth by which we see that so many men are not saved because God does not will it, although men do.

How can the human will deserve to have grace given to it, if it is given freely[50] to those to whom it is given, that it may be truly grace? What weight can the merits of the human will have in the matter, when those to whom this grace is not given differ by no merit, by no act of will, from those to whom it is given, but share with them the same just reason for receiving it, yet it is not given through a just judgment of God—for 'there is no injustice with God'?[51] Thus, those to whom it is given are to understand how freely

---

49 1 Cor. 15.22.
50 The argument turns on the connection between *gratuita,* 'freely given,' and *gratia,* 'grace,' which is not apparent in English.
51 Rom. 9.14.

it is given to them, when it could equally justly be withheld, since it is justly withheld from those who have the same claim to it.

How is it possible to attribute to anything but the grace of God the will not only to believe, but also to persevere to the end, when the very end of this life depends on the power of God, not of man, and God could certainly bestow on one who would not persevere the blessing of hurrying him out of the body, 'lest wickedness should alter his understanding'?[52] For man will not receive either good or evil except according to what he has done in the body, not according to what he would have done if he had lived longer.

How can anyone say that the grace of God is not given to some children, but is given to others, destined to die, because God foresees the future will which they would have had if they had lived, when each one receives either good or evil, as the Apostle has defined, according to what he has done in the body, not according to what he would have done if he had remained longer in the body? How can men be judged according to the future will which, it is said, they would have had if they had been longer detained in the flesh, when Scripture says: 'Blessed are the dead who die in the Lord'? Undoubtedly, their happiness is neither certain nor secure if God will also judge the things they have not done, but which they would have done if they had had a more extended life. So, also, he who is carried off 'lest wickedness should alter his understanding' receives no benefit, because he pays the penalty for that very wickedness from which, when it threatened him, he has probably been removed; and we should not rejoice over those who, as we know, have died in upright faith and a good life, because they may be judged according to some wicked deeds which they would perhaps have committed if they had lived. Those

---

52 Wisd. 4.11.

who have ended their life in unbelief and depraved morals should not be a subject of grief and detestation to us, because, perhaps, if they had lived they would have done penance and lived religiously, and so should be judged by this. In that case the whole book *On Mortality* by the most blessed martyr Cyprian[53] is to be censured and rejected, for in it his entire contention is that we know we should give thanks for the faithful who die a good death because they are taken away from the temptations of this life and will henceforth abide in assured blessedness. But, since this is not false and the dead who die in the Lord certainly are blessed, there should be only mockery and execration for the erroneous opinion that men are to be judged according to their future will—which dying men will not have.

How can they say that it is a denial of the free choice of the will to admit that every man who believes in God in his heart believes only through his own free will, when those who attack the grace of God through which the will is free to choose and do good are, rather, the ones who attack the freedom of the will? How can they say that the fulfillment of the words of Scripture: 'The will is prepared by the Lord,'[54] is accomplished by the law of God and the doctrine of the Scriptures and not, rather, by the secret prompting of the grace of God, when we pray to God with upright faith that those who contradict that same doctrine and refuse to believe may be willing to believe?

How can God wait on the will of men that they to whom He gives grace may forestall Him, when we give Him thanks —not without good reason—for those to whom He has advanced mercy, although they did not believe in Him and persecuted His doctrine with an evil will; whom He has converted to Himself with omnipotent ease, and whom from

---

53 *De mortalitate* 7.20-21.
54 Prov. 8.35 (Septuagint).

unbelievers He has made willing believers? Why give Him thanks for this if He has not done it? Why do we glorify Him in proportion to the joy we feel for those who had refused to believe but who have become believers, if the human will is not changed for the better by divine grace? The Apostle Paul says: 'I was unknown by face to the Churches of Judea which are in Christ, but they had heard only that he who persecuted us in times past doth now preach the faith which once he impugned; and they magnified God in me.'[55] Why did they magnify God if God, in the goodness of His grace, had not converted the heart of that man to Himself, when, as he himself admits, he had 'obtained mercy of the Lord to be faithful'[56] to that faith which once he impugned? And by that word which he used, whom, if not God, does he declare to have wrought this great good? What is the meaning of 'they magnified God' except 'they pronounced God great in me?' But how could they pronounce God great if He had not wrought that great deed of Paul's conversion, and how could He have done it but by changing his unwillingness into willingness to believe?

Assuredly, it is clear from those twelve statements—and you will not be allowed to deny that they form part of Catholic belief—that we confess the effect of them, separately and together, is to establish that the will of man is forestalled by the grace of God and that it is prepared by grace rather than rewarded in receiving it. But if you claim that any one of the twelve is not true—and I commend the number to you as making it easier to commit them to memory and to retain them more accurately—do not be slow to write and let me know, and I will answer you with whatever skill the Lord may give me. For my part I do not believe that you are a Pelagian heretic, and I am so anxious for you not to be

55 Gal. 1.22-24.
56 1 Cor. 7.25.

one that I want none of this error to pass into you or to be left in you.

Perhaps, however, among these twelve statements you will find something which you think can be either denied or doubted, and which you may consequently force me to discuss more painstakingly. But surely you will not forbid the Church to pray for unbelievers that they may be believers, for those who refuse to believe that they may be willing to believe, for those who are at variance with God's law and doctrine that they may submit to His law and doctrine, that God may give them what He promised by the Prophet: 'A heart for understanding Him and ears for hearing,'[57] which certainly those had received of whom the Saviour Himself spoke when He said: 'He that hath ears to hear, let him hear.'[58] And when you hear the priest of God at His altar exhorting the people to pray to God, and himself praying in a loud voice, that He would compel the unbelieving nations to come to His faith, will you not answer: 'Amen'? Or will you offer arguments opposed to the integrity of this faith? Will you object loudly or secretly that blessed Cyprian was wrong in this when he teaches us[59] to pray for the enemies of the Christian faith that they may be converted to it?

Finally, will you reproach the Apostle Paul for entertaining such wishes for the unbelieving Jews? Of them he says: 'The good will of my heart, indeed, and my prayer to God is for them unto salvation.'[60] He also says to the Thessalonians: 'For the rest, brethren, pray for us that the word of the Lord may run and may be glorified even as among you; that we may be delivered from importunate and evil men, for all men have not faith.'[61] How else could the word of God run

---

57 Cf. Bar. 3.21.
58 Matt. 13.9; Mark 4.9; Luke 8.8.
59 *De Dominica oratione* 17.
60 Rom. 10.1.
61 2 Thess. 3.1,2.

and be glorified except by the conversion to the faith of those
to whom it is preached, when he says to present believers:
'Even as among you'? Surely he knows that this is effected
by Him to whom he wishes prayer to be made that this may
be so, and also that he may be delivered from importunate
and evil men who certainly were not likely to believe because
of those who prayed. It is for this reason that he adds: 'For
all men have not faith,' as if to say: 'The word of God will
not be glorified among all, even at your prayer,' because
those who were likely to believe were the ones 'who were
ordained to life everlasting,'[62] predestined 'unto the adoption
of children through Jesus Christ unto himself,' and chosen
'in him before the foundation of the world.'[63] No one is so
unlearned, so carnal, so slow of wit as not to see that God
does what He commands us to ask Him to do.

These and other divine testimonies, which it would take
too long to enumerate, show that God by His grace takes
away the stony heart[64] from unbelievers and forestalls merit
in men of good will in such wise that their will is prepared
by antecedent grace, but not that grace is given through
antecedent merit of the will. This is shown both by thanksgiving and by prayer: prayer for unbelievers; thanksgiving
for believers. Prayer is to be made to Him that He may do
what we ask; thanksgiving is to be offered when He has done
it. Hence, the same Apostle says to the Ephesians: 'Wherefore
I also hearing of your faith that is in Christ Jesus, and of your
love towards all the saints, cease not to give thanks for you.'[65]

But now we are speaking of the very beginnings when
men who were opposed and hostile are converted to God,
and begin to will what before they did not will and to have

---

62 Acts 13.48.
63 Eph. 1.5,4.
64 Ezech. 11.19; 36.26.
65 Eph. 1.15,16.

the faith which they did not have. That this may be accomplished in them, prayer is offered for them, even though no prayer is offered by them, for 'how shall they call on him in whom they have not believed?'[66] But, when what is asked has been accomplished, thanksgiving is made both for them and by them to Him who has accomplished it. In the matter of prayers which the faithful offer for themselves and for other faithful that they may advance on the course which they have begun, and of thanksgiving for the advance they make, I think there is no point of controversy with you, for you and I are at one in that controversy against the Pelagians. They, indeed, attribute everything which has to do with a faithful and devout life in man to the free choice of the will, so as to imagine that we have it of ourselves; we do not have to ask it of God. But you, if what I hear of you is true, will not admit that the beginning of faith, in which is the beginning of a good, that is, of a religiously inclined, will, is the gift of God, and you contend that we derive the beginning of belief from ourselves, while you agree that God by His grace gives the other gifts of the devout life to those who ask, seek and knock according to their faith.[67] In this you do not observe that prayer is made to God for unbelievers that they may believe, since God also gives faith, and thanksgiving is offered to God for those who do believe for the same reason that God also gives faith.

Therefore, to bring this talk with you to an end sometime, if you say that prayer is not to be made for those who refuse to believe, that they may be willing to believe; if you say that thanks are not to be given to God, when those who refused to believe have become willing to believe, you must be dealt with in some other way that you may not remain in the wrong, or, if you persist in being wrong, that you may not

---

66 Rom. 10.14.
67 Matt. 7.7,8; Luke 11.9,10.

drive others into error. But if, as I think more likely, you see
and you agree that we ought to pray to God, and we usually
do, for those who refuse to believe, that they may be willing
to believe, and for those who oppose and contradict His law
and doctrine, that they may yield to it and follow it; if you
see and you agree that we ought to thank God, and we
usually do, for such as are converted to His faith and doctrine,
whose wills changed from opposition to consent—then you
must necessarily confess without doubting that the will of
man is forestalled by the grace of God, and that when we
pray to God to do this He makes men will the good which
they had not willed; and we know that it is right and just
for us to give Him thanks when He has done this. May the
Lord give you understanding in all things, lord and brother.

218. Augustine to his beloved lord and dearly cherished son, Palatinus[1] (426 or 427)

Your stronger and more fruitful intercourse with the Lord
our God has brought us great joy. You have chosen his
instruction from youth that you may find wisdom unto your
grey hairs.[2] 'For the understanding of a man is grey hairs
and a spotless life is old age.'[3] May the Lord grant you this
as you ask, seek and knock, who knows how to give good
gifts to His children.[4] Although advisers and advice are yours
in plenty, to bring you to the way of salvation and of eternal
glory, and although the grace itself of Christ has spoken to
you so fruitfully in your heart, I offer this additional en-

1 A young man who had just started to live a religious life and needed
some warning against Pelagian ideas.
2 Eccli. 6.18.
3 Wisd. 4.8,9.
4 Matt. 7.7,8,11; Luke 11.9,10,13.

couragement in returning your greeting as a token of the affection which I owe you, and I send it not so much to rouse you from sloth or sleep as to challenge you and urge you on as you run your course.

You must, my son, have wisdom to persevere as you have had wisdom to choose. Let this be the object of your wisdom to know whose gift it is.[5] 'Commit thy way to the Lord and trust in him; and he will do it. He will bring forth thy justice as the light, and thy judgment as the noonday.'[6] 'He will make thy courses straight and he will bring forward thy ways in peace.'[7] As you have despised what you once hoped for in the world, that you might not glory in the multitude of your riches,[8] which you had begun to covet in the fashion of the children of this world, so now, in taking up the yoke of the Lord and His burden, do not trust in your own strength and His yoke will be sweet, His burden light.[9] Those 'that trust in their own strength and those that glory in the multitude of their riches'[10] are both rebuked, as you know, in the psalm. And so you did not yet have glory in your riches, but you very wisely put away what you were desirous of having. Take care not to let trust in your own strength steal upon you, for you are a man, and 'Cursed be every one that putteth his hope in man.'[11] But put your trust fully and with your whole heart in God and He will be your strength; trust Him lovingly and gratefully and say to Him humbly and faithfully: 'I will love thee, O Lord, my strength,'[12] because that very charity of God, which when perfected in us 'casteth

5 Wisd. 8.21.
6 Ps. 36.5,6.
7 Prov. 4.27.
8 Ps. 48.7.
9 Matt. 11.29,30.
10 Ps. 48.7.
11 Cf. Jer. 17.5.
12 Ps. 17.2.

out fear,'[13] is poured forth in our hearts, not by our own strength, that is, human strength, but, as the Apostle says, 'by the Holy Spirit who is given to us.'[14]

Watch, therefore, and pray, that you enter not into temptation.[15] Indeed, that very prayer warns you that you need the help of your Lord that you may not put your hope of living a good life in yourself. For you no longer pray that you may receive the riches and honors of the present life or any object of human vanity, but that you may not enter into temptation. Obviously, if a man could endow himself with this by willing it, he would not ask it in prayer. Therefore, if the will sufficed to prevent us from entering into temptation, we should not have to pray for it, but, if we had no will, we should not be able to pray. Granted, then, that we will it, let us pray that we may be able to do what we have willed, when, by His gift, we have attained the right wisdom. The good work that you have begun is a subject for thanksgiving. 'For what hast thou that thou hast not received? And if thou hast received it, take care not to glory as if thou hadst not received it,'[16] that is, as if you could have it of yourself. Knowing, then, from whom you have received it, ask of Him to accomplish it as He gave you to begin it. 'With fear, therefore, and trembling, work out your salvation. For it is God who worketh in you both to will and to accomplish, according to his good will;'[17] since 'the will is prepared by the Lord,'[18] and by Him 'shall the steps of a man be directed and he shall like well his way.'[19] This holy thought will keep you that your wisdom may be piety, that is, that you may have your

13 1 John 4.18.
14 Rom. 5.5.
15 Matt. 26.41; Mark 14.38; Luke 22.46.
16 Cf. 1 Cor. 4.7.
17 Phil. 2.12,13.
18 Prov. 8.35 (Septuagint).
19 Ps. 36.23.

goodness from God and may not be ungrateful to the grace of Christ.

Your parents long for you, but in the spirit of faith they congratulate the better hope which you have begun to have in the Lord. We, however, whether you are physically present or absent, desire to have you in one Spirit,[20] through whom 'His charity is poured forth in our hearts,' so that, wherever our bodily presence may be, our souls cannot be separated. We have received with great pleasure the hair shirts which you sent, whereby you have first reminded us of practising and preserving humility in our prayers.

219. *Aurelius, Augustine, Florentius and Secundus,[1] bishops, give greeting in the Lord to their beloved lords and honorable brothers and fellow priests Proculus and Cillenius[2] (426 or 427)*

Our son, Leporius,[3] who had been deservedly and properly disciplined by your Holiness for his presumptuous error, came to us after he had been expelled by you, and, finding him wholesomely troubled, we have taken him in with the intention of setting him right and healing him. For, as you have obeyed the Apostle by 'rebuking the unquiet,' so have we by 'comforting the feeble-minded and supporting the weak.'[4] When 'a man is overtaken in any fault,'[5] and that no slight one, and one concerning the only-begotten Son of God, because, 'in the beginning was the Word, and the Word was

---

20 Phil. 1.27; 1 Cor. 12.9; Eph. 2.18.

1 African bishops.
2 Gallic bishops.
3 A monk who had been expelled by the Gauls for his Nestorian ideas on the Incarnation.
4 1 Thess. 5.14.
5 Gal. 6.1.

with God and the Word was God,'[6] but, 'when the fullness
of the time was come,'[7] 'the Word was made flesh and dwelt
among us,'[8] if that man were to deny that God was made
man, his wisdom would not embrace right objects nor would
he understand the truth. Manifestly, the reason could be his
fear lest some unworthy change or depreciation might come
upon the divine substance by which He is equal to the
Father,[9] but he does not see that he is thereby introducing a
fourth person into the Trinity and that is entirely opposed
to the integrity of faith and the truth of the Catholic creed.
With the Lord's help, as best we could, we have instructed
the brother 'in the spirit of meekness,' more particularly
after he saw that the 'vessel of election'[10] added: 'considering
thyself, lest thou also be tempted.'[11] And lest any should
rejoice at having attained an advanced spirituality so as to
imagine that they could no longer be tempted as men, he
added still further the wholesome and peaceful sentiment that
we should bear one another's burdens, because thus we shall
fulfill the law of Christ: 'For if any man think he is something
whereas he is nothing, he seduceth himself,'[12] beloved and
honorable brothers.

But perhaps we should never have been able to complete
his conversion if you had not previously condemned the
fallacious ideas he held. Therefore, the same Lord, our
physician, making use of His vessels and ministers, who said:
'I will strike and I will heal,'[13] struck his swelling pride through
you and healed his suffering through us; the same governor

6 John 1.1.
7 Gal. 4.4.
8 John 1.14.
9 John 5.18; Phil. 2.6.
10 Acts 9.15.
11 Gal. 6.1.
12 Gal. 6.2,3.
13 Deut. 32.39.

and provider of His house destroyed through you what was badly built, and built up through us what was to be erected; the same loving husbandman rooted out, through you, the sterile and harmful plants of His estate, and planted, through us, what is useful and fertile. Let us not, therefore, give glory to ourselves, but to His mercy, for both we and our words are in His hand.[14] And just as our humility has praised your ministry in the case of this aforementioned son of ours, so let your Holiness give thanks for our ministry. With a fatherly and brotherly heart receive him from us, corrected with merciful meekness, as we received him from you, chastised with merciful severity. And although your course of action is different from ours, one charity has made both courses necessary to the salvation of our brother: 'For one God has done it, since God is charity.'[15]

As he has been welcomed by us in person, let him be welcomed by you in his letter. We have thought it advisable to sign his letter with our own hand as a testimonial to him. After being warned by us, he saw easily that God became man because 'the Word was made flesh, and the Word was God,'[16] and the Apostle taught him that He accomplished this, not by destroying what He was, but by taking on what He was not, for 'He emptied himself,' not losing the form of God, but 'taking the form of a servant.'[17] When he refused to admit that God was born of a woman, that God was crucified, and that He suffered other human woes, what he feared was that divinity might be believed to have suffered change in becoming man, or to have been tainted by its admixture with man; his fear arose from his filial love, but his mistake from his lack of advertence. His filial love saw that divinity can

14 Deut. 33.3.
15 1 John 4.8.
16 John 1.14,1.
17 Phil. 2.6,7.

undergo no change, but in his inadvertence he assumed that
the Son of man could be separated from the Son of God, so
that there would be a difference between the one and the
other, and that either Christ was neither of them or that
there were two Christs. But after he had recognized that the
Word of God, that is, the only-begotten Son of God, became
the Son of man without either nature being changed into
the other, but both remaining with their own substance, so
that God in man suffered human vicissitudes while His divinity
remained unchanged in Him, he confessed without any fear
that Christ is God and man, having a greater fear of the
addition of a fourth person to the Trinity than of any loss
of substance in the divinity. We do not doubt that your
Charity accepts the news of his correction with gratitude and
that you give notice of it to those whom his error scandalized,
because those who came here with him have been corrected
and healed with him. This is hereby made known by their
signatures which were written in our presence. It remains
for your Beatitude to be so kind as to show your joy by your
reply and thereby to give us joy in turn. We pray, beloved
and honorable brothers, that you may enjoy good health in
the Lord and that you will remember us.

*220. Augustine to his son, lord Boniface,[1] that he may be
guarded by God's mercy for his welfare now
and forever (427)[2]*

Up to the present I have not been able to find a more
trustworthy man to carry my letter, or one who had readier
access to your presence, than the servant and minister of

---

1 Cf. Letter 189 n. 1.
2 This letter was written after his disgrace, but before he invited the
Vandals to Africa.

Christ whom the Lord has now provided, the deacon Paul, a man very dear to both of us. Thus I am able to say something to you, not about the power and position which you hold in this evil age, nor about the well-being of your corruptible and mortal body—because that is a passing thing and it is always uncertain how long it will last—but about the salvation which Christ has promised us. For the sake of it He was dishonored and crucified on earth that He might teach us to despise rather than cherish the goods of this world, and to love and to expect from Him what He showed forth in His Resurrection, for He rose again 'from the dead, and he dieth now no more; death shall no more have dominion over him.'[3]

I know you have no lack of men devoted to you, according to the life of this world, and who, according to it, give you advice, sometimes useful, sometimes useless, because they are only human and they do what they can in the light of today's wisdom, unaware of what may happen on the morrow. But it is not easy for anyone to advise you according to God, that your soul may not be lost, not because you have no friends to do this, but because it is difficult for them to find a time to speak to you of such things. I have always had a great longing to do so, but I have never found the time or the place to deal with you as I ought to deal with a man whom I love so deeply in Christ. For you know how I was when you saw me at Hippo at the time of your kind visit to me, how I could scarcely speak through fatigue and bodily exhaustion. But now, my son, listen to me while I speak to you by letter, at least, a message I was never able to send to you in the midst of your dangers because of the risk to the bearer and the need of caution that my letter should not fall into the hands of those whom I would not have it reach. I ask you to pardon me if you think I have been more fearful than I should have been; however, I admit it, I was fearful.

---

3 Rom. 6.9.

Hear me, then, or, rather, hear the Lord our God speaking through me, His weak minister; recall what you were when your first wife of pious memory was still in the flesh and how, just after her death, you recoiled from the vanity of this world and longed to enter the service of God.[4] We know, we are witnesses of what you said to us at Tubunae[5] about your state of mind and your intention, when brother Alypius and I were alone with you. I do not think the earthly cares with which you are overwhelmed have prevailed so far that they could entirely wipe out that memory from you. You wanted, in fact, to give up all the public business in which you were engaged, to retire into a holy retreat and to live the life of a servant of God as the monks live it. What kept you from doing it? Nothing but the thought, urged by us, of the great benefit to the churches of Christ of what you were doing, provided you did it with the sole intention of defending them from the incursions of barbarians,[6] so that they might 'lead a quiet and peaceable life,' as the Apostle says, 'in all piety and chastity';[7] but also on condition that you sought nothing from this world beyond what was necessary to sustain your own life and that of your household, fastening about you the girdle of the most chaste continence, and putting on, along with the armor of the body, the surer and stronger armor of the spirit.

While we were rejoicing over this proposal of yours, you sailed away and you married a wife. Your voyage was a matter of obedience, which, according to the Apostle, you owed to higher authority,'[8] but you would not have married a wife if you had not been overcome by concupiscence and given up

---

4 That is, to become a monk.
5 A town of Mauretania, modern Tobna.
6 Not the Vandals or Goths, but African tribes, as is indicated later.
7 1 Tim. 2.2.
8 Rom. 13.1.

the continence you had undertaken to keep. When I heard it, I admit I was dumbfounded with amazement, but I found some consolation for my sorrow when I heard that you had refused to marry the woman until she first became a Catholic.[9] In spite of that, the heresy of those who deny the true Son of God had such influence in your household that your daughter was baptized by them. But now, if the rumors that have reached us are not false—and would that they were false!—that even maidens consecrated to God have been rebaptized by those same heretics, with what floods of tears should we weep over so great an evil! People are also saying that even your wife is not enough for you, but that you have defiled yourself by intercourse with some unnamed concubines. It may be that this is a lie.

What shall I say of the many and great evils, matters of public knowledge, which have resulted from your actions since your marriage? You are a Christian, you have a conscience, you fear God. Look into yourself and you will find what I shrink from saying of the many evil deeds for which you ought to do penance. I believe this is why the Lord spares you and delivers you from all dangers, that you may do penance as it should be done, but on condition that you hearken to what is written: 'Delay not to be converted to the Lord, and defer it not from day to day.'[10] You say that your cause is just.[11] I am no judge of that, as I am unable to hear both sides, but whatever your cause, about which at present there is no need of inquiry or discussion, can you deny before God that you would not have become involved in these straits if you had not loved the goods of this world,

9 She was an Arian named Pelagia, and relapsed into her heresy after her marriage.
10 Eccli. 5.8.
11 He had been recalled from Africa in disgrace by Empress Placidia at the treacherous instigation of Aetius, who later betrayed her, also.

which, like the servant of God we knew you formerly to be, you should have despised entirely and have counted as nothing? If they were offered, you should have accepted and used them to further your love of God; if they were denied or entrusted to you to administer, you should not have sought them out with such eagerness as to let yourself be drawn into the present dilemma in which, because vanity is loved, evil is done, not, in many cases, by you, but more on account of you, and because some things are feared which injure for a short time, if they do injure, other things are done which really injure for eternity.

To cite one of several instances, who can fail to see that many men rally around you to protect your power and your personal safety, who may all be faithful to you and you may not have to fear treachery from any of them, yet their aim is to attain through you to those goods which they love for worldly motives, not for the sake of God, and thus you are forced to satisfy in others the covetous desires which you should have curbed and controlled in yourself? To accomplish this, you are obliged to let many things be done which are displeasing to God. And not even this way is such covetousness satisfied, for it is easier to cut it off in those who love God than to satisfy it partially in those who love the world. It is for this reason that Scripture says: 'Love not the world nor the things which are in the world. If any man love the world, the charity of the Father is not in him; for all that is in the world is the concupiscence of the flesh and the concupiscence of the eyes, and the pride of life, which is not of the Father but is of the world. And the world passeth away and the concupiscence thereof; but he that doth the will of God abideth forever, as God abideth forever.'[12] When will you be able, with so many armed men whose cupidity has to be humored, whose barbarity is to be feared, when, I repeat,

_____
12 1 John 2.15-17.

will you be able, I say not to satisfy the covetousness of those who love the world, which is utterly impossible, but to appease it partially in order to prevent the loss of everything, without doing what God forbids and what He threatens to punish in those who do it? As a consequence, you see that there has been so much pillage that hardly anything, however worthless, is left to be plundered.

What shall I say of the ravaging of Africa, which is being carried on by African barbarians with no one to oppose them as long as you are so absorbed in your own difficulties that you take not steps to ward off this disaster? Who would have believed, who would have feared that the barbarians could have dared so much, advanced so far, ravaged so widely, looted so much property, made a desert of so many places which had been thickly peopled, when Boniface had been appointed Count of the Household and of Africa, with so great an army and with such power, whereas while a tribune, with a few provincial forces, he had subdued all those tribes by aggressive and repressive measures? Was it not common talk that, as soon as you took on the authority of count, the African barbarians would not only be subjugated but would become tributaries of the Roman Empire? And now you see how men's hopes have been cheated by contrary happenings. There is no need of speaking any more to you about this, for you can think of more things than I can say.

Perhaps your answer to this is that the blame is to be laid, instead, on those who have injured you, who have not given you the recognition befitting the strength of your administration, but have done the very opposite. These pleas I am unable to entertain and to judge; rather, it is for you to look at and to look into your own case, which, as you know, concerns your relations with God, not with any men whatever. If you live as one of Christ's faithful, He is the one you ought to fear to offend. I am thinking of higher reasons which should induce men to attribute to their own sins the fact that Africa endures such misfortunes. However, I do not want you to be included in the number of those evil and wicked men whom God uses to scourge His chosen ones with temporal punishments, for He reserves for these wicked men, whose malice He justly uses to inflict temporal evils on others, eternal torments if they do not amend their lives. As for you, turn your attention to God; meditate on Christ who has bestowed such great goods and endured such great wrongs. All who wish to belong to His kingdom and to live a life of eternal bliss with Him and under Him love even their enemies, do good to those who hate them, and pray for those by whom they are persecuted;[13] and if at any time they display a harsh severity in the exercise of discipline, they do not for that fail to preserve the most sincere affection. If, then, benefits, however earthly and transitory, have been conferred on you by the Roman Empire, for it is itself an earthly not a heavenly power and it can only bestow what it has at its disposal, if, then, these goods have been conferred on you, do not render evil for good; nor, if evils have been inflicted on you, render evil for evil.[14] Which of the two is the case I neither wish to discuss nor am I able to judge. I am speaking to a Christian. Do not render evil for good or evil for evil.

You say, perhaps: 'What would you have me do in such straits?' If you ask my advice concerning your worldly interests, namely, how your transitory safety may be secured and your power and wealth may either be preserved as they now are or increased, I do not know what answer to give you, for, indeed, such uncertainties cannot produce a specific plan.[15] But if you consult me on a matter concerning God, how to save your soul from loss, and if you fear the words of Truth

---

13 Matt. 5.44; Luke 6.27,28.
14 Rom. 12.17; 1 Thess. 5.15; 1 Peter 3.9.
15 Terence, *Eunuchus* 57-63.

when He says: 'What doth it profit a man if he gain the whole world and suffer the loss of his own soul?'[16] I do indeed have something to say; I have advice which you should hear. There is no need of my saying anything different from what I said above: 'Love not the world, nor the things which are in the world. If any man love the world, the charity of the Father is not in him. For all that is in the world is the concupiscence of the flesh and the concupiscence of the eyes and the pride of life, which is not of the Father but is of the world. And the world passeth away and the concupiscence thereof, but he that doth the will of God abideth forever, as God abideth forever.'[17] Here is your advice; seize it and act upon it. Let this show whether you are a strong man; conquer the impulses which make you love the world; do penance for your past misdeeds when you were overcome by your impulses and taken captive by vain passions. If you take this advice, if you hold to it and keep it, you will attain to the goods which are certain and keep your soul safe as you pass through present uncertainties.

But perhaps you ask me again how you are to do that while you are entangled in such great distresses in this world. Pray earnestly and speak to God in the words of the psalm: 'Deliver me from my necessities.'[18] For those necessities are brought to an end when the passions are overcome. He who has heard your prayers and ours as we prayed for you that you might be delivered from so many great perils of visible and corporeal wars, where the sole danger is to this life doomed to end sometime—but the soul does not perish unless it is held captive by malign passions—will Himself hear your prayer that you may win an invisible and spiritual victory over your interior and invisible enemies, that is, those same

16 Matt. 16.26; Mark 8.36; Luke 9.25.
17 1 John 2.15-17.
18 Ps. 24.17.

passions; and that by so using this world as if you used it not[19] you may do good with its good things instead of becoming evil yourself. For these things are good in themselves and are not given to men except by Him who has power over all things in heaven and on earth. Hence, they are given to the good that they may not be considered evil, and they are given to the evil that they may not be considered the great or supreme good. In like manner, they are taken away from the good in order to test them; from the evil, in order to punish them.

Who does not know, who is so foolish as not to see, that the health of this mortal body and its perishable parts, strength and victory over men who are our enemies, and honor and temporal power and all such earthly goods are given equally to the good and the evil, and taken away equally from the good and the evil? But the health of the soul, together with the immortality of the body, and the strength of justice, and victory over the passions which are our enemies, and glory and honor and peace forever are granted only to the good. These are the things, therefore, to love, to desire, and to seek by every possible means. To secure them and hold them, give alms, pour out your prayers, practise fasting, as far as you can do it without bodily harm, but withdraw your love from those earthly goods, however abundant they may be. Use them to do much good through their means, but do no evil because of them. All such things will surely pass away, but good works do not pass away even though performed by means of goods which do pass away.

If you had no wife, I should tell you what we told you at Tubunae, namely, that you should live in chastity and continence, and I should add what we then forbade you to do, that you should withdraw from those warlike pursuits as far

19 1 Cor. 7.31.

as might be without risk to the peace of mankind; that you should devote your time to that life you then desired to lead in the company of holy men, where the soldiers of Christ wage war in silence, not for the purpose of killing men, but of overthrowing 'principalities and powers and the spirits of wickedness.'[20] These are the enemies whom the saints conquer, enemies whom they cannot see, yet they conquer their invisible enemies by triumphing over the objects of their senses. I cannot now urge you to that life, for your wife is an obstacle to it, and without her consent it is not allowable for you to live in continence, because, although you should not have married her after what you said at Tubunae, she nevertheless married you in all innocence and sincerity, knowing nothing of all that. I wish you might be able to induce her to live in continence so that without hindrance you might render to God what you owe Him. But if you are unable to reach that agreement with her, at least preserve your conjugal chastity and ask God to deliver you from your necessities, so that you may be able to do at some other time what you cannot do now. However, that you may love God, you must not love the world; even in the midst of warfare, if you still have to engage in it, hold fast to the faith, seek peace, do good with the goods of this world, and do no evil for the sake of this world's goods. A wife is not or ought not to be a hindrance to that. It is my affection for you, dearly beloved son, that has prompted me to write you thus, because I love you according to God, not according to this world, and because when I call to mind what is written: 'Rebuke a wise man and he will love thee, rebuke a fool and it will increase his hatred for thee,'[21] I certainly ought to think of you as a wise man, not a fool.

---

20 Cf. Eph. 6.12.
21 Prov. 9.8 (Septuagint).

221. *Quodvultdeus,*[1] *a deacon, to Bishop Augustine, his deservedly revered lord and truly saintly father* *(426 or 427)*

For a long time I was afraid and I kept putting off to another time this daring act of mine, but the thing that chiefly spurred me on, as they say, was the kindness of your Beatitude, so universally displayed. Considering that I was even more afraid that the Lord might judge me proud for not asking, indolent for not seeking, and slothful for not knocking, I might have believed that my will was sufficient for me up to a certain point, if I had not been able to attain my object, but since I know for certain that heavenly grace has opened the door of divine speech[2] to your Reverence, and that your holy mind, possessed by Christ, is ready to open it not only to those who wish it but even to those who do not, and to urge them not to be slow in entering in, I shall not interrupt your Reverence's busy life by idle chatter, but shall make known briefly the much desired object of my petition.

From my own observation I gather that some of the clerics of this populous city are uninformed and I submit what I ask to the consideration of your Holiness as a subject of discussion which would be advantageous to the clergy. For I presume, unworthy as I am, that I shall share in the privilege of all who profit by your spiritual labors, deservedly revered lord and truly saintly father. Therefore, I ask your Piety please to make a list of all the heresies that have existed and still exist, from the time when the Christian religion received the name promised as its inheritance: what errors they have introduced and still do introduce; what views they hold against the Catholic Church; what they hold about

---

1 A cleric of the church at Carthage, whose request was later complied

faith, the Trinity, baptism, penance, Christ as man, Christ as God, the Resurrection, the New and Old Testaments, and, in general, every point in which they differ from the faith; which heresies have baptism, which ones do not, so that the Church in baptizing after them does not rebaptize; how she receives heretics when they come to her, and what answers she makes to each according to law, authority, and reason.

Your Beatitude must not believe that I am such a fool as not to realize how many and how enormous the volumes needed to solve these questions would be. But that is not what I ask; I do not doubt it has been done in great detail, but I want something brief, to the point, a summary. I ask that the teaching of each heresy be set down, and that as much as is needful for instruction of the contrary teaching of the Catholic Church be set under it, so that, if anyone wants fuller, more detailed, more extensive information on any objection or conviction, he may be referred from this memorandum, derived, so to speak, from all sources, to those rich and splendid volumes in which the subject is known to have been treated by various authors, and especially by your Reverence in the same field. Such a memorandum will be adequate for the learned and the unlearned, the idle and the busy, and to those promoted to the ministry of any rank in the Church from any other rank, so long as he who reads much remembers the facts briefly, and, if forgetful, is reminded by the summary so as to know what to hold, what to avoid, what to refuse to do, what to try to do. But, perhaps, if what I think is true, even this short work against the evil minds and deceitful lips of calumniators[3] will not fail to be a glory in your crown among its other splendors, and those to whom the field of deceit is wide open, being hemmed in by the strong and all-embracing boundaries of faith, and assailed on all sides by every kind of weapon of truth, or even

---

3 Ps. 11.3,4; 16.1; 30.19.

laid low by one inclusive weapon, may not dare to breathe out their carrion breath.

I see how vexatious I am to a holy old man who is thinking of higher things, administering more important things and suffering bodily ailments. But I ask it by the Lord Christ who has ungrudgingly granted you a share of His wisdom, that you may do this favor to the unlearned in the Church, for you recognize that you are a debtor to the wise and the unwise, and with right and justice you will say: 'See that I have not labored for myself only but for all that seek out the truth.'[4] I could have added many pleading prayers and have joined crowds of the unlearned with me, but I would rather rejoice in what you dictate than keep you busy reading any longer.

222. *Augustine to his beloved son and fellow deacon, Quodvultdeus (427-428)*

I have received the letter of your Charity in which you expressed a lively wish that I should write a compendium of all the heresies which have spawned against the teaching of the Lord our Saviour from the time of His coming, and I am taking advantage of an opportunity offered by my son Philocalus, a leading citizen of Hippo, to answer almost at once, explaining what a difficult task that is. I am using this present opportunity to write again and to explain briefly the difficulty of the task.

A certain Philastrius,[1] Bishop of Brescia, whom I myself saw at Milan with the saintly Ambrose, has written a book on this subject, which includes even the heresies which arose

---

4 Eccli. 24.47; 33.18.

1 His *Liber de haeresibus* appeared between 386 and 391.

among the Jewish people before the coming of the Lord; he estimated these at twenty-eight, and those after the coming of the Lord at 128. Epiphanius,[2] a Cyprian bishop, who also wrote on this subject, in Greek, is widely praised as an expounder of the Catholic faith. His list for both periods includes eighty heresies. Both of them set out to do what you ask of me, but you see from the number of sects what a difference there is between them. This would surely not have happened if what appeared heresy to one of them had also appeared heresy to the other. It is not to be imagined that Epiphanius was ignorant of some heresies which Philastrius knew, because Epiphanius has a much higher reputation for learning that Philastrius has. We should rather say that many were unknown to him if the former had enumerated more and the latter fewer. But, undoubtedly, when there was question of deciding what constitutes a heresy they did not see it the same way. As a matter of fact, this is an extremely difficult definition to formulate, and when we try to enumerate all of them we have to be on our guard not to pass over some which are really heresies or to include some which are not. See, then, whether I ought not perhaps to send you the book of holy Epiphanius; I think he has spoken more learnedly on this subject than Philastrius. There might be someone at Carthage who can translate it into Latin easily and fluently so that you may, instead, furnish us with what you ask of us.

I earnestly recommend the bearer. He is a subdeacon from our diocese from the estate of Orontius, a nobleman who is a great friend of ours. I have written to the latter on his behalf and that of his father, by whom he was adopted. When your Christian Benignity reads this letter, I ask you to be so kind as to further my request by your intercession with the

with by Augustine in the composition of his *De haeresibus*.

---

2 He lived from 315 to 413, was Bishop of Constantia, Cyprus, and became involved in the Origenist controversy. His *Panarion* included pagan philosophies among the heresies.

aforementioned man. I have sent with him a man from our church in case access to your Holiness might be difficult for him. I am not a little anxious about him, but I hope the Lord will free me from this anxiety through the medium of your Charity. I ask you not to fail to let me know what progress is made in the Catholic faith by that Theodosius by whom several Manichaeans were reported, and whether those whom we think he reported have been converted. If you happen to have heard anything about the journey of the holy bishops, let me know. May you live to God.

223. *Quodvultdeus to Augustine, his deservedly revered lord and truly blessed and holy father (427 or 428)*

I have received one communication from your Reverence, the one you were so kind as to send by the cleric, but the one which your Beatitude said had been sent previously through the honorable Philocalus has not yet reached me. Although I have always been conscious of my own sins, I now recognize clearly that, when it is a case of gaining the favor which I asked, my character is a hindrance to the whole Church. But I firmly trust that He who deigned to blot out the sins of the human race by the grace of His only Son will not permit mine to prevail for the destruction of others, but will, instead, make His grace to abound where sin had abounded,[1] deservedly revered lord and truly blessed and holy father. I was not unaware of the difficulty of the work, and I forewarned you of it, but I humbly asked your Beneficence to undertake it for the instruction of the unlearned like me, and with a true heart I presumed on the fullness of the divine fount which the Lord has bestowed on you.

Even though it is proved that Philastrius and Epiphanius,

---

1 Rom. 5.20.

venerable bishops, wrote something of the sort, which among other things or, rather, among all things, is unknown to me, I still do not think they showed care and diligence in setting down the contrary answers after each one of those opinions or in appending the method [of rebuttal]. Moreover, it is probable that the work of neither of them will have the brevity which I desire. It is useless to recommend Greek style to a man who has not learned it in Latin, because I asked not only your advice but also your help. Why should I remind your Reverence of the difficulty as well as the obscurity caused by interpreters, when you have a full and clear recognition of it yourself? Besides there are some heresies which, as we hear, have arisen since the death of those two writers, of which they have made no mention.

For these reasons, I throw myself on the mercy of your Piety as if you were my personal patron, and I appeal to your devoted and holy heart, disposed to compassion. The voice is mine, but the longing is universal. Leaving aside those foreign dainties, you will not refuse me, after recalling the text of your previous letter, the African bread which our province always has to perfection, fashioned, as it is of heavenly manna. I knock late,[2] but I suffer hunger, and I assure you I will not cease knocking until you grant to my unwearied persistence what no merit of mine can claim as a prerogative.

224. Augustine to the lord Quodvultdeus, his sincerely beloved brother and fellow deacon (427 or 428)

An opportunity of writing to you has presented itself, thanks to a priest from Fussala,[1] whom I recommend to your

---

2 Cf. Luke 11.5-8.

1 A Numidian town forty miles from Hippo, where Punic was used more than Latin.

Charity, and I have reviewed your letter in which you ask me to write something on the heresies which have contrived to break out from the time of the announcement of the Lord's coming in the flesh. I have tried to examine whether I ought to undertake the actual work now and send you an excerpt from it to show you that your wish to have it short adds greatly to its difficulty. But I was not able to do even this, hampered as I am by such overwhelming cares, of which I cannot possibly make a secret for they have drawn me off from a work which I had in hand.

This work is my reply to the books of Julian,[2] of which he published eight after I had refuted the first four. Brother Alypius found this out at Rome, and although he had not secured a copy of all the books, he did not want to let slip an opportunity of sending me five, promising to send the other three speedily and insisting strongly that I should not delay to refute them. Forced by his insistence, I have had to slacken on what I was doing, and, in order not to slight either work, I do one in the daytime and the other at night, as far as I can get any respite from other demands which come upon me ceaselessly from all sides. I have been engaged on a work which is extremely urgent, for I am revising all my works, and if there is anything in them which displeases me or could offend others, I have been making clear, partly by correcting and partly by defending, what can and ought to be read. I have finished two volumes of *Retractations* after having gone over all my writings. I had no idea how many there were and I find that they amount to 232. There yet remain the letters and the popular tractates which the Greeks call homilies. I had already read most of my letters, but had not yet dictated anything on them, when these books of Julian began to claim my attention; and I have now begun my answer to the fourth. When I have finished it and have

2 Cf. Letter 101 n. 1.

answered the fifth, I intend, if the Lord wills, and if the last
three books do not come to hand, to begin the work you ask,
working at both at once, that is, this one and the revision of
my writings, dividing my time between them, one by day
and one by night.

I am making this known to your Holiness that you may
the more fervently ask help for me from the Lord, according
to the greatness of your desire to receive what you ask, and
that I may be of service to your praiseworthy zeal as well as
helpful to those whom you think this work may benefit, my
lord and sincerely beloved brother. I again commend to you
the bearer of my letter and the business which is the cause of
his trip. When you learn with whom he has to deal, I ask you
not to be slow to help him, for we cannot neglect the needs
of men like him, who are not only our tenant farmers, but
much more our brothers; they have a claim on our care in
the charity of Christ. May you live to God.

*225. Prosper[1] to Augustine, his saintly lord, indescribably
wonderful and incomparably honorable prelate
and illustrious patron (427 or 429)*

Although I am not personally acquainted with you, I am
known to you to some extent, if you remember, in mind and
speech, for I have sent and received letters through my holy
brother, the deacon Leontius. Now, however, I take the
liberty of writing to your Blessedness, not only for the pleasure
of greeting you as I did then, but because of my zeal for the
faith by which the Church lives. Knowing that your watchful
care is ever on guard to protect all the members of the body
of Christ against the snares of heretical doctrines, and ever

---

1 St. Prosper of Acquitaine (390-463), a sympathetic admirer of Augustine, and, although a layman, one of his best interpreters.

ready to fight in the strength of truth, I think I need not fear being burdensome to you or importunate in a matter which touches the salvation of many and therefore is of concern to your Piety. In fact, I believe I should incur guilt if I failed to bring such an extremely dangerous situation to the attention of the outstanding defender of the faith.

Many of the servants of Christ who live in the city of Marseille,[2] having read the writings which your Holiness published against the Pelagian heretics, think that your argument on the calling of the elect according to the design of God is contrary to the opinion of the Fathers and the tradition of the Church. And while they have chosen for some time past to blame their own slowness of comprehension rather than criticize what they do not understand, and some of them wanted to request of your Blessedness a plainer and clearer explanation of this matter, it happened, by the disposition of God's mercy, that you published a book, full of divine authority, on *Amendment and Grace*,[3] at a time when similar doubts assailed certain monks in Africa. When this work had been brought to our knowledge by an unhoped-for chance, I thought that all the complaints of our opponents would be quieted, because your answer in that work was as complete and as final, on all points on which your Holiness had been consulted, as if you had in mind the special aim of allaying the disturbance that had arisen among us. But after they had studied this book of your Blessedness, those who had formerly followed the holy and apostolic authority of your teaching became more enlightened and much better instructed, while those who were held back by the darkness of their own prejudice went away more opposed than they had previously been. We have to fear this headlong separation

---

2 At the monastery of St. Victor.
3 *De correptione et gratia*, addressed to the monks of Hadrumetum; cf. Letters 214, 215.

of theirs, first for their own sake, lest the spirit of Pelagian impiety make sport of men so clear-minded and so exemplary in the pursuit of all virtues; and second, for the more ordinary souls, who hold the former in high esteem because they see their uprightness, lest they think that the safest opinion they can hold is the one they hear asserted by the others whose authority they follow without reflection.

This is a summary of what they profess: All men have sinned in the sin of Adam and no one can be saved by regeneration through his own efforts, but through the grace of God. Moreover, the propitiation which is found in the mystery of the Blood of Christ was offered for all men without exception; hence, all who are willing to approach to faith and baptism can be saved. God foresaw before the foundation of the world[4] those who would believe or who would stand firm in the faith, which thereafter would be seconded by grace; and He predestined to His kingdom those whom He called freely, of whom He foresaw that they would be worthy of election and would depart from this life by a good death. Therefore, every man is warned by divine enactments to believe and to perform good works, so that none need despair of laying hold on eternal life, since a reward is prepared for voluntary consecration. But they claim that this calling by God according to His design by which a distinction between the elect and the reprobate is said to have been made—either before the beginning of the world or in the act of creating the human race, so that, according to the pleasure of the Creator, some are created vessels of honor, others vessels of dishonor[5]—deprives the lapsed of a motive for rising from their sins, and affords good Christians an excuse for luke-warmness, if the reprobate cannot enter heaven by any effort of his own, or the elect be cast out for any negligence.

---

4 Eph. 1.4; Matt. 25.34.
5 Rom. 9.21.

However they act, the outcome for them cannot be other than what God has determined, and in this uncertainty of hope there can be no constant course of action, because the effort of man's striving is useless if the choice of God's predestination rules otherwise. This has the effect of undermining effort and doing away with the virtue, if the purpose of God is antecedent to the human will, and thus under the name of predestination a certain inevitability of fate is introduced; or else the Lord is described as the Creator of different natures, if no one can become different from what he was made. To sum up briefly and completely what these men think: whatever your Holiness has set down in this book from the thought of your opponents as something to refute, and whatever you have quoted in the books against Julian of his own words on this question, as something to be most powerfully attacked, these holy men have carefully put together into a whole and are raising an outcry against. And when to refute them we offer writings of your Blessedness, furnished with the most cogent and innumerable proofs from the divine Scriptures, and when we imitate the form of your reasoning by building up an argument strong enough to hem them in, they defend their obstinacy by an appeal to antiquity. Quoting what the Apostle Paul wrote in his Epistle to the Romans[6] as proof of divine grace antecedent to the merits of the elect, they declare that these words have never been understood by any ecclesiastical writer as they are now understood. When we ask them to explain this passage as it is understood by those to whom they refer, they say they have not found the statement they want, and they enforce silence about those whose lofty heights no one can scale. They have reached such a pitch of stubbornness that they define our faith in a way to disedify their hearers, saying things which, even if true, ought not to be said aloud;

6 Rom. 9.14-21.

they make dangerous statements which are not to be accepted, and without any risk they pass over in silence what is unintelligible.

Some of them, indeed, are so far from forsaking Pelagian paths that when they are forced to admit that the grace of God forestalls all human merits—because if it is given as a reward of merit it is wrongly called grace—they hold that it comes to each single man in this way. Before man exists and is therefore incapable of merit, the grace of the Creator makes him a rational being endowed with free will; then, through his ability to discern good from evil,[7] he can direct his will to the knowledge of God and the observance of His commandments; by asking, seeking, and knocking,[8] through the use of that natural faculty, he attains to that grace by which we are reborn in Christ, and he receives, he finds, and he enters in because he makes a good use of a good gift of nature; thus, with the help of the initial grace he merits to attain to the grace of salvation. The proposition of the grace of election they define entirely in this way: that God has determined to admit none to His kingdom without the sacrament of regeneration, but that all men without exception are called to this gift of salvation either by natural law or by written law or by the preaching of the Gospel; that all who will may become sons of God, and that there is no excuse for those who refuse to be of the number of His faithful; that the justice of God consists in this, that those who do not believe in Him are doomed, but His goodness is shown by the fact that He excludes no one from life, but 'will have all men' without distinction 'to be saved and to come to the knowledge of the truth.'[9] At this point they offer evidence according to which the admonition of the

---

7 Heb. 5.14.
8 Matt. 7.7,8; Luke 11.9-10.
9 1 Tim. 2.4.

divine Scripture rouses the wills of men who, of their free
choice, either do what they are commanded or fail to do it.
They think it follows that, as the sinner's disobedience is
attributed to his lack of will, so there is no doubt that the
faithful man has been obedient because he willed it; that
each one has as much potentiality for evil as for good, and
that the mind moves with equal inclination to vice and to
virtue; that, finally, the grace of God supports the soul when
it seeks what is good, but a just condemnation overtakes the
one who pursues evil.

When we offer as an objection to these arguments the
unnumbered throng of little children who are cut off by a
decree of God, who, except for the taint of original sin under
which all men are equally born to share in the condemnation
of the first man, have as yet no will, no actions of their own,
who are to be carried off before any experience of this life
gives them a discernment of good and evil, of whom some are
enrolled among the heirs of the heavenly kingdom because
of their regeneration, while others, without baptism, pass
over as debtors to eternal death, they say that such children
are lost or saved according to what the divine knowledge
foresees they would have been in their adult years if they
had been preserved to an active life. They do not observe
that they are thereby debasing the grace of God which they
represent as a companion, not a forerunner, of human merits,
making it subject to those wills which they admit are forestalled by it according to their own fanciful idea. But in
making the free choice of God subject to certain imaginary
merits they invent a future which is not going to exist, as the
past also does not exist, and by a new kind of absurdity God
foresees what is not going to happen and what is foreseen
does not happen. Certainly, they imagine they are affirming
this foreknowledge of God in human merits, according to
which His grace of election operates, when they come to

consider those nations of past ages which were given up and allowed to enter upon their own ways, or which are even now going to destruction in the impiety of an ancient ignorance, without any enlightenment of law or Gospel to shine upon them. But when and inasmuch as the gate is opened and a way made for preachers [of truth], when the people of the Gentiles who sat in darkness and in the shadow of death have seen a great light,[10] and those who were not His people are now the people of God, while those on whom He had no mercy, on them He now has mercy,[11] these objectors say that the Lord foresaw that they would believe and that He dispensed to each nation the times and services of rulers so that the faith of their collective good will should come into being, and they confidently assert that 'God will have all men to be saved and to come to the knowledge of the truth.' But there is no excuse for those who are indeed able to be instructed by their natural intelligence in the worship of the one true God, but who do not hear the Gospel because they would not accept it if they heard it.

Our Lord Jesus Christ, they say, died for the whole human race, and thenceforth no one is excluded from the redemption wrought by His Blood, not even a man who should spend his whole life in a state of hostility to Him, because the mystery of divine mercy includes all men. The reason why many do not receive a new life is because God foresees that they have the will not to receive it. Therefore, as far as God is concerned, eternal life is prepared for all; but as far as the freedom of the will is concerned, eternal life is won by those who believe in God by their own choice and who receive the help of grace as a reward of their belief. Those whose contradictions displease us turned eagerly to that manner of preaching grace as soon as they had better thoughts about it,

10 Isa. 9.2; Matt. 4.16.
11 Osee 2.24; Rom. 9.25; 1 Peter 2.10.

because, if they were to admit that grace was antecedent to all those good merits and that these are made possible and conferred by it, they would necessarily have to concede that God acts according to His plan and the determination of His will by a hidden purpose and a manifest act 'to make one vessel unto honor, another unto dishonor,'[12] because none is justified except by grace and none is born except in sin. But they shrink from admitting this and they have a dread of designating the merits of the saints as the work of God; they do not agree that the predestined number of the elect can be neither increased nor diminished, because in that case they would have no ground among unbelieving and careless souls for the incentives of their preaching; the tax on their effort and industry would be fruitless and their zeal would be brought to nought if free choice ceased to exist. For they assert that anyone can be roused to conversion or to spiritual progress if he knows that he can be good by his own effort, and that therefore his liberty will be assisted by the help of God if he chooses what God commands. Thus, as there are two causes which bring about human salvation, namely, the grace of God and the obedience of man, those who give the preference of time in this matter to free will insist that obedience comes before grace. In this case we should have to believe that salvation is initiated by the one who is saved, not by the One who saves, and that the will of man procures for itself the help of divine grace, not that grace subordinates the human will itself.

As we have learned by the enlightening mercy of God and the instruction of your Blessedness that this is a most evil belief, we can indeed be firm in refusing to accept it, but we are no match for the authority of those who hold such theories, because they far surpass us in prestige and some of them outrank us by having recently been raised to the honor of the

---

12 Rom. 9.21.

episcopate,[13] so it would not be easy for any but the few fearless lovers of perfect grace to refute the arguments of men so far above us. As a consequence, there is increasing danger not only for those who listen to them, but even for themselves, because of their rank, since respect for them holds many in an unprofitable silence or carries them along in an uncritical assent, so that statements which are not challenged by any refutation seem to them perfectly safe. Since, then, there is no small trace of poison in these survivals of Pelagian error, if the beginning of salvation is wrongly ascribed to man; if the human will is impiously set above the divine will so as to claim that man is helped because he has willed it, not that he wills because he is helped; and if it is wrongly believed that man, sinful in his origin, receives the first beginnings of good, not from the Supreme Good but from himself; but, since it is true that man can please God only through the bounty of God, grant us your help in this cause, most holy prelate and excellent father; let your Piety put forth its utmost effort with the Lord's help, and be so good as to expound to us with your clearest explanations all that is obscure in these questions and too hard to understand.

In the first place, as there are many who think that the Christian faith is not harmed by this difference of opinion, I should like you to make clear the danger in this point of view; next, explain how the freedom of our will is not hindered by this forestalling and co-operating grace; next, whether the foreknowledge of God remains constant according to His purpose, so that those same things which are determined by Him are to be accepted as foreknown or whether they undergo change through different kinds of causes and

---

13 Honoratus and Hilary had been Bishops of Arles during this time, and Augustine's teaching on grace and predestination met some opposition in Gaul, especially at the monastery of Lérins, from which Hilary had come.

varieties of persons, and because there are different ways of election among those who are saved without any future activity on their part so the purpose would seem to be preeminent in them, whereas in those who are destined to perform good works the purpose could depend on the foreknowledge; or, on the other hand, whether these two forces act in one and the same manner, and although the foreknowledge cannot be separated from the purpose by a distinction of time, yet the foreknowledge in point of order depends on the purpose; and, as there is no form of activity which the divine foreknowledge has not foreseen, so there is nothing good in which we take part which is not originated by God. Finally, if those who are preordained to eternal life become believers through this preaching of the purpose of God, how is it that none of those who are to be exhorted are hindered or have any opportunity of being negligent if they despair of being predestined? We ask you, then, to bear with our foolishness and show us how that argument can be demolished, because, after reviewing the opinions of our predecessors on this matter, we find that almost all of them are reducible to one and the same statement in which they set forth the purpose and predestination of God according to His foreknowledge, in the sense that He made some to be vessels of honor and others vessels of dishonor because He foresaw the end of each one and knew beforehand what each would be like in will and action under the help of His grace.

After you have disentangled all these knotty points and discussed many others over and above which, with your deeper insight, you see can have a bearing on this case, we believe and hope that not only will our insufficiency be strengthened by the strong protection of your arguments, but also that those men, distinguished by merits and honors, whom the fog of this opinion wraps in darkness, may receive the most pure light of grace. Your Beatitude must know that one of them, a man of eminent authority and ability in spiritual studies, the saintly Hilary, Bishop of Arles, is an admirer and follower of your teaching in all other matters, and that he has long been anxious to consult your Holiness on his attitude to this question, which has brought him into the controversy. But as it is not certain whether he will do this, or for what purpose he will do it, and as the weariness of all of us is refreshed by the vigor of your charity and your knowledge, under the provident grace of God in the present age, lend your learning to the humble, give your rebuke to the proud. It is necessary and even useful to write what has been written, lest we esteem too lightly what is infrequently debated. People think that absence of pain betokens health and they do not feel a wound covered over with skin, but let them understand that the body which has a swelling tumor will have to be cut. May the grace of God and the peace of our Lord Jesus Christ crown you for all time and glorify you forever as you progress from virtue to virtue, my lord and most blessed prelate, my indescribably wonderful and incomparably honorable, most illustrious patron.

226. Hilary[1] to his father, Augustine, his most holy lord, longed for with all affection and greatly cherished in Christ (428 or 429)

The researches of learned men are generally acceptable to opponents when their own objections fail, because by them they also learn things which it is not dangerous not to know, but I think the care we have devoted to our report will be

---

1 Not the Bishop of Arles spoken of in Letter 225, but a layman, as is clear from his references to himself in this letter. The reply to these two young Gauls was made in Augustine's *De praedestinatione sanctorum*.

still more acceptable, and although it points out things mentioned by certain men which are contrary to the truth, it
contents itself, on the advice of your Holiness, with taking precautions against them, not so much for its own sake as for
the sake of those who are both the disturbers and the disturbed, most saintly lord, worthy of all our affection, and our
greatly cherished father.

These, then, are some of the views that are being aired at
Marseille or even in some other places in Gaul: that it is a
new theory and one useless for preaching which says that
some are to be of the elect according to the purpose [of God],
but that they are able neither to grasp nor to hold this salvation
except through the will to believe which has been given to
them. They think that all the force goes out of preaching if
it is said that there is nothing left in man which can be
aroused by it. They agree that all men died in Adam and
that no one can be saved from that death by his own will,
but they assert that it is consistent with truth, or at least con-
sonant with their preaching, to say that when the opportunity
of gaining salvation is made known to human nature, laid
low and never likely to rise by its own strength, it can be
cured of its weakness through the merit by which it wills and
believes, and that an increase of faith and a complete restora-
tion follow as an effect. But they admit that no one can be
fully capable of beginning this work, much less of carrying
it through to completion. The fact that everyone who is sick
wills, with a frightened and suppliant will, to be cured, should
not, they think, be ascribed as a reason for the cure. Taking
the words, 'Believe and you shall be saved,' they assert that
one of these represents something demanded as payment, the
other something offered; with the result that if there is payment of what is demanded, then what is offered is attributed
to it. They think it follows that faith is to be manifested by
man, since this concession has been made to his nature by

the will of the Creator, and that this nature is not so debased or destroyed that it ought not or cannot will to be healed. Therefore, man is either cured of his illness or, if he does not will it, he is punished by being left with it. They say it is not denying grace to predicate such an act of will as its precursor, a will which only seeks its physician but is not able to do anything for itself. Referring to passages such as: 'According as God hath divided to every one the measure of faith,'[2] and the like, they try to make them mean that he who has begun to will is helped, not that the grace is given to make him will. They exclude from this gift some equally guilty, who could likewise be saved if the will to believe were imparted to them as it is imparted to others equally unworthy. According to them, if such a will exists in all men so that each one is able to reject or to obey it, they think that the final casting up of accounts of the elect and the reprobate depends on the use that each one makes of the merit of free will which is given to him.

When they are asked why the faith is preached or not preached to some or in some places, or whether it will now be preached, although in the past nearly all peoples were left without preaching, as some are today, they say it is a consequence of the divine foreknowledge and that truth was or is made known at that time and place and to those people when and where God foresaw that it would be believed. They claim to prove this not only from the testimony of other Catholics, but even by an earlier argument of your Holiness in which with no less transparency of truth you expounded this same grace, as, for instance, in that passage where your Holiness refuted Porphyry on the question of the temporal beginning of the Christian religion and said that 'Christ willed to appear among men and to preach His doctrine to them at the time when and the place where He knew there would be souls

---

2 Rom. 12.3.

to believe in Him.'[3] In that other passage from your book on
the Epistle to the Romans at this place: 'Thou wilt say
therefore to me: Why doth he then find fault? for who
resisteth his will?'[4] you say: 'He answers this query so as to
make us understand that the first merits of faith and impiety
are clear to spiritual men, and even to men who do not live
like carnal men, and he shows how God in His foreknowledge
chooses those who will believe and condemns unbelievers, yet
does not choose the former according to their works, nor
condemn the latter according to their works, but makes it
possible for the faith of the former to do good works and
hardens the impiety of the latter by abandoning them to their
evil works.'[5] Again in the same book you say in an earlier
passage:[6] 'All are equal prior to the existence of merit, and
among things that are equal it is utterly impossible to speak
of choice. But since the Holy Spirit is given only to believers,
God does not indeed choose the works which He Himself
makes it possible for us to do when He gives the Holy Spirit
that we may do good works for love; nevertheless He does
choose the faith of the recipient, because unless a man believes
and is steadfast in his will to receive he does not receive the
gift of God, that is, the Holy Spirit, through whose infused
love he is able to do good works. Therefore, by His foreknowledge He does not choose anyone for the works which
are to be His own gift, but He chooses according to His
foreknowledge of a man's faith, and He chooses the one
whose faith He foreknows in order to give him the Holy
Spirit, that by performing good works he may attain eternal
life. For the Apostle says: "It is the same God who worketh

---

3 Cf. Letter 103.
4 Rom. 9.19.
5 *Expositio quarundam propositionum ex epistula ad Romanos* 62 (*PL*
35.2080).
6 *Ibid.* 60 (*PL* 35.2078).

all in all."[7] But nowhere does he say: "God believes all in all, for what we believe is our own doing but what we do is His." ' There are other passages in the same work which they say they accept and approve as being in accord with the truth of the Gospel.

For the rest, they assert that foreknowledge and pre-destination or purpose amount to this, that God foreknows or predestines or proposes to choose those who will believe. Of this belief it is not possible to say: 'What hast thou that thou hast not received?'[8] since it remains in the same nature which was whole and perfect when it was given but is now vitiated. When your Holiness says that no one perseveres unless he receives the strength to persevere, they accept it in a limited sense as meaning that when this grace is given even to a sluggish soul it is to be attributed to a prior will of man's own, which they say is free only to this extent that it can will or not will to admit its physician. But they profess to abominate and condemn those who think that any strength remains in anyone by which he can return to health. They do not want this perseverance preached in the sense that it cannot be won by prayer or lost by obstinacy. They are unwilling to yield themselves to the unknown purpose of God's will when it is evident to them, as they think, that they have some beginning of will, whatever it may be, by which they may obtain or receive [grace]. That other quotation you gave as proof: 'He was taken away lest wickedness should alter his understanding,'[9] they dispose of as being uncanonical and therefore to be disregarded. Thus, the foreknowledge which they accept is to be understood as a foreknowledge of a future faith, and they claim that the perseverance which is granted to anyone is not a grace to keep him from sinning,

---

7 1 Cor. 12.6.
8 1 Cor. 4.7.
9 Wisd. 4.11.

but a grace from which man of his own will can fall away
and thus become weakened.

They assert that the custom of exhorting anyone is useless
if it is said that nothing was left in man which could be
aroused by correction. They admit an innate residue left in
nature[10] in virtue of which, when truth is preached to the
ignorant, this grace is attributed to the existent will. For,
they say, if men are so predestined to either side that no one
can go from one to the other, what is the use of that external
pressure of correction if it does not rouse perfect faith in a
man, even though he has sorrow and compunction for his
weakness or is frightened by the demonstrated danger of
death? If a man cannot fear where there is cause for fear,
except by that will which is presumed to exist, no blame is
to be attached to him because of his present unwillingness, but
there is blame in and with the one whose unwillingness has
lasted for some time, so that he deserves this punishment for
himself and his posterity of never willing to seek what is
upright but always what is depraved. But if there is some kind
of sorrow which is aroused by the exhortation of the preacher
who rebukes, they say this is the very reason why one man is
rejected and one is saved, and thus there is no need of
setting up two classes of men to or from which it is impossible
either to add or to subtract.

In the next place they are displeased because a distinction
is made between the grace given in the beginning to the
first man and that which is now given to all, and that Adam
received perseverance 'not as something to make him such
that he would persevere, but as something without which he
could not persevere of his own free will, whereas now the
perseverance given to the saints predestined by grace for the
kingdom [of heaven] is not that kind of help, but the perseverance given to them is not only such that they could not

---

10 That is, after original sin.

persevere without that gift, but it is even such that they could not help but persevere through that gift.'[11] They are so disturbed by these words of your Holiness that they say a kind of despair is thereby set before men. For, they say, if Adam was helped so that he could remain steadfast in justice or fall away from justice, and if now the saints are helped so that they cannot fall away if once they have received that perseverance of will which prevents them from doing anything else, or if some are left unhelped so that they either do not approach [to the faith], or if they have approached they also fall back, they say that the usefulness of preaching or of threatening appeals to that will which maintains the free power of persevering or of giving up, but not to the will which is constrained by the inevitable necessity of refusing justice; with the exception of some who were created, along with those condemned as part of the universal clay, with the provision that they would be saved through the grace of redemption. Hence, they are willing to make this single distinction between the first man and the rest of human nature that this grace, without which he could not persevere, aided in him a will acting with unimpaired vigor; but for the rest of mankind with lost and ruined strength it not only raises up believers when they are prostrate, but also supports them as they walk. Outside this, they contend that whatever help is given to the predestined can be lost or retained by the force of their own will. This conclusion would be false if they thought it true that certain souls received such a grace of perseverance as made it impossible for them not to persevere.

That is why they do not accept that view which admits a fixed number of elect and reprobate,[12] and that they do not support the explanation of that opinion which you set forth. Their view holds that all men are saved, not merely those who

11 Augustine, *De correptione et gratia* 12.34 (*PL* 44.937).
12 *Ibid.* 13.39; 14.44.

will belong to the number of the saints, but absolutely all, making no exception of any. And in this there is no danger of anyone saying that some are lost against God's will; but, they say, in the same way that He does not will sin to be committed or goodness forsaken, yet it is constantly forsaken and sin is committed contrary to His will, so He wills to save all men, yet all men are not saved. The proofs from Scripture which you adduced concerning Saul or David[13] have nothing to do with this question which concerns preaching, they say, but they offer others which, according to their interpretation, favor grace in this sense that each one is helped after his will has acted, even to that election which is offered to the unworthy. They profess to prove this by passages both from your works and from those of others, which it would take too long to enumerate.

They do not admit that the case of children can be used as an example for adults. They say that your Holiness carried the argument to the point of wishing it to be undecided and preferring to leave the question of their penalty in doubt. You remember that in Book III of your treatise *Free Will* you left it so phrased that it could give them this ground.[14] They do this also with the works of others whose authority is recognized by the Church, and, as your Holiness observes, this can be no slight help to the other side unless we produce greater, or at least equal authorities. Your most prudent Piety is not unaware how many there are in the Church who hold their opinions or change them according to the weight of names. Finally, now that all of us are weary of it, their discussion or, rather, their complaint comes to this, that they say—and those who do not venture to disapprove of this definition of doctrine agree with them—what need was there to disturb the hearts of the less intelligent by an unresolved

---

13 *Ibid.* 14.45.
14 *De libero arbitrio* 3.23,66-68.

argument like this? They also say that the Catholic faith was no less usefully defended without this definition for so many years, by so many writers of treatises, in so many previous books both yours and others', against other heretics and especially against the Pelagians.

These are some of the things they say, my father, and there is an endless list of others which, to avow my inmost wish, I should have preferred to have you receive through me, or, since I have not deserved this honor, at least to have more ample time in which to collect and send you all the arguments by which they are influenced, so that I might hear what rebuttal is made on these matters, how far they can be refuted, or, if that is not possible, how much of it is allowable. But, since neither of these plans has worked out according to my wish, I have decided to do the best I could and send you this summary rather than remain entirely silent about this great opposition on the part of several. Some of them are persons of such importance that laymen are required by Church custom to show them the greatest respect. With God's help, we have tried to observe this without, at the same time, passing over in silence the points which our limited ability has been gathering together in order to give you a general idea of this question. So now, by way of reminder, I have sketched out these points in a summary fashion, as far as the haste of the bearer has allowed. It will be for your holy Prudence to discover what has to be done if the charge of these men, of such character and influence, is to be overcome or modified. I think it will be of little use for you to plead your case unless some authority is adduced which their tireless passion for argument cannot withstand. Certainly I ought not to refrain from telling you that they profess to admire your Holiness in all your deeds and words with this exception. You will have to decide how this opposition of theirs is to be met. Do not be surprised that I have added something of a different tenor in this letter which, as far as I can recall, I did not include in my last one. This is the nature of their present pronouncement, except for what I have perhaps omitted through haste or forgetfulness.

I ask that as soon as they are published we may deserve to have the books in which you are revising all your writings;[15] their authority will be of the greatest use to us, and in our anxiety to safeguard the honor of your name we shall no longer have to suppress anything that may not have been satisfactory to you. We have no copy of your *Grace and Free Will;* it remains for us to deserve to receive it, because we trust it will be of use in this controversy. However, I should not like your Holiness to think that I am writing this as if I were doubtful of the works which you have just published. Let it be penalty enough for me, exiled as I am from the sweetness of your presence which I used to drink in as life-giving nourishment, to be tormented by my separation from you as well as by the inflexibility of certain men who not only reject what is evident but even criticize what they do not understand. But I free myself from this suspicion so far as to reflect that my own weakness is so excessive that it makes me bear such men with too little patience. However, as I said, I leave it to your wisdom to decide what kind of measures to take. On my side, I have felt that as a return for that charity which I owe to Christ and to you I should not fail to speak of these matters which are in controversy. We shall gratefully welcome as an expression of that grace which all of us, both little and great,[16] admire in you, whatever decision you wish or are able to make, and it shall have for us a most beloved and revered authority. Because of the urgency of the bearer I greatly fear that I have not been able to cover everything, or that I have not done justice to what

---

15 The *Retractations.*
16 Ps. 103.25.

I have said, for I am aware of my own limited ability; consequently, I have arranged with a man[17] renowned for character and fluency of style and learning to include all the details he could collect in his letter. I have taken steps to despatch his letter with mine. He is a man whom your Holiness might well judge worthy of your acquaintance, even aside from this emergency. The holy deacon Leontius, an admirer of yours, joins with my parents in sending you cordial greetings. May your Paternity be mindful of me and may our Lord Christ deign to give you to His Church for many years, my lord and father.

I should like your Holiness to know that my brother and his wife, for whose sake we are leaving here, have vowed perfect chastity to God by mutual consent, and we ask your Holiness kindly to pray that the Lord may deign to strengthen and preserve them in this holy purpose.[18]

227. Augustine to the primate, Alypius[1] (After Easter, 428 or 429)

Brother Paul[2] has arrived safe; he reports a favorable turn in his affairs; the Lord will grant that this may be the end of it. He gives you cordial greetings and tells us the glad news that Gavinianus[3] has won that case of his by the mercy of God, and not only has become a Christian but a very good one. He was baptized last Easter, and professed with heart and mouth[4] the grace which he received. How can I tell you

---

17 Prosper, writer of Letter 225.
18 Indicated by editors as a postscript.

---

1 The missing inscription is supplied by editors.
2 Probably the bearer of Letter 120.
3 Not otherwise known.
4 Rom. 10.8.

how much I long to see him? But you know how much I love him. Dioscorus,[5] the chief physician,[6] also obtained that grace and became a faithful Christian at the same time. This is how it happened, for he would never have bowed his neck or subdued his tongue except in consequence of a miraculous happening. His only daughter, the joy of his life, fell ill and her cure was completely despaired of. Even her father had given up hope. There is a report—and it is true because Count Peregrinus,[7] a fine man and a good Christian, who was baptized at the same time with them, told us of it before brother Paul's return—there is a report, then, that this old man turned at length to implore the mercy of Christ, binding himself by a vow to become a Christian if he saw her cured. It happened. But he kept putting off the execution of what he had vowed. His hand[8] was still high. He was suddenly stricken with blindness and his mind at once pointed out the cause. He cried out, confessing his sin, and again vowed that if he recovered his sight he would fulfill his former vow. He recovered, he fulfilled it, but his hand was still high. He had not memorized the Creed,[9] or perhaps he refused to memorize it and excused himself on the ground of his inability. God knows. But after all the celebrations of his reception into the Church he became partly or almost totally paralyzed, and being warned in a dream, he confessed in writing that he had been told that this had befallen him because he had not recited the Creed. After that confession he recovered the use

5 Not the Dioscorus of Letters 117, 118.
6 *Archiater* was a public health official who received a salary from the town.
7 From his title a public official, but not otherwise known.
8 That is, his pride; cf. Exod. 14.8; Num. 33.3.
9 The recitation of the Creed is part of the ceremony of baptism. In the earlier ages of the Church it was forbidden to write it down; neophytes had to memorize it by ear. Cf. Augustine, *Sermones* 212.2; 58.1; *Retractationes* 1.17.

of all his faculties except his tongue. However, under that trial, he announced in writing that he had learned the Creed and could now remember it. Then, all that trifling with God fell away from him, which, as you know, was a blot on his natural goodness and made Christians think of him as insulting and sacrilegious. What shall I say to the Lord except: 'Let us sing a hymn, and let us exalt him above all forever'?[10] Amen.

228. Augustine gives greeting in the Lord to his holy brother and fellow bishop, Honoratus[1] (428 or 429)

By sending your Charity a copy of the letter which I wrote to brother Quodvultdeus[2] I thought I had discharged the obligation laid upon me when you asked my advice on the course of conduct you ought to pursue in the midst of the dangers which our times have brought upon us. Although I wrote briefly, I think I did not leave anything out of that letter which could serve as an answer to a query or a reply to a question. As a matter of fact, I said that those who wish and are able to move into fortified places should not be prevented from so doing, but, at the same time, that there should be no shirking of the duties of our ministry laid upon us by the charity of Christ, which oblige us not to desert the Churches to which we owe our service. Here is what I wrote in that letter:[3] 'It remains then,' I said, 'for us whose ministry

---

10 Judith 16.15; Dan. 3.57.

1 Bishop of Thiave, alarmed at the approach of the Vandals.
2 A bishop of this name is listed in Letter 175 as one of those present at the Council of Carthage in 416. The Quodvultdeus of Letters 221-224 was a deacon and therefore not to be identified with this one.
3 The letter is not extant.

is so necessary for the small remnant of the people of God,
wherever we are, that they would not persevere without it,
to say to the Lord: "Be thou unto us a God and protector,
and a place of refuge." [4]

But this advice is not enough for you, as you write, lest
we attempt to act contrary to the command or example of
the Lord when He warns us to flee from city to city, for we
recall the words He said: 'When they shall persecute you in
this city, flee into another.'[5] But who could believe that the
Lord meant by this that the flocks which He has purchased
with His Blood should be deprived of the indispensable ministry without which they cannot live? Surely He did not do
this when as a little child He fled into Egypt in the arms of
His parents.[6] Could we say that He had deserted the Churches
which He had not yet founded? And the Apostle Paul, when
he was let down from the window in a basket[7] so that his
enemy might not capture him, and so escaped from his hands,
did he deprive the Church, which was there, of a necessary
ministry, and was that duty not discharged by other brethren
appointed for that purpose? The Apostle so acted in deference
to their wishes that he might save himself for the Church,
since he was the only one whom the persecutor was seeking.
Therefore, let the servants of Christ, the ministers of His
word and of His sacrament, do what He has commanded or
permitted. Let them by all means flee from city to city when
any one of them is personally sought out by persecutors, so
long as the Church is not abandoned by others who are not
thus pursued, and who may furnish nourishment to their
fellow servants, knowing that otherwise these could not live. But
when the danger is common to all, that is, to bishops, clerics,
and laity, those who depend upon others are not to be forsaken

4 Cf. Ps. 30.3.
5 Matt. 10.23.
6 Matt. 2.14.
7 Acts 9.25; 2 Cor. 11.33.

by those on whom they depend. Therefore, either all should move to places of refuge, or those who have to stay should not be abandoned by those who should minister to their spiritual needs; thus, all may equally live and suffer whatever the Master of the household wishes them to endure.

If this happens, whether all suffer equally or some more, others less, it is plain to see which of them suffer for others, namely, those who were able to escape from such dangers by flight, but who chose to remain in order to supply the needs of others. In this case, there is the greatest proof of that charity commended by the Apostle John when he said: 'As Christ laid down his life for us, so we ought to lay down our lives for the brethren.'[8] For those who flee, or those who are unable to flee because they are bound by circumstances, do not suffer for the brethren, but for themselves, if they are caught and made to suffer; but those who refuse to forsake the brethren who depend on them for their salvation as Christians, and who suffer in consequence, unquestionably do lay down their lives for the brethren.

In regard to that sentiment which we have heard uttered by a certain bishop:[9] 'If the Lord has commanded us to flee from persecution in which the palm of martyrdom might be won, how much more should we flee from unprofitable sufferings when a barbarian enemy threatens invasion!' it is true and admissible, but only for those who are not bound by ecclesiastical duty. The man who is able to escape the horrors of invasion, but does not flee because he will not forsake the ministry of Christ, without which men can neither become nor live as Christians, wins a greater reward for his charity than the one who flees for his own sake, not for his brethren, but who is caught, refuses to deny Christ, and wins martyrdom.

---

8 Cf. John 3.16.
9 Not otherwise identified.

What was that sentence you wrote in your former letter? You say: 'If we have to stay in our churches, I do not see what good we can do for ourselves or for our people; it will be nothing but men being killed, women violated, churches burned, and ourselves fainting under torture when we are asked for what we have not.' God is certainly able to hear the prayers of His family and to turn away these evils which we fear, but in any case we should not desert the plain duties of our office, which are certain, for the sake of contingencies which are uncertain, for without us there is bound to be sure destruction for our people, not of things which belong to this life but of what pertains to the other life, which should be the object beyond compare of our constant and anxious care. If it were certain that the evils which are feared in the places where we live were going to happen, all those for whom we are bound to stay would leave first and would free us of the necessity of staying, for no one would say that the ministers ought to stay in a place where there are no longer any who need their services. It was thus that certain holy bishops fled from Spain after their flocks had been partly scattered in flight, partly slain, partly starved to death by siege, partly carried off in captivity, but many more remained to face the same array of dangers because their flocks remained and they stayed with them. If any did forsake their flocks, this is what we say should not happen, for such conduct is not authorized by divine teaching, but is due to the deceit of human error or the overpowering force of fear.

Why do they think they have to offer undiscriminating obedience to a command when they read that they must flee from city to city, and they do not fear to be the 'hireling who seeth the wolf coming and flieth . . . because he has no care for the sheep'?[10] Why do they not try to understand those two true statements of the Lord: the one permitting or

10 John 10.12,13.

commanding flight, the other blaming and reprehending it?
They would not be found contradictory, for they are not
contradictory. And how is this discovery made, except by
noting, as I have already proved above, that at the outbreak
of persecution we ministers of Christ must flee from the
places where we are when there is either no flock of Christ
to require our services there or the requisite services can be
furnished by others who have not the same reason for flight.
An example of this, as I mentioned before, was the Apostle
who was let down in a basket and escaped when he was being
individually pursued by the persecutor, while others who
had not the same necessity for flight were far from forsaking
the ministry of the Church in that place. In the same way,
St. Athanasius, Bishop of Alexandria,[11] took to flight when
Emperor Constantius[12] planned to arrest him alone, while the
Catholic people who lived in Alexandria were by no means
abandoned by other ministers. But when the people stay
and the ministers flee, and the ministry is withdrawn, what
shall we call it but a culpable flight of hirelings who have no
care for the sheep? For the wolf will come—not man, but the
Devil—and he has won over many of the faithful to apostasy
where the daily ministry of the Lord's Body has been lacking
and 'through thy ignorance, not thy knowledge, the weak
brother shall perish for whom Christ hath died.'[13]

When, however, there is question of men not so much led
astray in this matter by wrong thinking as overpowered by
panic, why do they not instead fight strongly against their
fear, with the Lord's merciful help, lest incomparably worse
evils befall them which are much more to be dreaded? This
is brought about when the charity of God burns brightly, not
when the covetousness of the world smoulders. For charity

11 A.D. 295-373.
12 Reigned 353-361.
13 Cf. 1 Cor. 8.11.

says: 'Who is weak and I am not weak? who is scandalized
and I am not on fire?'[14] But charity is from God. Let us pray,
then, that He may grant what He commands and by it may
we have greater fear for the sheep of Christ that they be
pierced to the heart by the sword of spiritual wickedness than
that they be stabbed in body by the steel, where, when, or by
whatever kind of death they are destined to die. Let us have
greater fear that the purity of faith be destroyed by corruption
of the inner senses than that women be violently raped in
the flesh, for chastity is not destroyed by this violence if it is
preserved in the heart, nor is it even violated in the flesh
when the will of the victim does not desecrate its own body,
but submits without consent to what is done by others. Let
us have greater fear that the living stones[15] be destroyed by
our desertion than that the stones and wood of earthly build-
ings be burned before our eyes. Let us have greater fear that
the members of Christ's body be starved of their spiritual
food than that the members of our body be bound and
tortured by enemy violence, not because these alternatives
cannot be avoided—for they can—but because it is better to
endure them when they cannot be avoided without disloyalty
to God. I suppose no one is likely to argue that a minister is
not disloyal who withdraws the ministry necessary to loyalty
at a time when it is most necessary.

Do we not recall what happens when that climax of misfortunes is reached and there is no possibility of escape, how
great a throng of both sexes and every age there always is in
the church, some asking for baptism, some seeking reconciliation, some the sacrament of penance, all looking for the
comfort to be found in the administration and distribution of
the sacraments? But if the priests are lacking, what a terrible
doom awaits those who leave this world without regeneration

---

14 2 Cor. 11.29.
15 1 Peter 2.5.

or laden with sin! How deep the grief of their kindred among the faithful, who will not have their loved ones with them in the repose of eternal life! Finally, what mourning on the part of all, and what curses on the part of some, over the absence of ministries and priests! See what temporal evils are caused by fear and what an increase of eternal woe results from it. If, however, the priests are at hand, they bring succor to all, according as the Lord furnishes them strength; some are baptized, some are reconciled to the Church, none is deprived of communion of the Lord's Body, all are comforted, edified, encouraged to ask God, who is all-powerful, to turn away what they fear, but equally prepared, if that chalice cannot pass away from them,[16] to accept the will of Him who cannot will any evil.

Surely, you now see what you wrote that you did not see: what a blessing it is for our Christian people not to be deprived of the presence of Christ's priests in the midst of the present dangers. You see, too, the evil effects of their absence, when they 'seek the things that are their own, not the things that are Jesus Christ's';[17] when they do not have that charity of which the Apostle says: 'it seeketh not its own,'[18] nor imitate him who said: 'not seeking that which is profitable to myself but to many that they may be saved.'[19] He would not have fled from the snares laid for him by the prince, his persecutor,[20] except that he wished to save himself for others who needed him, and that is why he said: 'But I am straitened between two: having a desire to be dissolved and to be with Christ, a thing by far the better; but to abide still in the flesh is needful for you.'

At this point, someone may say that the priests of God

16 Matt. 26.42.
17 Phil. 2.21.
18 Cf. 1 Cor. 13.5.
19 1 Cor. 10.33.
20 2 Cor. 11.32,33; Acts 9.23-25.

ought to flee from such threatening dangers in order to save themselves for the service of the Church in more peaceful times. It is right for some to do this when others are not lacking to supply the ministry of the Church, so that it is not wholly abandoned. This is what Athanasius did, as I said before; for the body of Catholic believers knew how necessary and how profitable it was for the Church to retain in the flesh a man who had defended it by words and heart's love against the Arian heretics. But when the danger is common to all and there is more reason to fear that the priest's escape may be attributed to a dread of death rather than an intention of future help, and when he does more harm by the example of his flight than he would do good by his preservation, there is no justifiable reason for doing it. Finally, there was holy David, who did not trust himself to the dangers of battle lest the lamp of Israel, as it is there said, 'should be put out';[21] but he did not take this course himself—he did it because his followers begged him to do it. Otherwise, he would have had many cowardly imitators who would believe that he acted thus at the bidding of his own fear, not for any motive of usefulness to others.

Sometimes another objection arises which we ought not to despise. If this motive of usefulness is not to be brushed aside, and if some priests may flee from an immediately threatening disaster so as to be saved in order to minister to such survivors as they may find after the calamity, what will happen if it seems likely that all will perish unless some escape? Well, what? If the fury rages in such wise as to seek our priests of the Church alone, what am I to say? Is the Church to be forsaken by runaway priests lest it be more sadly left alone by their death? But if the laity are not being persecuted to death, they can manage somehow to hide their bishops and priests, with the help of God who has power over all things,

21 2 Kings 21.17.

who can show His marvellous power by preserving the priest who does not run away. However, we are inquiring into what we ought to do so that we may not be guilty of tempting the Lord by expecting divine miracles at every turn. This storm in which the danger is common to clergy and laity is not like the common danger of merchants and sailors on the same ship. Yet, God forbid that this ship of ours should be held in such doubtful esteem that the sailors, and especially the pilot, should forsake it in its peril, even though they could escape by leaping into a small boat or by swimming. But the death we fear for those who might perish if we desert them is not a temporal death, which is bound to happen some time; we fear their eternal death, which can happen if we do not guard against it and can be averted if we do guard against it. In the midst of the common dangers of this life, whenever a hostile invasion threatens, why do we imagine that all the clergy are going to die and not all the laity, also, so that they who need the clergy may have done with life all together? On the other hand, why do we not hope that some of the clergy will survive as well as some of the laity to whom they will be able to furnish the necessary ministry?

Yet, if there should be contention among the ministers of God as to who should remain with the flock and who should take flight—Oh, let the Church not be left untended by the flight of all or by the death of all! Certainly there will be such rivalry among them when both groups burn with charity, and both are pleasing to charity. And if this contention cannot be otherwise settled, then, it seems to me, those who are to stay and those who are to go should be chosen by lot. Then the ones who will say that they ought to be chosen for escape will be shown up either as cowardly because they refuse to bear the impending misfortune or arrogant because they think themselves indispensable to the Church and therefore more worth saving. Again, it might happen that those who are more highly gifted might choose to lay down their lives for their brethren, and those who will be saved by flight might be men whose survival would be less useful to the Church because they have less skill in planning and governing. If these latter have any heavenly wisdom, they will oppose the former in their choice, because they will see that those who would rather die than flee are the ones who ought to live. Therefore, as it is written: 'The lot suppresseth contentions and determineth even between the might,'[22] for it is better for God to decide in uncertainties of this kind than for men, whether He deigns to call the better ones to a share in His passion and to spare the weak, or to strengthen the former to bear these evils and to withdraw from this life those whose survival cannot be as beneficial to the Church as theirs would be. It will be an unusual thing to proceed in this matter by drawing lots, but, if it is done, who will dare to judge it adversely? Surely, everyone but the envious or those ignorant of this appropriate quotation will praise it. But, if this plan is not acceptable because no example of it comes to mind, then let no one take flight, and let the ministry, which is supremely necessary to the Church and is an obligation in a time of such peril, not be found wanting. Let no one make so much of himself that he pronounces himself more worthy of life, and therefore of escape, because he seems to excel in some good quality. Whoever thinks this is too great an admirer of himself, whoever goes so far as to say it is hateful to all.

There are some, to be sure, who think that when bishops and priests do not flee from such dangers but remain among them they lead their flocks astray, since these latter do not flee because they see their superiors remaining. It is easy enough to refute this objection, or evil thought, by addressing the flocks and saying to them: 'Do not be led astray by our not leaving this place; we are not staying on our own account,

---

22 Prov. 18.18.

but on yours, that we may not fail in the ministry which we
know is needful for your salvation which is in Christ. If you
choose to flee, you will release us from the obligations which
keep us here.' And I think this ought to be said whenever it
seems really advantageous to move to safer places. If, after
hearing this, all, or even some, say: 'We are in the power
of God, whose anger no one escapes wherever he may go;
whose mercy can be found by anyone wherever he may be,
who does not wish to go anywhere because he is bound by
certain obligations or who is unwilling to spend his effort in
seeking an uncertain place of refuge which is less likely to
end his dangers than to change them,' there is no doubt that
these are not to be deprived of Christian ministrations. But,
if, after hearing what the bishops say, they choose to go, there
is no obligation for the priests to stay on their account, because
there is no longer anyone there for whose sake they should
stay.

Therefore, if anyone takes flight in such wise that no
necessary ministry is lacking to the Church through his flight,
he does what the Lord commands or permits. But, if anyone
flees in such wise as to withdraw from the flock of Christ the
nourishment necessary for their spiritual life, he is a hireling
'who seeth the wolf coming and fleeth because he hath no
care for the sheep'. I have written this to you, dearest brother,
because you asked my advice, and I have spoken with what
I believe to be truth and unfeigned charity, but I do not
prescribe that you should not follow a better opinion if you
find one. But we cannot find anything better to do in the
midst of these dangers than to pray to the Lord our God that
He may have mercy on us. Some prudent and holy men
have won merit by the grace of God by doing this very thing,
that is, not forsaking their churches, and have stood against
the teeth of their detractors without the least diminution of
their strength of purpose.

229. Augustine to his very dear son in Christ, his deservedly
honored and most distinguished lord Darius[1] (c. 429)

I have heard of your character and high rank from holy
brothers and fellow bishops, Urban[2] and Novatus,[3] one of
whom had the good fortune to meet you in the town of
Hilaris[4] near Carthage, and also recently at Sicca; the other,
at Sitifis. They have made it possible for me to consider you
as no stranger. The fact that I am not permitted to speak to
you face to face, owing to my physical weakness and the dual
cold of winter and of age, has not prevented me from seeing
you, for the latter of these friends was kind enough to visit
me and to give me a personal description, not of your physical
appearance, but of the face of your heart, while the former
did the same by letter. Thus, I see you inwardly with all the
more pleasure. This face of yours both you and I, by the
favor of God, look upon with great joy in the holy Gospel as
in a mirror, where the words are written by Truth itself:
'Blessed are the peacemakers for they shall be called the
children of God.'[5]

But the truly great and those who have their own glory
are not only the bravest warriors but the most faithful—and
this is a source of truer praise. These are the men by whose
toils and perils, with the help of God's protection and support,
an invincible foe is subjugated, peace is won for the state as
well as for the provinces, restored to order. But it is a greater
glory to destroy war with a word than men with a sword,
and to secure and maintain peace by means of peace rather

---

1 A court official of Valentinian III, sent to Africa to arrange a
reconciliation with Count Boniface and avert war with the Vandals.
Cf. Letter 189 n. 1.
2 Bishop of Sicca, a former monk of Augustine's monastery at Hippo.
3 Bishop of Sitifis, brother of the deacon Lucillus mentioned in Letter 84.
4 Not otherwise known. A textual error is suspected.
5 Matt. 5.9.

than by war. There is no doubt that those who fight are also
seeking peace, if they are good men, but they are seeking it
through bloodshed, whereas you have been sent to prevent
blood from being shed. On others rests the necessity of killing;
on you, the blessedness of forestalling the taking of life.
Therefore, deservedly distinguished and most honored lord,
my dearly beloved son in Christ, rejoice in that great and
true blessing which is yours, and enjoy it in God to whom
you owe it that you are such a man and that you are
undertaking such a worthy task. May God confirm what He
has wrought in us[6] through you. Accept this greeting from
me and be so kind as to repay it with one of your own. As
brother Novatus has informed me, he has contrived to make
me known in my writings also to the learning of your Excellency. If, then, you have read the works he gave you, I, too,
have become known to your interior perceptions, not too
unpleasing, I think, if you have read with greater inclination
to charity than to severity. It is not much to ask, but it would
be a great favor if you would send me just one letter in
return for my writing both this one and the others. I give
greeting, also, with the affection which I owe him, to that
pledge of peace,[7] whom you have happily recovered by the
grace of the Lord our God.

230. Darius gives greeting to his Augustine (c. 429)

How I wish, my lord and holy father, that as my name has
been carried to your ears and those of your fellow bishops,
Urban and Novatus, by the favoring help of God, as you

---

6 Cf. Ps. 67.29.
7 This expression is generally taken to refer to Verimodus, son of
Darius, who was supposedly a hostage held by the Vandals to ensure
the signing of peace by the Romans. The words of Darius at the end
of Letter 230 confirm this supposition.

say, so the God of all, your God, would set me before your
hands and eyes, not that the finer file of your judgment might
show me greater than I am or even such as the flattering
speech and commendatory letters of such eminent men had
made me, but rather that I might savor from your mouth
the true and immortal fruits of your wisdom, and might drink
in the sweetness, as it were, of pure water from the very
source of the everlasting spring! Oh, thrice and four times
happy should I be—as someone has said[1]—or, rather, a
thousand times or times beyond all numbering, if it were
granted me to behold in person your truly starry countenance,
and, if it were permitted me, not only by a mental effect, but
also by the sweetness of actual hearing, to receive and to
drink in your divine voice uttering divine words! I would
surely think that I was taking on some of the conditions of
immortality not merely as if I received them from heaven,
but as one already established in heaven itself, and hearing
certain words of God, not from His temple afar but through
the one who stands at the very tribunal of God.

Perhaps I might deserve that this should be my lot because
of the ardor of your desire, but as far as my conscience is
concerned I confess that I do not deserve it. However, even
in my separation from you I have derived no little fruit of
good desire, and of secondary goods this is to me the ultimate
climax of good. I have been commended to one whom I
wished to know by the word of two holy priests,[2] living in
different places: one, as I said, has spoken kindly of me and
has given me a personal testimonial, so to speak; from the
other, flying words, written in the same strain and in a
similar tenor, have come to you. These great men have decked
me in your eyes with a garland, not of full-blown flowers,
but by the testimony of their complimentary words they have

---

1 Vergil, *Aeneid* 1.94.
2 Urban and Novatus; cf. Letter 229.

woven one with the tender buds of an immortal fame. I pray
to the most high God for you, and I beg your intercession,
holy father, that it may fall to me, at least sometime, to be a
man like that, since I am conscious that I am far from being
the man of such a testimonial. But, surely, all those drawbacks
of my absence have not prevailed, since you now deign to
speak to me, to write to me and to greet me; since you do not
allow absence to exist between us. I was grieving that I had
not been seen by the one who is my saviour after God my
Saviour; yet, as you say, you look not at my physical appearance but at the face of my heart, and the more you look
upon me inwardly the more pleasing I seem to you. God
grant, my dear father, that I may measure up to your estimate
and that I may not blush before my own conscience when I
look within and see myself unlike that picture which you
have made for yourself.

In that divine and heavenly letter of yours, with your
eloquence furnishing you material for praise, as is your way,
you say that I—I repeat, that I—destroy war with a word.
My holy father, this expression made my mind emerge from
the dark clouds of thought, as if it recognized its true praise.
And now, to make a complete, brief and simple avowal to
your Blessedness, if we have not stamped out war, we have
certainly postponed it, and by the help of God, the Ruler of
all, the evils which had increased to a very climax of calamity
have been quelled. Moreover, I hope to obtain from Him
from whom we ought to hope everything that is good—nay,
rather, I augur from the blessing of your own letter, so
generous, so assured—that this postponement of war which
I mentioned may have and hold the constant and abiding
stability of peace You said, and you based your statement on
the eternal law of God, that I should rejoice in what you
called my great and true good, that I should enjoy it in God
from whom you say I receive as a gift both to be such as I

am and to undertake such worthy tasks. Then you add this:
May God confirm, you say, what He has wrought for you
through me. These are prayers uttered not only for me but
for the welfare of all! For that glory of mine cannot be
separated from the welfare of all; for me to be happy according to your prayers it is imperative that all be happy with me.
My dear father, may you long keep up and recite such
prayers for the Roman Empire, for the common weal of
Rome, and for those whom you may deem worthy. When you
return late into heaven,[3] may you leave them as a legacy to
your successors and enjoin them on those who follow you.

I have done fairly well, perhaps, as was my duty, but it is
certain that my words fall far short of what I want to say.
I admit it, while writing to you, I picture your countenance
to myself as if you were here, and although my speech is
untutored and my stammering tongue fails me, I cannot have
enough of talking and babbling to you as if I were with you.
Hence, from this, also, you can measure my longing for you.
Although the wordiness of my letter's page, probably tiresome
to you, has long since deserved an end, I turn my back on
modesty and think only of my desire, because I have a
feeling that to bring an end to my speech is the same as going
away from you. It is not that I do not want to stop, but that
I cannot. If you will believe me, father, you have been
enshrined in my feelings and in my innermost being ever
since the time when, not satisfied with the report of your
great and renowned fame, I chose to look upon you in your
writings, when your one short letter to me enkindled such a
flame and blaze of ardor. Consequently, I beg of you and I
entreat you with my whole heart that, as I have despised
pagan rites more completely and unequivocally than ever
before as a result of reading you—although I inherited the
religion of Christ from my parents, my grandparents and the

---

3 Cf. Horace, *Odes* I.2.45.

earliest ancestor of my race, nevertheless the proud conceit of this extravagant superstition has often invaded my senses— I now ask you again to be so good as to send me the gift of the books you wrote entitled *Confessions*. For if others, also, of accommodating mind and kindly heart, have given me your writings, how how much less excuse have you to refuse me your own!

There is a story about a letter which a certain foreign potentate or king[4] wrote to the Lord Christ whom he addressed as God, and sent to Him while He was sojourning in the country of Judea before He had ascended to His own heaven. Because the writer was hindered by illness from going or making his way to Christ and because he believed that he could not otherwise be cured, he begged the Saviour of the world and its Healer to come to Him if He should deem it worthy. And that he might not seem to demean a majesty so great, which the king without knowing it had represented to himself with prophetic but not perfectly enlightened mind, they say also that he praised his own country in order that God, attracted by the beauty of the city and the hospitality of the king, might not disdain the prayer of the suppliant. God was favorable to the king who was cured, and He gave a twofold answer to the petition by letter. He not only sent health to His suppliant, but gave him security as a king, and over and above He commanded that his city should be safe from enemies forever and ever. What more could be added to these benefits? I, also, am a humble servant of kings, and I beg of you, my lord, not to fail to intercede daily with that same Christ the Lord and supreme God of all to pardon my sins, and I ask you not to weary in praying for me and pleading for whatever you yourself choose.

If you are bored with this long letter of mine, try to bear

---

4 His name was Abgar of Mesopotamia and his letter is given by Eusebius, *Ecclesiastical History* 1.13.

it with your generous patience and lay the blame on yourself, because you gave the orders. I beg and entreat you over and over to write to me again; that will make it possible for me to suspect that the receipt of my letter has given you pleasure. May God grant your Holiness to stay with us for many years, that you may pray for us, my lord and truly holy father. My son Verimodus sends cordial greetings to your Blessedness; he was just now congratulating himself that you are so kind as to mention him in your letter to me. I am giving the holy priest Lazarus some remedies to take to you; we received them from the chief physician who is with us; this estimable man assures us that they will be most effective in relieving your suffering and curing your illness.

231. Augustine, servant of Christ and of the members of Christ, gives greeting in Him to his son, Darius, a member of Christ (c. 429)

You wanted my answer to be a sign that your letter had given me pleasure. See, I am answering; yet I cannot make my answer a sign of that, either in this or in any other letter, whether I write briefly or at great length, for neither in few words nor in many is it possible to signify what cannot be signified in words. Indeed, even in saying much I express myself inadequately, but I do not admit that any man, be he ever so eloquent, could express in a letter of whatever kind or length the feeling which your letter aroused in me. I could not do it and neither could he, even if he could see this feeling in my heart as I do. It devolves on me, then, to give you some sign of what you wanted to know, so that you may feel what my words do not utter. What shall I say, then, but that your letter pleased me very much? The repetition of this word[1] is not a mere repetition, but a constant utterance; since it is not possible to keep on saying it all the time, at least I can accomplish something by repeating it; in this way, perhaps, it is possible to say what defies utterance.

Hereupon, if anyone should ask me what, after all, gave me such intense pleasure in your letter, whether it was its literary style, I shall answer: 'No'; and he perhaps will come back with: 'Then it was your own praise,' and to this I shall also answer: 'No.' But this will not be for the reason that those two things were not found in your letter, for its style is so fine that it shows quite evidently both the excellence of your natural gift and the polish given by literary training; in addition, your letter is full of my praises. 'And so,' some imaginary person may say, 'such things give you no pleasure?' On the contrary, 'My heart is not horny,' as someone says,[2] that I should be insensible to such things or should take no pleasure in them. They do give me pleasure, but what bearing have they on my having said that I was very pleased? It is true, your literary style gives me pleasure because it is so gravely sweet and sweetly grave; and as to my praises— although I do not take pleasure in every kind or from every- body, but only in those of which you judge me worthy and those from men like you who love the servants of Christ for His sake—I cannot deny that I was also pleased with the praises of me expressed in your letter.

Let serious and learned men consider what they should think of the famous Themistocles—if I am really referring to the right man—who refused to play on the lyre at a banquet, a practice which was customary among the distinguished and cultured men of Greece. He was consequently rated as a man of low taste, but, as he showed his contempt for all that kind of amusement, they asked him: 'What, then, do you like to

---

1 In Latin, *valde,* a strong intensifier.
2 Persius, *Satires* 1.47.

hear?' And he is reported to have answered: 'My own praises.'
Let such men reflect on what they think was the purpose or
object of his words and why he said them. He was, in the
eyes of the world, an eminent man, for, when they asked him
this further question: 'What then, do you know?' he said:
'How to make a great state of a small one.'[3] For my part,
however, I think that the saying of Ennius, 'All men yearn
to be praised,'[4] is partly to be approved and partly to be
distrusted. Thus, as truth is to be sought after as being beyond
doubt uniquely worthy of praise, even though it is not praised,
so the vanity which easily steals over the praise of men is to
be shunned. That is the case when those good qualities
which deserve praise are considered not worth having, unless
a man is praised by his fellow men, or when a man desires
great praise for something in him which is worthier of slight
praise or even of rebuke. Hence, Horace was more moderate
than Ennius when he said: 'Are you swollen with love of
praise? There are certain charms which can restore you if
you read the book through three times.'[5]

So he thought that the swelling caused by love of praise
was to be, as it were, charmed away like a serpent's bite, by
healing words. Therefore, our good Master has taught us by
His Apostle not to live right and do right in order to be
praised by men,[6] that is, not to make the praise of men our
motive for doing what is right,[7] yet for the sake of men we
are to seek the praise of men. When good men are praised,
the benefit falls on those who praise, not on those who are
praised. For, as far as the latter are concerned, it is enough
for them that they are good, but the former, whose advantage
it is to imitate the good, are to be congratulated when they

---

3 Cicero, *Pro Archia* 9.20; Plutarch, *Themistocles* 2.
4 Ennius, *Annales* 560.
5 Horace, *Epistolae* 1.1.36,37.
6 1 Thess. 2.4; Matt. 5.16.
7 Cf. Persius, *Satires* 1.48.

praise the good because they give evidence that those whom they praise sincerely are pleasing to them. Thus, the Apostle says in a certain passage: 'If I pleased men, I should not be the servant of Christ,'[8] and likewise in another passage he says: 'Please all men in all things as I also in all things please all men,' but he gives the reason: 'not seeking that which is profitable to myself but to many that they may be saved.'[9] See what he was seeking in the praise of men when he said: 'For the rest, brethren, whatsoever things are true, whatsoever modest, whatsoever chaste, whatsoever holy, whatsoever lovely, whatsoever of good fame, if there be any virtue, if any praise, think on these things, which you have both learned and received and heard and seen in me; these do ye and the God of peace shall be with you.'[10] So, the other things which he mentioned above he included in the word virtue when he said, 'if there be any virtue.' But he followed up that other expression which he used, 'whatsoever of good fame,' by saying 'if there be any praise.' Thus, when he says: 'If I pleased men I should not be the servant of Christ,' it is to be taken as if he said: 'If I made human praise the motive of the good I do, I should be swollen with love of praise.' The Apostle wanted them to please all men and he took pleasure in pleasing them, not because he swelled up interiorly at their praise, but because by being praised he edified them in Christ. Why, then, should I not rejoice in being praised by you, since you are a good man—unless I am wrong about you—and you praise the things which you love and which it is profitable and beneficial for you to love even if they are lacking in me? This is a gain not only for you, but also for me. For, if these qualities are lacking in me, it is good for me to be ashamed and to burn with a desire to have them.

8 Gal. 1.10.
9 1 Cor. 10.33.
10 Phil. 4.8,9.

And so I rejoice in possessing the qualities which you praise
in me which I recognize as my own, and also in having you
love them and me because of them. But those that I do not
recognize in myself I yearn to acquire, not only to possess
them for myself, but also that those who truly love me may
not be wrong when they praise me.

See how much I have talked and I have not yet said what
it was that delighted me in your letter far more than your
literary style, far more than your praise of me. What else do
you think it is, good sir, except that I have won the friendship
of a man of your worth, even without seeing you, if I ought
to say I have not seen you when I have seen your mind if
not your body in your letter, and can now depend on my
own impression of you and not, as previously, on the testimony
of my brethren? I had already heard what manner of man you
are, though I had not yet experienced what you were to me.
But I am sure that from this friendship of yours even my
praise—of which I have already explained enough why it
gives me pleasure—will be much more fruitful for the Church
of Christ, since you possess and read and admire and extol
my works in defense of the Gospel against the remainder of
impious devil-worshipers to such an extent that I become
that much better known in proportion to your high position.
Illustrious as you are, you give lustre to my lowly works;
famous as you are, you add fame to them;[11] and wherever
you see that they can do good you will not allow them to
remain altogether unknown. If you ask how I know this, it
is from your letter that I get such an impression of you. You
can see from this how great pleasure your letter was able to
afford me, if, with the good opinion you have of me, you
reflect on how greatly I rejoice in the gains made for Christ.
And when you declare that you yourself, who have had the

---

11 There is here a double play on the words: *inlustris, inlustras; clarus
declaras.*

ability, as you write, of inheriting the Christian religion from your parents, your grandparents, and the earliest ancestor of your race, were yet helped by my works as by nothing else in your conflict with pagan practices, should I think it a slight thing that through your commendation and public support my writings are able to do so much good to others both numerous and high-born, and through them to reach out so easily and profitably to still others to whom such works are serviceable? With that in mind I cannot but be filled with a gladness made up of no slight or insignificant satisfactions.

Since, then, I have not been able to express in words the greatness of the joy which your letter gave me, I have spoken of the reason for my joy, and I leave you to conjecture for yourself what I have not been able to describe, namely, the greatness of my joy. Receive, then, my son, receive, good sir and good Christian that you are, not on the surface only but with Christian charity, receive, I say, the books of my *Confessions* which you longed for; in them behold me and praise me not beyond what I am; in them believe what I say of myself, not what others say of me; look upon me there and see what I was in myself and of myself. If anything in me pleases you, join me in praising Him to whom I wish praise given for what He has done for me, and do not praise me, for 'He made us and not we ourselves';[12] we, indeed, had destroyed ourselves, but He that fashioned us also re-fashioned us. When you find me in those pages, pray for me that I may avoid defection and reach perfection;[13] pray, my son, pray. I feel deeply what I am saying, I know what I am asking; do not think it unfitting or beyond your merits; you will cheat me of a great help if you do not do it. And not only you, but let all who have learned to love me from your words pray for me. Tell them that I have asked this, or, if

12 Ps. 99.3.
13 Another elaborate play on words: *fecit, refecit; deficiam, perficiar.*

you have this much regard for me, consider my request a command. In any case, grant my request, all of you, or obey my command: pray for me. Read the word of God and you will find that the very rams,[14] our Apostles, asked this of their sons, or enjoined it on their hearers. For my part, as you have asked me to do the same for you, He who hears our prayers sees how earnestly I do it, as He saw that I did it before; in this matter pay me an equal service of love. We are your guardians, you are the flock of God;[15] reflect and see that our perils are greater than yours and pray for us. This befits both us and you that we may give a good account of you to the Prince of pastors[16] and our universal Head, that we may likewise escape the flattery of this world, more dangerous than its afflictions, except when its peace produces for us what the Apostle advised us to pray for, that is, 'that we may lead a quiet and peaceable life in all piety and charity.'[17] But if piety and charity should be lacking, what is peace and respite from these and other evils of the world but a source of self-indulgence and destruction, or at least an incitement or help thereto? So, in order that we may have a 'quiet and peaceable life in all piety and charity,' do you ask in prayer for us what I do for you, wherever you are, wherever we are, for He is everywhere 'whose we are.'[18]

I am also sending some other books which you did not ask for: *Faith in Things Not Seen, Patience, Continence, Providence,* and a large volume on *Faith, Hope, and Charity.* If you read all these while you are in Africa, send me your opinion of them; either send it to me or despatch it to a place from which it can be sent to me by my lord, the primate Aurelius. However, I hope to have letters from you wherever

---

14 That is, the leaders of the flock.
15 1 Peter 5.2; Jer. 13.17.
16 1 Peter 5.4.
17 1 Tim. 2.2.
18 Cf. Acts 27.23.

you are, and you shall have them from me as long as I am able. I have received with gratitude the things you sent, both the remedies for my health—of body, it is true, since you wish me to be free of any hindrance of ill-health so as to devote myself to God—and the help you so kindly furnish for our library so that books can be either prepared or repaired. May the Lord repay you both here and in the life to come with the blessings which He has prepared for such as He has willed you to be. I ask you again to give greeting, as you did before, to the pledge of peace,[19] restored to you and very dear to us both.

*231A[1]   Augustine gives greeting in the Lord to the dis-
tinguished and justly honored lord, Firmus,[2] his
cherished son*

I am sending, as I promised, the books of the *City of God* which you have been anxiously demanding of me. I have revised them, as your brother, my son Cyprian,[3] has insisted on my doing, with God's help, of course, but his insistence has not been displeasing to me.

There are twenty-two fascicles, which are a good many to reduce to one volume. And if you want it done in two volumes, they should be divided so that one has ten books; the other, twelve. For in the first ten there is a refutation of

---

19 Cf. Letter 229 n. 7.

---

1 This letter, written after 426, was found serving as a foreword in two manuscripts of the *City of God*. It was published in 1939 and discussed by C. Lamlot in *Revue Bénédictine,* 51, pp. 109-121.
2 A close friend of both Jerome and Augustine. He traveled back and forth between them and carried letters for both. This letter tells us that he resided at Carthage. Cf. Letters 81, 82, 172, 184A, 191, 200, 248.
3 A cleric of the church at Hippo, bearer of letters to Jerome. Cf. Letters 71, 73, 82. The revision mentioned would seem to be the first general one, since the work was completed in 426.

the vain pretensions of the wicked; in the last twelve our religion is proved and defended; although this same theme is also treated in the former books where it is relevant, and the former theme is similarly treated in the latter books.

However, if you want more than two volumes, then you ought to make five, the first to contain the first five books, in which a rebuttal is built up against those who maintain that it is the worship of demons, not of gods that conduces to happiness in this life.[4] The second volume should contain the next five books against those who think that such gods, or many more like them, should be worshiped with rites and sacrifices for the sake of the life which is to come after death.[5] The three other volumes which are left will have to have four books each,[6] for I have arranged this part so that four books show the origin of that City and the same number its progress or, we might rather say, its outcome; the last four describe the respective and due destinies of the two cities.

If you are as assiduous in reading these books as you have been in getting them, you will understand by your own experience rather than by my promise how helpful they are. However, our brothers there at Carthage have not yet acquired the books belonging to this work on the *City of God*. I ask that you graciously and willingly permit those who ask to transcribe it. You will not, however, give it to many, but to about one or two, and they will give it to the others. You will see for yourself how to share it with your friends, either those among the Christian people who wish to be instructed, or those in bondage to one or other superstition from which it seems possible that they may be set free through this work of mine, by the grace of God.

If the Lord wills, I shall take care to inquire often how far

---

4 Cf. Letter 184A; *De civitate Dei* 6.1.
5 *Retractationes* 2.69; *De civitate Dei* 6.12.
6 Cf. *Retractationes* 2.69; *De civitate Dei* 10.32.

you agree with what I have written as you read it. As a scholarly man you are not unaware how much repeated reading helps one to understand what is read. For there is no difficulty in understanding or at least very little, where there is ease in reading, and this becomes greater as the text is used over and over again so that by constant use what . . .[7] had been unripe. . . .

My distinguished and justly honored lord and cherished son, Firmus, I ask you to let me know how you got possession of those books which, as I mentioned in our recent conversation, I wrote on the Academics,[8] since you let me know in previous letters that they were known to your Excellency.

An enclosed brief resume[9] will indicate the general content of the twenty-two books.

232. Augustine to his esteemed lords and beloved brothers,[1] the citizens of Madaura,[2] whose letter I have received through brother Florentius[3]

If by any chance it is those among you who are Catholic Christians who have written me a letter of this kind, I only wonder that they sent it to me under the name of their

---

7 There is a lacuna in the text. A suggested reading is *maturescat quod indiligentia,* that is: 'what had been unripe through lack of attention becomes ripe through repetition.'

8 *Contra Academicos,* Augustine's first work after his conversion, of which, according to this letter, he did not even have a copy.

9 This *breviculus* was not a table of contents, but a collection of brief summaries to be incorporated at appropriate places in the text.

---

1 This is the first letter of Class IV, consisting of letters for which no sure date can be assigned. From references to imperial edicts against idolatry it would appear that this letter was probably written between 399 and 408.

2 An important Numidian town in which paganism continued to flourish long after the Empire became officially Christian.

3 Not otherwise known, probably one of Augustine's monks.

office[4] rather than their own. But if, as a matter of fact, all
or almost all of you, members of the town council, have
condescended to write to me, I am surprised at your addressing
me as 'Father,' and giving me 'greeting in the Lord,' for I
note with deep grief of heart your superstitious worship of
idols, idols against which it is easier to close your temples[5]
than your hearts, or, rather, the idols are not more enshrined
in your temples than in your hearts. But perhaps you are at
length giving serious thought to that salvation[6] which is in
the Lord, and which you wished me in your greeting. If
that is not the case, I ask you, esteemed sire and beloved
brothers, what injury, what offense I have done to your
Benevolence that you should think fit to mock me rather
than honor me by addressing me as your bishop?

For, when I read your words, 'To Father Augustine, eternal
welfare in the Lord,' I was suddenly lifted up with such
hope that I believed you had already turned to the Lord and
to His eternal salvation or that you were eager to turn to
Him through my ministry. But when I read the rest, my
heart was chilled; however, I asked the bearer of the letter
whether you were now Christians or wished to become so.
Upon learning from his answer that you were far from being
converted, I grieved more deeply that you thought fit not
only to reject, but, even in addressing me, to mock at the
name of Christ to which you now see that the whole world
submits. For I could not think of any other lord but the
Lord Christ under whom a bishop could be called 'Father'
by you, and, if there had been any uncertainty on this score
about the meaning of your phrase, it would have been removed by the closing sentence of your letter in which you
wrote plainly: 'We pray that you, sir, even surrounded by

4 They were members of the town council called *ordo* or *curia*.
5 This was done by imperial edicts in 399 and 408.
6 *Salus* means both greeting and health of body or soul.

your clergy, may rejoice for many years in God and in His Christ.' After having read and pondered over all this, what else could I, what else can anyone, think but that these words were written as either a truthful or a hypocritical expression of the sentiment of the writers? If you write these words as your true sentiment, who has cut off your way to this truth? Who has strewn it with sharp thorns? What enemy has thrown down steep rocks to block it? Finally, who has shut the door of the Church when you wished to enter, that you refuse to share with us the same Lord through whom you salute us? If, however, you write these words in a spirit of hypocrisy and derision, is that the way to impose the care of your interests on me by failing to exalt with due respect the name of Him through whom I am able to do anything, and daring to toss that name about with insulting flattery?

You must know, my dear sirs, that I say this with an indescribable pang of heart for you, for I know that you will have to render a heavier and more damning account to God if what I say has no effect on you. All that has happened in times past to the human race, as our ancestors have recorded it and handed it down to us, all that we ourselves experience and hand down to posterity, especially all that concerns the seeking and holding of the true religion, all this divine Scripture has spoken of, and everything comes to pass exactly as it was foretold that it would come to pass. You see plainly that the Jewish people have been torn from their native land and have been dispersed and scattered through almost all countries; and the origin of this same people, their growth, their loss of power, their dispersal in all directions, has come to pass exactly as it was foretold. You see plainly that the word of God and His law coming forth from that same people through Christ who was miraculously born of them have laid hold upon the faith of all nations and have possessed them; we read that all these happenings were foretold as

we see them accomplished. You see plainly that many have
been cut off from the root of Christian society, which, through
the apostolic sees and the recognized succession of bishops
has spread throughout the world, and although they are now
like withered branches which we call heresies and schisms,
they still boast of the external likeness of their origin under
cover of the name of Christian; all this has been foreseen,
and written down. You see plainly some of the temples of
idols fallen into ruin and left unrestored, some destroyed, some
closed, some turned to other uses, and the idols themselves
broken or burned or buried or destroyed; and the very powers
of this world who at one time persecuted the Christian
people for the sake of their idols have been defeated and
conquered not by revolting but by dying Christians, and have
now turned their attacks against the same idols for whose sake
they once put Christians to death; and you also see the highest
ruler of this far-famed Empire put off his crown[7] and make
supplication at the tomb of Peter the fisherman.

The divine Scriptures which are now accessible to all
testified long ago that all these things would happen; our
joy in seeing everything fulfilled is based on a faith that is
all the stronger as we find everything foretold in the sacred
writings with more impressive authority. I ask you, then, are
we to suppose that the only decree of God that will not
come to pass, the only decree of God, will be the one which
we read in those same writings as being about to judge
between believers and unbelievers,[8] when everything else that
we read has happened as it was foretold? On the contrary,
it will come to pass as all those other prophecies came to
pass. Then there will be no man of our times who will be
able at that judgment to find an excuse for his unbelief when

---

7 Probably a symbolic expression, but it calls to mind the case of St.
Ambrose and Emperor Theodosius.
8 Cf. Eccle. 3.17.

everyone shall call on Christ: the upright man for justice, the perjurer for deceit, the king for power and the soldier for battle, the husband to maintain his authority and the wife to show her submission, the father for command and the son for obedience, the master for his right to rule and the servant for his subjection, the humble man for piety and the proud for ambition, the rich man to distribute and the poor to receive, the drunkard at his wine cups and the beggar at the gate, the good man that he may excel in virtue and the bad one that he may cheat, the Christian worshiper and the pagan sycophant—all have the name of Christ upon their lips, and, with whatever intention and formula they invoke Him, without doubt they shall render an account of it to Him whom they invoke.[9]

There is something invisible from which as from a creative principle all things that we see come into being, supreme, eternal, unchangeable, and able to be expressed to itself alone. There is something by which that supreme Majesty expresses and declares itself: the Word, equal to that which begets and utters Him, by which He who begets the Word is made known. There is a certain Holiness, sanctifier of all holy things that are created, an inseparable and indivisible bond of union between the unchangeable Word through which the First Principle is uttered and that Principle which utters itself in equality with the Word. Who would be able, with untroubled and pure mind, to contemplate this Totality which I have tried to express by not expressing it and not to express by expressing it, and from that contemplation draw perfect happiness, fainting away and forgetting himself, so to speak, in that which he contemplates, pressing on to the vision which makes a man worthless in his own eyes, which

---

9 Salvian, in *Gubernatio Dei* 4.15.71 deplores this too common and profane use of the name of Christ, and Augustine, *Sermones* 180.10, confesses his own excesses in his youth.

means to be clothed with immortality and to possess that
eternal salvation which you think fit to wish me in your
salutation—who could do this but he who has laid low all
the swellings of his pride by confessing his sins and has cast
himself down in meekness and humility to receive God as
his teacher?

Since, therefore, we must first be brought down from the
vanity of pride to humility that we may rise thence and attain
to a true loftiness, His spirit could not be breathed into us—
the more gentle for its very greatness—so that our native
savagery might be tamed by persuasion rather than by force,
if that Word, through whom God the Father reveals Himself
to the angels,[10] who is His strength and wisdom, who could
not be seen by the human heart, blinded by its passion for
visible things, had not deigned to show Himself and act His
part in human form so as to make man more afraid of being
puffed up by human glory than of being humbled after the
example of God. Therefore, the Christ who is preached
throughout the whole world is not a Christ adorned with
earthly royalty, not a Christ rich in earthly goods, not a
Christ resplendent with any earthly blessedness, but Christ
crucified, a subject of mockery first for proud peoples,[11] and
still a subject of mockery for a remnant of them. Few
believed in Him at first, but now the nations believe, because,
when Christ crucified was then preached to affirm the faith
of the few and oppose the mockery of the nations, the lame
walked, the dumb spoke, the deaf heard, the blind saw, the
dead rose again.[12] So at length the pride of earth was convinced that nothing on earth was as powerful as divine
humility, so that even the most salutary humility of man

10 1 Cor. 1.24.
11 1 Cor. 1.23.
12 Matt. 11.5; Luke 7.22.

may find refuge in the protection of that divine example against the scornful attacks of pride.

Awake at last, my brothers and my kinsmen[13] of Madaura! It is God who has given me this opportunity of writing to you. I did as much as I could to support and help in the case of Florentius by whom you sent your letter, but the affair was such that it could easily have been settled even without my help. Almost all the men of that household who are at Hippo know Florentius and sympathize deeply with his bereavement. However, since you sent me a letter, it is not presumptuous of me to write to you and I have taken advantage of the opportunity to speak of Christ to worshipers of idols. But I beg of you, if your mention of Him in your letter to me was not idle words, let not what I have written to you be idle words. On the other hand, if you intended to make fun of me, fear Him whom the proud world first mocked at and condemned but now submissively awaits as its Judge. For the affection of my heart for you, which I have expressed as best I could on this page, will be a witness against you at His judgment, when He will confirm those who believe in Him and confound those who do not. May the one true God set you free from all the vanity of this world and convert you to Himself, estimable lords and beloved brothers.

233. *Augustine to Longinianus*[1]

They say that among the ancients who were convinced that they should desire nothing so much as to be good men,

---

13 Madaura was not far from Tagaste, Augustine's birthplace, and was the scene of his early schooling. Its citizens might be called by courtesy his kinsfolk.

---

1 A pagan philosopher.

a certain one said that for these what remained to learn was easy. This statement—Socratic, if my memory serves me— was expressed in prophetic form long before, teaching men briefly and completely not only to aim at goodness, but also how they might become good: 'Thou shalt love the Lord thy God,' it says, 'with thy whole heart, with thy whole soul and with thy whole mind,'[2] and 'Thou shalt love thy neighbor as thyself.'[3] Whoever was convinced of this would not find other learning easy, but so long as he accepted the whole doctrine he would find it profitable and helpful. For there are many schools of learning—if, indeed, they can be called learning—either useless or baneful. Christ, bearing witness to the ancient books, says: 'On these two commandments dependeth the whole law and the prophets.'[4] Consequently, as I seem to have seen in the mirror, as it were, of my conversation with you that you choose above all things to be a good man, I venture to inquire how you think God is to be worshiped, since there is nothing more perfect than He and it is from Him that the human soul draws its power to be good. I ask also what you think of Christ. I have noted that your esteem for Him is not slight, but I should like to know whether you think happiness can be attained solely by the way which was pointed out by Him, but on which for some reason you delay to travel, without actually refusing to do so; or whether you imagine there is another or several other ways to attain that precious and supremely desirable possession, and you think you are now entering on one of them. I think I am not taking a liberty in asking this, as I have a great affection for you, for the reason which I mentioned above, and I think I am not presumptuous in supposing that

---

2 Deut. 6.51; Matt. 22.37; Mark 12.30; Luke 10.27.
3 Lev. 19.18; Matt. 22.39; Mark 12.31; Luke 10.27.
4 Matt. 22.40.

you return my affection. Now, among men who are kindly
disposed to one another, more fruitful discussion is neither
engaged in, nor sought for, nor offered, nor accepted on any
other topic than on the origin of goodness and happiness.

*234. Longinianus to his revered lord, his truly deservedly
cherished and holy father, Augustine*

That you have considered me worthy of being overwhelmed
by the honor of your divine address has made me happy
and has now illumined me with the pure light of your brilliant
virtue. But, estimable lord, by your inquiries and by expressing
such thoughts just at this time in terms of my opinion, that
is, the opinion of a pagan, you lay on me a heavy burden and
a particularly difficult task of answering you. It is true there
is an abundance of questions, either on what has been partly
agreed on between us up to this time, or on what is now
being more and more agreed upon in repeated letters, about
the precepts, I do not say only of Socrates, or yours, truly
best of Romans, or of the Prophets, or the few Jewish ones,
but also those of Orpheus and Agis and Trismegistus[1]
originated long ago by the gods in those ancient and almost
primitive times and revealed to the whole earth, divinely
divided by fixed boundaries into three parts, before Europe
had taken its name or Asia had received or Libya possessed
a good man such as you, upon my honor, have been and will
be. Not in the memory of man, unless you agree that the

1 Orpheus was credited with having introduced religion and worship of
the gods into Greece, and with having founded certain cults called
mysteries. Agis, King of Sparta (244-240 B.C.), tried to restore the
institutions of Lycurgus and to set up an ideal state. Trismegistus, an
Egyptian priest of very early date, was said to have written out the
revelation of Hermes. He was credited with 20,000 works on universal
principles, celestial beings, astrology, medicine, etc.

parable of Xenophon[2] is like the figure of a fable, have I heard or read or seen anyone, except you, or at least only one, of whom I could call God to witness with good and safe hazard, that you always strive to know God, and that you are able to follow Him with ease because of the purity of your mind and your victory over the weight of the body, and that with the hope of a perfect conscience you possess Him with sure faith.

But, by whatever way He can be attained, it is better that you should not be ignorant and should give me some instruction, although I am an outsider and not initiated, than that you should learn anything from me, worshipful lord. Because then, I confess, in order to make my way into the abode of this good I am gathering provision for my journey, a quite inadequate one, but as much as I am able, as the priesthood of my religion requires. I will set forth in a few words, as best I can, what I hold and keep as holy and ancient tradition. There is a better way to God by which a good man, proved by his godly, just, pure, chaste, true words and actions, hastens to go, not moved by any vicissitudes of changeful times, guarded by the company of gods or, at any rate, by powers in the service of God, filled with the strength of the one universal, incomprehensible, indescribable, unwearied Creator—in your cult you call these angels—or whatever other power there is after God, or with God, or from God, or tending to God with intensity of mind and soul. There is a way, I repeat, along which those who are purified by godly precepts and refined in soul and body by the most pure expiations and temperate observances constantly hasten.

But about Christ, a God of flesh and spirit according to your belief, through whom you find a sure way to the

---

2 The reference here is probably to his *Cyropaedeia*, a historical romance on the life of Cyrus, in which he depicted the ideal man and ruler.

supreme, blessed and true Father of all, I do not dare nor
am I able to express what I think, because I believe it is
extremely difficult to define what I do not know. I take it as
sufficient token of a good life that you have been so kind as
to make known to me, an admirer of your virtues, as if I had
long known it, that you hold me in your affection, and on
this account I take care not to displease you who daily
place yourself and your soul before God. You understand, of
course, that I also hold you in sweetest affection, since I receive
and keep the model and outline of the estimate you have
formed of me. But, above all, I ask you to be indulgent to my
utterly insignificant opinion and readily to overlook my language to you—negligent, perhaps, and ill-chosen—because you
obliged me to write, and to be so kind as to inform me what
you think of these ideas and what your own opinion is, if I
deserve to receive your writings, sweeter, as the poet says, not
than honey but than nectar.[3] May you enjoy the goodness of
God, my lord and father, and may you please God, as you
must, by your unending holiness.

235. *Augustine to Longinianus*

My letter bore fruit in the reply of your Benevolence. I
see from it that there has arisen between us the beginning of
a fine crop of argument on a matter of great importance.
That was the first thing I wanted and God will help me to
the second which I still want, namely, that this beginning
may be concluded by a due and profitable end. Moreover, I
make no difficulty about attributing to the natural disposition
of a pagan mind your thought that you should not pronounce
for or against Christ without reasonable ground. I shall

3 Cf. Ovid, *Tristia* 5.4.29,30.

certainly not say 'No' to your desire to be taught by my writings on this matter, and I shall not cease to comply with the requests of your upright will which is so dear to me. But the first task is to clarify somewhat and to render intelligible your statement about ancient forms of worship, when you said there was a better way to God 'by which a good man, proved by his godly, just, pure, chaste, true words and actions, hastens to go, not moved by any vicissitudes of changeful times, guarded by the company of gods, or at any rate, by powers in the service of God, filled with the strength of the one, universal, incomprehensible, indescribable, unwearied Creator—in your cult you call them angels—or whatever other power there is after God, or with God, or from God, or tending to God with intensity of mind and soul'—you recognize these words from your letter—you then said by way of addition: 'There is a way, I repeat, along which those who are purified by godly precepts and refined in soul and body by the most pure expiations and temperate observances constantly hasten.'

In these words I understand, if I mistake not, that you do not seem satisfied with a way to God by which a good man serves the gods by godly, just, pure, chaste, true words and actions, and hastens to approach the supreme God, Creator of all things, under the protection of their company, unless he is purified by the godly precepts and expiations of ancient sacrifices. Therefore, I should like to know what you think needs purifying by sacred rites in the man who has served the gods by living a godly, just, pure, and truthful life and through them approaches that one God of gods. If a man is still in need of purification by sacrifices he surely is not pure, and if he is not pure he has not lived a godly, just, pure, chaste life. But if he has so lived he is now pure. Besides, what need is there of purifying by sacrifices one who is already pure and undefiled? This, then, is the knotty point of our discussion; once this is untangled, we shall see what follows: Either a man lives well that he may be purified by sacrifices or he is purified by sacrifices that he may live well; either he is not yet ready for the happiness which is received from God, unless the help of these sacrifices is added, however great measure of right living exists in him, or it is a part, so to speak, of right living to partake of these sacrifices, so that there is no difference between the good life and the consecrated life, and the good life is enclosed within the boundaries of the consecrated life. I ask you not to shrink from letting me know which of these four alternatives you most approve. For it is very important in this question which we have undertaken to settle by mutual argument that time needed for other things should not be wasted on futilities, as it would be if I should labor to refute many unnecessary points as if you believed them, when, perhaps, you do not believe them. I have not wanted to load this letter with details, so that we may quickly get to work on other points when you reply.

236. Augustine gives greeting in the Lord to his saintly lord, Deuterius,[1] his reverend and dear brother and fellow bishop

I think the best thing I can do is to write directly to your Holiness, so that my negligence may not allow the Enemy to lay waste the flock of Jesus Christ in your province, for

---

1 A bishop of Mauretania, one of Augustine's early contemporaries. As he wrote nothing against the Manichaeans for the last twenty-five years of his life, this letter would seem to belong to an earlier period.

he never ceases to lay snares to destroy the souls bought at so dear a price. It has come to my knowledge that a certain Victorinus, a subdeacon of Malliana,[2] is a Manichaean, and that he hides his sacrilegious error under the name of cleric. He is also a man of advanced age. He was so well known that I questioned him before he could be arraigned by witnesses; he could not deny the accusation, for he knew that there were many such to whom he had incautiously given himself away. He would have appeared altogether too bold, not to say out of his mind, if he had tried to deny it. He admitted that he was indeed a Manichaean hearer but not an elect.[3]

Those who are called hearers among them eat flesh meat, till the soil, and, if they wish, have wives, but those called elect do none of these things. The hearers kneel before the elect that these may lay a hand on the suppliant, and this is done not only toward their priests or bishops or deacons, but toward any of the elect. Like these, they adore and pray to the sun and moon. Like them, they fast on Sunday;[4] like them, they believe all the blasphemies for which the heresy of the Manichaeans is to be abominated; denying, for example, that Christ was born of a virgin, claiming that His Body was not real but apparent, and for this reason insisting that His passion was apparent, too, and that there was no resurrection. They revile the patriarchs and prophets. They say that the Law given through Moses, the servant of God, did not come from the true God, but from the Prince of darkness.

2 Or Manliana, a town in Mauretania.
3 Or perfect, like the adepts of pagan mysteries. These ascetics lived a life similar to that of Buddhist monks, except that they were always itinerant, being forbidden to possess house or home, to own property, to eat meat or drink wine, to marry, to engage in any servile occupation, commerce, or trade. Their number was, naturally, small.
4 Cf. Letter 36.

They think that the souls of men as well as of beasts are of the substance of God and are, in fact, pieces of God. Finally, they say that the good and true God fought with the tribe of darkness and left a part of himself mingled with the Prince of darkness, and they assert that this part, spread over the world, defiled and bound, is purified by the food of the elect[5] and by the sun and moon; and whatever is left of that part of God which cannot be purified is bound with an everlasting and penal bond at the end of the world. As a consequence, they believe that God is not only subject to violation, corruption, and contamination, since it was possible for a part of Him to be brought to such an evil pass, but the whole God cannot even be purified from such foulness and filthiness and misery even at the end of the world.

That subdeacon, posing as a Catholic, not only believed those intolerable blasphemies as the Manichaeans do, but he taught them as vigorously as he could. He was discovered by his teaching when he trusted himself, so to speak, to his pupils. Indeed, he asked me, after he had confessed that he was a Manichaean hearer, to lead him back to the way of truth of Catholic doctrine, but I confess I was horrified at his duplicity under his clerical guise and I took steps to have him confined and driven from the city. And I was not satisfied with that until I had notified your Holiness by letter that he should be known to all as a person to be shunned, having been degraded from his clerical rank with fitting ecclesiastical severity. If he seeks an opportunity for repentance, let him be believed if he will make known to us the other Manichaeans whom he knows, not only at Malliana but in the whole province.

---

5 By eating certain foods, such as melons and other fruits, the elect could set free the light particles which had been lost by God and had become imprisoned in darkness.

237. Augustine gives greeting in the Lord to his saintly lord, Ceretius,[1] his deservedly revered brother and and fellow bishop

It seems to me, after reading the letter your Holiness sent me, that Argyrius has gone headlong over to the Priscillianists,[2] either unwittingly, that is, not knowing at all whether they are Priscillianists, or as one entangled in the nets of that heresy. I have no doubt that those Scriptures are a Priscillianist version. I could scarcely find a minute, with one emergency after another coming upon me without intermission, but at least one of those two volumes was read to me in its entirety. The other one has gone astray somehow or other and the most careful search among my books has not been able to turn it up, my saintly lord and deservedly revered father.

As for the hymn which they attribute to our Lord Jesus Christ and which roused deep veneration in you, it is commonly found in the apocryphal scriptures. These are not specifically Priscillianist, but other heretics of several sects make use of their vain ungodliness, interpreting them variously among themselves, each group following its own different heresy. However, in their diversity they have these scriptures in common and they make a great practice of consulting them, although they do not accept the Old Law or the canonical writings of the Prophets. Like the Manichaeans, the Marcionites,[3] and others who have adopted this damnable blasphemy, they say that these Scriptures are not consistent with a good God or with Christ His Son. Even in the canonical Scriptures of the New Testament, that is, in the true Gospels

---

1 Probably a Spanish or Gallic bishop, since he had trouble with Priscillianism, which was confined largely to Spain and Acquitania.

2 A heretical sect originating in Spain at the end of the fourth century, which preached a Gnostic-Manichaean dualism of light and darkness. Cf. St. Augustine, Letters, Vol. I, p. 162.

3 Followers of Marcion (d. 170), whose system was based on the opposition between the Law, work of a just God, and the Gospel, work of a good God.

and the apostolic writings, they do not accept everything, but only what they want, and they choose the books they will accept, rejecting the others. And in each of the books they accept they pick out the passages which they think are in accord with their errors. Some of the Manichaeans reject the canonical book entitled Acts of the Apostles. For they fear its too evident truth where it is clear that the Holy Spirit was sent as He had been promised in the true Gospel by our Lord Jesus Christ.[4] Under the name of this Spirit to whom they are utterly opposed they deceive the untutored hearts of men, asserting with an astonishing blindness that this same promise of the Lord was fulfilled in the person of their Manichaean heresiarch. Other heretics called Cataphrygians[5] do the same thing, saying that the Holy Spirit whom the Lord promised to send came in the person of some demented persons—Montanus, for example, and Priscilla,[6] whom they regard as their own special prophets.

The Priscillianists, it is true, accept all the Scriptures, both canonical and apocryphal together, but they change everything that is contrary to their teaching, twisting it to their own perverted meaning, sometimes by a clever and subtle explanation, sometimes by an absurd and stupid one. They do not go so far as to believe the truth of those points which they explain to men unacquainted with their sect; otherwise, they either would be Catholics or would not be far removed from the truth, since even in their apocryphal scriptures they find or seem to want to find Catholic meanings. But, although among their own they hold other views, and among their own teach or study what they do not dare to make public, since these doctrines are hateful and abomin-

---

4 Acts 2.2-4; John 14.16; 26.15,16.
5 Also called Montanists; an adventist sect of the second century and after.
6 A reformer who founded the Cataphrygians. Priscilla was one of his wives. They believed that the Second Coming was near at hand.

able, still, to those whom they fear they do teach the Catholic faith, which they do not hold, but under which they hide. It is possible, perhaps, to find some heretics more immoral, but none to compare with them for trickery. Some, indeed, with the usual failing of men, lie because it is a custom of this life or through frailty, but these are said to have it as a commandment, in the hateful teaching of their heresy, to lie even with a false oath to keep the secret of their dogma. Men who have had experience of them and have belonged to them, but have been delivered from them by the mercy of God, recall these words of this commandment: Swear truly or falsely, but betray not the secret.

Therefore, in order to make clear without difficulty that they do not hold the opinion they pretend to express about the apocryphal scriptures, we must examine the explanation they seem to give which attributes an almost divine authority to those same scriptures, or, what is worse, even prefers them to the canonical books. You have their words in that volume expressed thus: 'The hymn of the Lord which He spoke secretly to the holy Apostles, His disciples, because it is written in the Gospel: "A hymn being said, He went unto the Mount," '[7] and also that 'it is not included in the canon because of those who, according to Him, do not understand as the Spirit and the truth of God require, and also because it is written: "It is good to hide the secret of a king, but honorable to reveal the works of God." '[8] That is the great reason they give why that hymn is not in the canon, because it was to be hidden, like the secret of a king, from those who understand according to the flesh and not according to the Spirit and the truth of God.[9] Therefore, the canonical Scriptures do not belong to the secret of the king, which it seems

7 Matt. 26.30; Mark 14.26.
8 Tob. 12.7.
9 Cf. Rom. 8.5.

to them should be hidden, and they are written for those who understand according to the flesh and not according to the Spirit and the truth of God. Is this not the same as to say that the holy canonical Scriptures are not wise according to the Spirit of God and do not belong to the truth of God? Who could accept that? Who could bear the horror of such impiety? If the canonical Scriptures are understood spiritually by the spiritual and carnally by the carnal, why is that hymn not found in the canon if the spiritual understand it spiritually and the carnal carnally?

Finally, why is it that the Priscillianists try to explain that same hymn in terms of the canonical Scriptures? If it is not found in the canonical Scriptures because those Scriptures are for the carnal, but that hymn was written for the spiritual, how can that hymn, which is not for the carnal, be explained by means of Scriptures which are for carnal men? Suppose, for example, these words are sung and recited in that hymn: 'I wish to release and to be released,' because, as they explain these words, the Lord Christ has released us from intercourse with the world that we may not again be entangled in it, certainly we have learned from the canonical Scriptures that the Lord has freed us from intercourse with the world and that we ought not to be entangled in it again. What else is meant by: 'Thou hast broken my bonds,'[10] or what else by: 'The Lord looseth them that are fettered?'[11] The Apostle also admonishes the fettered by saying: 'Stand fast and be not held again under the yoke of bondage,'[12] and the Apostle Peter says: 'For if flying from the pollutions of the world through the knowledge of our Lord and Saviour Jesus Christ, they be again entangled in them and overcome, their latter state is become unto them worse than the former,'[13] thus

---

10 Ps. 115.16.
11 Ps. 145.7.
12 Gal. 5.1.
13 2 Peter 2.20.

proving that when we have been set free we should not again be entangled in the world. Since, then, it is manifest that these words are in the canon, both from these passages which I have cited and from many others, and since they are constantly read and recited, what is the purpose of these men in saying that this hymn in which the words—to quote them, very obscure words—are used is not in the canon lest these words be revealed to carnal men, when we see that they are revealed in the canon, but in this hymn they are entirely veiled, as they admit? It is much more believable that it is not these words, but some others which they obscure more successfully by their explanation and which they shrink from revealing.

Surely, if they meant by these words that the Lord has released us from intercourse with the world so that we may not again be entangled in it, they would not say: 'I wish to be released,' but: 'I wish to release and I do not wish those whom I have released to be bound.' If He transforms His members, that is, His faithful into Himself, instead of saying: 'I was hungry and you gave me to eat,'[14] He should rather have said: 'I wish to be released and I do not wish to be bound.' Or if He Himself releases and is Himself released because, if the head releases, the members are released—those members which were being persecuted by him to whom He cried out from heaven: 'Saul, Saul, why dost thou persecute me?'[15]—that interpreter of these words did not say that, but even if he had said it we could answer him what we answered awhile ago, that we read this in the canonical Scriptures, we understand it there, from there we declare it and preach it daily. What, then, is the reason for saying that that hymn is not put in the canon because it is withheld from carnal men, when what is hidden in the hymn is revealed in the

14 Matt. 25.35.
15 Acts 9.4; 22.7; 26.14.

canon? Are they so far gone in folly or, rather, madness that they dare to say the secret of the king is hidden from the spiritual in that hymn, but is revealed to the carnal in the canon?

This can also be said of further words of the same hymn, where it says: 'I wish to save and I wish to be saved.' For if, as they explain it, these words mean that we are saved by the Lord through baptism and we save, that is, we guard in us the Spirit given us by baptism, does not the canonical Scripture fairly shout that meaning when we read: 'He saved us by the laver of regeneration,'[16] and when it says: 'Extinguish not the spirit'?[17] How, then, is that hymn kept out of the canon so that it may not be known by the carnal, when what is obscure in it is crystal clear in the canon, unless it is because under this so-called explanation, which they display for others, they try to hide what they themselves know? They are so blind as to offer words from the canon to explain a hymn which they say is not in the canon lest the secret of the king be revealed to carnal men. Why, then, do they let it be known that the ideas are more clearly expressed in the canon through which the obscurities of their hymn are revealed?

If, as they say, we are to understand that hymn where it says: 'I wish to be begotten,' to mean what is written in the canonical Epistle of the Apostle Paul: 'Of whom I am in labor again until Christ be formed in you';[18] if we are to understand that hymn where it says: 'I wish to sing,' to mean what is written in the canonical psalm: 'Sing ye to the Lord a new canticle';[19] if we are to understand that hymn where it says: 'Dance, all of you,' to mean what is written in the canonical Gospel: 'We have piped to you and

16 Titus 3.5.
17 1 Thess. 5.17.
18 Gal. 4.19.
19 Ps. 95.1; 97.1; 149.1.

you have not danced';[20] if we are to understand these words
of that hymn: 'I wish to mourn, beat your breast, all of you,'
to mean what is written in the Gospel song: 'We have
lamented and you have not mourned';[21] if the words in that
hymn: 'I wish to adorn and I wish to be adorned,' mean
what is written in the canon: 'That Christ may dwell by
faith in your hearts';[22] and 'You are the temple of God and
the Spirit of God dwelleth in you';[23] if the words in that
hymn: 'I am a lamp to thee, thou who seest me,' mean what
is written in the canonical psalm: 'In thy light we shall see
light';[24] if these words in that hymn: 'I am a door to thee,
whoever thou art who knockest at me,' mean what we read
in the canonical psalm: 'Open ye to me the gates of justice,
I will go in to them and give praise to the Lord,'[25] and in
another psalm: 'Lift up your gates, O ye princes, and be ye
lifted up, O eternal gates, and the King of Glory shall enter
in';[26] if the words in that hymn: 'Thou who seest what I do,
be silent about my deeds,' mean what is written in the Book
of Tobias: 'It is good to hide the secret of a king'[27]—why is
it said that that hymn is not in the canon so that the secret
of the king may be hidden from the carnal, when the
thoughts expressed in that hymn are also read in the canon
and are there found to be so clear that these obscure phrases
are explained by them? What other reason except that they
have explanations on the words of that hymn under cover
of which they hide, and their real meaning is one which they
fear to disclose to strangers?

20 Matt. 11.17; Luke 7.32.
21 *Ibid.*
22 Eph. 3.17.
23 1 Cor. 3.16.
24 Ps. 35.10.
25 Ps. 117.19.
26 Ps. 23.7.
27 Tob. 12.7.

It would take too long to prove all the rest by argument, but from what I have said it is very easy to examine the rest and to see that what they offer as an honest and sincere explanation of this hymn is also found in the canon. Consequently, that is not a reason, but a subterfuge by which they explain that their hymn is kept out of the canon because the secret of the king must be hidden from carnal men. From this we draw a not undeserved conclusion that by their explanations they do not seek to reveal what they read, but to conceal what they think. This is not surprising, since they believed that in this hymn the Lord Jesus Himself was speaking, not by the mouths of Prophets or Apostles or angels, but by their own deceitful mouth, rather than as a teacher of truth. Certainly, when they attribute divine authority to this hymn in which the obscure author of this same hymn pretended that He had said: 'By a word I made sport of all things and I am never made sport of,' let them answer, if they can, these eminently spiritual men, where we are to go, to whom we are to give ear, in whose speech we are to have faith, in whose promise we are to put hope, if by a word Christ has made sport of all things, if by a word the omnipotent Master has made sport of all things, if, by a word, He who is the only-begotten, the Word of God the Father, has made sport of all things. What more can I say of such depraved, lying seducers of minds, first of their own, then of other men's, whom they have succeeded in allying with themselves, predestined to eternal death? I have written to your Reverence much more seriously than I intended and more at length than I had planned. You do well to guard watchfully against wolves, but you must also labor with the same pastoral care, and with the help of the Lord of pastors, to heal the sheep if, perchance, the wolves have broken in and have wounded them.

238. *Augustine*[1] *to Pascentius*[2]

At your request and insistence—may you kindly remember
it—nay, rather, at your command, which accords more with
your age and rank, I had wished to confer with you, face to
face, about the Christian faith, as far as the Lord might
grant me the ability. But as you disavowed after lunch what
had been agreed between us in the morning, namely, that
our words be taken down by secretaries, so that you might
not say afterward, what I hear that you do not fail to say, that
I had not dared to declare my faith to you, receive it now in
this letter which you may read and give to whomsoever you
wish to read, and answer in turn whatever you wish to write.
For it is unfair for anyone to wish to judge another and
refuse to judge himself.

Indeed, from our prior agreement, which you refused to
carry out at the specified noon hour, it can easily be deduced
which of us had no confidence in his faith: whether it was
the one who wished it to be declared and feared that it might
be held, or the one who was so anxious for it not to be withdrawn from the decision of debate that he wanted it committed to writing and preserved for the memory of readers,
so that no one, either conjecturing what was forgotten or
annoyed by disagreement, could say either that what was
said between us was not said or that something was said
that was not said. In these cases, men who are more eager
for contention than for truth usually seek out hiding places
for their own defense. This could not have been said either
by you or by me, or about you or about me, if you had kept
faith with your agreement, especially as you changed the
words in which you pronounced your belief as often as you

---

1 There is no formula of address.
2 An Arian count, member of the royal household and an energetic
tax-collector.

repeated them, but I believe this happened through forgetfulness, not by any deliberate deceit.

For at first you said that you believed in 'God the Father almighty, invisible, unbegotten, incomprehensible, and in Jesus Christ, His Son, God, born before ages, through whom all things were made, and in the Holy Spirit.' On hearing this, I answered that thus far you had not said anything that conflicted with my belief, and thus, if you had written it, I could have signed it. Somehow or other the matter progressed so far that you took a sheet of paper and said you were willing to set down in writing with your own hand all that you had said. When you gave it to me to read I noticed that you had left out 'Father' when you 'wrote God almighty, invisible, unbegotten, unborn.' When I called it to your attention, after considerable objection you added 'Father,' but in your writing you omitted 'incomprehensible,' which you had said orally. I made no observation on that.

Then, when I said that I was ready to sign it and that those words could still be mine, I first asked you, so as not to let slip what had come into my mind, whether the words 'unbegotten Father' are found anywhere in the divine Scriptures. I did this because at the beginning of our conversation when Arius[3] and Eunomius[4] were mentioned, not by me but by my brother Alypius, who wanted to know which of them had the support of Auxentius,[5] whom a short time before you had praised with no slight enthusiasm, you called down anathema on both Arius and Eunomius. Thereupon, you at once demanded that we should anathematize *homooúsion,* as if it were some man who was called this, like Arius and Eunomius. After that, you violently insisted that we show

---

3 Originator of Arianism, a complicated heresy concerning the divinity of the second Person of the Holy Trinity.
4 Bishop of Antioch (*c.* 361), an Arian whose apologetical book was refuted by St. Basil.
5 A fourth-century writer of pronounced Arian bias.

you this word in the Scriptures, and you would then join our communion. We answered that we spoke Latin and that word was Greek, and that we should first ask what *homo-ousion*[6] means, and then you could demand that it be shown in the sacred books. You, on your side, kept repeating that word over and over, making an odious show of it, recalling that it was written in the councils of our predecessors, and insisting that we should point out that very word *homooúsion* in the holy books. We replied again and again that our language was not Greek and that, first, there should be an interpretation and explanation of what *homooúsion* means, and then it should be sought for in the divine writings, because, even if the word itself is not found, perhaps the thing it stands for might be found; for what is more obstinate than to wrangle about the name while agreeing about the thing?

Therefore, as we had already argued these points and had reached the agreement, as I mentioned, that you should write out your creed, although I saw nothing in these words opposed to our faith, and had said that I was ready to subscribe to it, I asked, as I said, whether the Scriptures of God contained this expression, that the Father was unbegotten, and when you replied that it did I asked insistently to have it pointed out. Then one of the bystanders, a sharer in your belief, as far as I could discover, said to me: 'What, then! Do you say that the Father is begotten?' 'I do not say so,' I replied. And he said: 'Then, if He is not begotten, He is surely unbegotten.' To this I answered: 'You see how possible it is for a word which is not in God's Scripture to be understood in such a sense as to be proved correct. So it is

---

6 That is, consubstantial. This word arose in the Trinitarian conflict of the third century; it was first accepted as orthodox, then rejected as heretical because it was not always given the same meaning. It was revived in the Arian heresy. Today it is accepted that the Son is consubstantial with the Father.

with *homooúsion,* which we are being pressed to prove by the authority of the divine books; even if we do not find the exact word, it is possible that we may find the truth to which in our judgment the word may be correctly applied.'

After saying this I waited to hear what you thought of it, and you said that there was good reason why the expression unbegotten Father was not used in the holy Scriptures, lest such a word should dishonor Him.' 'Then,' I said, 'He has just been dishonored and that by your hand.' On hearing this you began to admit that you should not have said it. But when I warned you that if you thought this word was such as to dishonor God, you ought to erase it from your written statement, you reflected, I suppose, that it was possible for it to be used correctly and to be justifiable, and you went on to say: 'Certainly I do say it.' Then I repeated what I had said before, that in the same way it was equally possible that the word *homooúsion* might not be found in the sacred pages, yet could be justified as an expression used in a profession of faith, just as we read nowhere in those books that the Father is unbegotten, yet the term is admissible. Then you took back the paper which you had given me and tore it up. And we agreed that secretaries should be present in the afternoon to take down our words and that we should have a more careful discussion on these points as far as it rested with us.

We came, as you know, at the appointed hour, we brought secretaries, we sat down and waited for yours to appear. You repeated your creed and among your words I did not hear 'unbegotten Father,' I suppose because you had reflected on what had been said about it in the morning and you wanted to be on guard. Then you asked that I should also declare my faith. Recalling our agreement of the morning I asked that you would first be so good as to dictate what you had said; whereupon you cried out that we were preparing a malicious charge against you and that was why we wanted to keep your words in writing. I do not care to recall what I answered and I pray you to forget it. However, I preserved the respect due to your rank and I did not count as an insult what I had to take, not because it was true, but because you were a person in power. However, I ask you to pardon me for repeating your own words and saying in a subdued voice: 'Do you mean that we are preparing a malicious charge against you?'

On hearing this, you again repeated your creed in a louder tone, and this time I did not hear the words 'God the Son,' which up to this time you had never left out however often you recited it. Hereupon I asked, as moderately as I could, that the agreement between us about taking down our words should be carried out, and I even pointed out its usefulness from our present experience, saying that you yourself had not been able to recall your own most common words since you had not succeeded in repeating them in a case where it was especially necessary for you not to leave anything out. How much less, I said, could those who were listening to us remember our words, so that if you should want to review and discuss anything I said or I wanted to do the same with anything you said, they would be able to recall clearly whether it was said or not. How easily the secretaries could help us out of this predicament by reading the record! Then you said indignantly that it would have been better if you had known me by reputation alone because you had found that I fell short of what my fame had spread abroad. Upon this I recalled that when we greeted you before luncheon, and you spoke to us of that fame, I said that it bore false witness of me. In this certainly you have admitted that I spoke the truth. Consequently, when two witnesses speak contrary things to you about me, when my fame says one thing and I say another, surely I ought to be better pleased that I rather than it should be found truthful. But since it is written: 'God alone is true, and every man a liar,'[7] I fear that I may have been rash in saying even this of myself, for we are not truthful in or of ourselves, but when we are so it is because He alone who is true speaks in His servants.

If you recall these proceedings as I have told them, you see how wrong you are to boast before men that I did not dare to declare my faith to you, since, in fact, you refused to keep faith with our agreement, and, influential man that you are, because of the faith that you owe to the state you do not fear the imprecations of the provincials, but because of the faith that you owe to Christ you do fear the false charges of bishops. Moreover, as you were anxious to have prominent men[8] present at our discussion, I wonder why in that very avoidance of false charge you fear to have your words taken down by secretaries and you do not fear to have them heard by illustrious witnesses as they fall from your mouth. Do you not see that it is difficult for men to suspect you of having any fear of false charge on our part, which was your reason for not wanting your words to be taken down, but when you remembered that you had been caught up on a word written by your own hand before luncheon, they might suspect you of thinking that you could not so easily destroy the tablets of the secretaries as you had torn up that piece of paper? But, if you say that the proceedings were not as I have related them, either you are wrong through forgetfulness—for I do not venture to say that you are a liar—or I am equally wrong or I am a liar. You see, then, how right I am in saying that the detail of these extremely important proceedings should be taken down and transcribed, and how right you would have been in accepting that if your afternoon fear had not broken down your morning agreement.

---

7 Rom. 3.4.
8 Possidius (*Life of Augustine* 17) says that their names were omitted in this letter 'through fear.'

Listen, then, to my profession of faith. The mercy of the Lord our God is powerful enough to enable me to say what I believe so as not to offend either His truth or your human sensibility. I confess my belief in almighty God, the Father, eternal with that eternity—by this I mean immortality—which God alone has. I believe this of His Son, the only-begotten in the form of God; I believe this also of the Holy Spirit of God, who is the Spirit of God the Father and of His only begotten Son. But, inasmuch as that only-begotten Son of God the Father, our Lord and God, Jesus Christ, 'when the fulness of time was come,'[9] received the form of a servant,[10] at the appointed day of our salvation, many things are said of Him in the Scriptures speaking of Him in the form of God and many of Him in the form of a servant. I cite two of these by way of example, one reference for each. According to the form of God He said: 'I and the Father are one';[11] according to the form of a servant: 'For the Father is greater than I.'[12]

But where it is written of God: 'who only hath immortality,' and: 'to the invisible, the only God, be honor and glory,' and other expressions of this kind, we take those to apply not only to the Father, but also to the Son, considering Him in the form of God, and likewise the Holy Spirit. For the Father and the Son and the Holy Spirit are one God, and He is the only true and the only immortal God in His absolutely immutable substance. Now, if it is said of the flesh of diverse sexes that 'He who is joined to a harlot is one body,' and if of the spirit of man, who is not the Lord, it is immediately added: 'But he who is joined to the Lord is one spirit,'[13] how much more God the Father in the Son and

---

9 Gal. 4.4.
10 Phil. 2.7.
11 John 10.30.
12 John 14.28.
13 1 Cor. 6.16,17.

God the Son in the Father, and the Spirit of the Father and the Son are one God in whom there is no diversity of nature, when it is said of diverse natures joined together that they are either one spirit or one body!

And since the union of body and soul is called one man, why should not the much closer union of the Father and the Son be called one God when they are inseparably joined as the body and soul are not? And since the body and the soul are one man, although they are not one thing, why should it not be much more true that the Father and the Son are one God, since the Father and the Son are one according to that word of truth: 'I and the Father are one?'[14] In like manner, although the inner man and the outer man are not one—for the outer man is not of the same nature as the inner, because the outer man is spoken of when we name the body, but by the inner man we understand the rational soul only—the two of them are not called two men, but one man: how much more are the Father and the Son one God, since the Father and the Son are one because they are of the same nature or substance or any other word that can be more fittingly used to express what God is, whence it is said: 'I and the Father are one!' Therefore, the one Spirit of the Lord and one spirit of man are not one, yet when man is joined to the Lord they are not two spirits, but one; and one inner man and one outer man are not one, yet, because of the union of the bond of nature, they are at the same time not two men, but one man—so it is much more true when the Son of God says: 'I and the Father are one' that the Father is one God and the Son is one God, yet at the same time they are not two gods but one God.

What happened in the case of many saints called to be joint heirs of Christ by the 'adoption of children,'[15] when

14 John 10.30.
15 Eph. 1.5.

one faith and one hope and one charity[16] made them of 'one heart and one soul'[17] toward God is especially effective in making us understand that the one and same nature of the Father and the Son—the nature, if it may be so expressed, of Godhead—is such that the Father and the Son who are one, inseparably one and eternally one, are not two gods but one God. For those holy men were one in their participation and unity of one and the same nature, by which they were all men, even though in the diversity of wills and sentiments and opinions and in the variety of characters they were not one, but they will be fully and perfectly one when they attain to the end 'that God may be all in all.'[18] But God the Father and His Son, His Word,[19] God with God, are always unutterably one, and much more are they not two gods but one God.

Men who have less understanding of the reason why something is said want to form their opinions in haste, and, without carefully searching the Scriptures, they take up the defense of some theory from which it is difficult or impossible to detach them, because they yearn to be thought rather than to be learned and wise. Thereupon, they want to refer to God as God the words used of God in the form of servant and again they want to interpret as terms meaning nature and substance the words that refer to the mutual relationship of the Persons. But it is our faith to profess and to believe that the Father and the Son and the Holy Spirit are one God; we do not say that He who is the Son is the Father or that He who is the Father is the Son; nor do we call Him either Father or Son who is the Spirit of the Father and the Son. What is meant by these names is to be referred to their mutual relationship, not to the substance by which they are one. For,

16 Rom. 8.17; 1 Cor. 13.13.
17 Acts 4.32.
18 1 Cor. 15.28.
19 John 1.1.

when He is called Father He is necessarily the Father of a Son, and when He is called Son it is understood that He is the Son of a Father, and He is called Spirit in a sense to be referred to Someone breathing, and the One who breathes breathes forth the Spirit.[20]

None of those concepts is experienced corporeally, nor are they to be understood in the customary sense in God, 'who is able,' as the Apostle says, 'to do all things more abundantly than we desire or understand,'[21] and if this is true of His action, how much more is it of His being! For the word spirit is not used to express a relationship to something, but its use here signifies its nature: every incorporeal nature is called spirit in the Scriptures; hence, the term is applicable not only to the Father and the Son and the Holy Spirit, but to every rational being and soul. Thus the Lord says: 'God is a spirit and therefore they that adore God must adore him in spirit and truth.'[22] It is also written: 'Who maketh his angels spirits,'[23] and of certain men it is said: 'They are flesh, a wind that goeth and returneth not,'[24] and the Apostle says: 'No man knows what is done in man but the spirit of a man that is in him.'[25] It is also written: 'Who knoweth if the spirit of the children of man goeth upward and if the spirit of the beast goeth downward into the earth?'[26] The word spirit is also used in Scripture to indicate a certain distinction in the single soul of an individual man, as when the Apostle says: 'That your whole spirit and soul and body may be preserved unto the day of our Lord Jesus Christ,'[27] and likewise in another passage: 'If I pray in a

20 *Spiritus* in Latin means 'wind' or 'breath.'
21 Eph. 3.20.
22 John 4.24.
23 Ps. 103.4.
24 Ps. 77.39.
25 Cf. 1 Cor. 2.11.
26 Cf. Eccle. 3.21.
27 Cf. 1 Thess. 5.23.

tongue my spirit prayeth but my understanding is without fruit. What is it then? I will pray with the spirit, I will pray with the understanding.'[28] But in a special sense the Spirit is so named because of His relationship to the Father and the Son, that He is their spirit. However, according to substance, since it was said once for all that 'God is a spirit,' the Father is a spirit and so is the Son and the Holy Spirit, yet there are not three spirits, but one spirit—just as there are not three gods, but one God.

Why do you wonder? Peace is worth so much, not the kind of peace we ordinarily mean, nor the kind which is praised in this life because of the concord and charity of the faithful, but that 'peace of God which,' as the Apostle says, surpasseth all understanding,[29]—and what understanding but our own, that is, of every rational being? Therefore, reflecting upon our weakness, and hearing the Apostle confess and declare: 'Brethren, I do not count myself to have apprehended,'[30] and 'If any man think that he knoweth anything he hath not yet known as he ought to know,'[31] let us carry on our discussion with the help of the divine Scriptures, to the best of our ability, peacefully, without strife, not striving to outdo each other in a vain and childish rivalry, that the peace of Christ may rather prevail in our hearts so far as He has given us to experience it in this life. And considering what that peace has effected among the brethren, of whom from so many souls and so many hearts He has made one soul and one heart,[32] toward God, let us believe with due filial love and much more intensely in that peace of God 'which surpasseth all understanding,' that the Father and the Son and the Holy Spirit are not three gods, but one God,

---

28 1 Cor. 14.14,15.
29 Phil. 4.7.
30 Phil. 3.13.
31 1 Cor. 8.2.
32 Acts 4.32.

and let us do this in a manner as much higher than that of those whose soul and heart were one as the peace which surpasseth all understanding is higher than that peace which the one heart and one soul of all maintained toward God.

But the same Person who is Son of God we also call Son of man, not, however, considering Him in the form of God in which He is equal to God the Father, but in the form of servant which He took,[33] in which the Father is greater than He. And because we say the same Person is the Son of man, we confess that the Son of God was crucified, not in the power of His divinity, but in the weakness of His humanity, not through the continuity of His own nature, but through His assumption of ours.

Consider now for awhile the passages of Scripture which force us to confess that the Lord is one God, whether we are asked about the Father alone, or the Son alone, or the Holy Spirit alone, or about the Father and the Son and the Holy Spirit together. Certainly, it is written: 'Hear, O Israel, the Lord thy God is one Lord.'[34] Of whom do you think that is said? If it is said only of the Father, then our Lord Jesus Christ is not God, and whence did those words come to Thomas when he touched Christ and cried out: 'My Lord and my God,'[35] which Christ did not reprove but approved, saying: 'Because thou hast seen, thou hast believed?'[36] Moreover, if the Son is Lord God and the Father is Lord God, and both are now two lords and two gods, how will it be true to say: 'The Lord thy God is one Lord?' Or is it, perhaps, that the Father is one Lord but the Son is not one Lord but only lord, in the sense that there are many gods and many lords, but not in the sense that He is one, of whom it is written: 'The Lord thy God is one Lord'? In that case, what

33 Cf. Phil. 2.6,7.
34 Deut. 6.4.
35 John 20.28.
36 John 20.27.

answer shall we give to the Apostle when he says: 'For although there be that are called gods either in heaven or on earth (for there be gods many and lords many), yet to us there is but one God, the Father, of whom are all things and we unto him; and one Lord Jesus Christ by whom are all things and we by him.'[37] Moreover, if what is said of one God the Father entails the exclusion from Him of the Son, let those who dare say that the Father cannot be considered lord because there is 'one lord, our Lord Jesus Christ.' For, if He is one, undoubtedly He is the only one; if He is the only one, how is the Father also Lord unless He and the Father are one God and the only God, not excluding the Holy Spirit? Therefore, the Father is God and with Him the Son is one God, although the Father is not one with Him; likewise, there is one Lord Jesus Christ and with Him one Lord, the Father, although Jesus Christ is not one with Him as if the Father were Jesus Christ, for this name was taken in the dispensation of mercy when He took our humanity.

But perhaps in the words of the Apostle: 'One Lord, our Lord Jesus Christ,' you do not wish the word 'one' to be attached to the word 'Lord,' but to what follows: 'by whom are all things,' so that we should have not 'one Lord,' but 'one by whom are all things.' In this case, it would not be the Father by whom are all things, but the Father alone of whom are all things, and the Son alone by whom are all things. If that is so, you must finally admit that the Father and the Son are one God our Lord. 'For who hath known the mind of the Lord? or who hath been his counsellor? or who hath first given to him and recompense shall be made him? For of him and by him and in him are all things, to him be glory.'[38] He did not say: 'of the Father all things and by the

---

37 1 Cor. 8.5,6.
38 Rom. 11.34-36.

Son all things,' but 'of him and by him and in him.' In whom?
None but the Lord, of whom he says: 'For who hath known
the mind of the Lord?' Of the Lord, therefore, and by the
Lord and in the Lord are all things, and not one way in
one and another way in another, but in one Lord, because
he did not say: 'To them be glory,' but 'to him be glory.'

But if anyone affirms that when the Apostle says: 'One
Lord Jesus Christ by whom are all things' he does not mean
'one Lord' or 'one by whom are all things,' but 'one Jesus
Christ' who is called 'one Lord Jesus Christ,' not in the
sense of 'one Lord' but 'one Jesus Christ,' what is he to say
when he hears the same Apostle exclaiming: 'One Lord, one
faith, one baptism, one God and Father of all'?[39] Since he is
referring to God the Father in this passage where he says:
'one God and Father of all,' surely when he said above 'one
Lord' whom else does he mean but the Lord Jesus Christ?
If, then, they agree to this, let the Father cease to be Lord,
because there is one Lord Jesus Christ. If it is senseless and
wicked to think that, let us learn to understand the unity of
the Father and the Son and the Holy Spirit, and in what is
said of one only God let us not be hindered from applying it
at once to the Son or to the Holy Spirit, because the Father
is indeed not the Son and the Son is not the Father and the
Spirit of both is not the Father or the Son, yet the Father
and the Son and the Holy Spirit are one who is the only
true Lord God.

As for the Holy Spirit, if He were either not God or not
the true God, our bodies would not be His temple. 'Know
you not,' says the Apostle, 'that your bodies are the temple of
the Holy Spirit who is in you, whom you have from God?'
and lest anyone should deny that the same Spirit is God, he
immediately follows up and says: 'You are not your own,
for you are bought with a great price. Glorify God, therefore,

---

39 Eph. 4.5,6.

in your body,'[40] that God, namely, whose temple he said our bodies were. Now, this would be a remarkable thing if what I hear you say is true, that the Holy Spirit is less than the Son as the Son is less than the Father. For, since our bodies are the members of Christ,[41] as the Apostle says, and our bodies are likewise the temple of the Holy Spirit, as the same Apostle says, I wonder much how the members of the greater are the temple of the lesser. But perhaps they are now pleased to say that the Holy Spirit is greater than the Lord Jesus Christ. There seems to be some support for that opinion in the following statement that 'Whoever shall speak a word against the Son of man, it shall be forgiven him, but he that shall speak against the Holy Spirit, it shall not be forgiven him, neither in this world nor in the world to come.'[42] It is more dangerous to sin against a greater than against a lesser, but it is not permissible to separate the Son of man from the Son of God, because it was the very Son of God who became the Son of man, not by changing what He was, but by taking on what He was not. But God forbid that such impiety should be believed, that the Holy Spirit is greater than the Son. Therefore, let such statements not lead us astray too easily as if they proved that one Person is greater than the other.

There are, indeed, certain passages which to men of little intelligence make it seem as if the Son Himself were greater than the Father. For, if anyone were asked: 'What is greater, the true or the truth?' would he not answer that truth is greater? Whatever is true is true because of truth. But it is not so in God. We do not say of the two that the Son is greater than the Father, yet the Son is spoken of as truth: 'I am,' He says, 'the way and the truth and the life.'[43] But you wish to apply to the Father only these words which He

40 1 Cor. 6.19,20.
41 1 Cor. 6.15.
42 Matt. 12.32; Luke 12.40.
43 John 14.6.

said: 'That they may know thee, the only true God and Jesus
Christ whom thou hast sent.'[44] where we mentally supply
'Jesus Christ, true God,' as if the passage read thus: 'That
they may know thee and Jesus Christ whom thou hast sent,
the one true God,' Thus we avoid the absurdity of saying
that Jesus Christ is not true God because it is said of the
Father: 'Thee the one true God,' or that the Father is not
Lord because it is said of Christ, 'one Lord.'[45] Nevertheless,
according to a perverted or rather erroneous understanding
of this, God truth is greater than God true, because true
derives from truth; therefore, the Son is greater than the
Father because the Son is truth, the Father is true. This
distorted idea is driven from the mind by the knowledge
that God the Father is true by begetting truth, not by being
part of it, and that the substance of the true Begetter is not
different from the substance of the Truth begotten.

But since the eye of the human heart is powerless to contemplate these truths, it happens that it is confused by controversy. And when will it see? The Scripture says that the
Son of God, our Lord and Saviour Jesus Christ, is the Word
of God, and truth and wisdom; and men say that before the
Incarnation in which He took flesh of the Virgin Mary He
was visible and mortal, without any assumption of corporeal
nature, in the very nature and substance by which He is the
Word of God and the wisdom of God; and they try thereby
to prove what they hold by saying that the words: 'To the
immortal, invisible, the only God'[46] were said only of the
Father! I ask you: The word of man is not visible, much less
the Word of God, but regarding that wisdom of which it is
said that she 'reacheth everywhere by reason of her purity,'
and 'no defiled thing cometh into her,' and 'remaining in

---

44 John 17.3.
45 1 Cor. 8.6.
46 1 Tim. 1.17.

herself she reneweth all things,'[47] and other like passages—if it is mortal, I know not what to say except that I mourn over human presumption and marvel at divine patience.

Since, then, it is said of wisdom that 'she is the brightness of eternal light,'[48] I do not imagine that your followers are now saying that the light of the Father—and what is it but His substance?—existed at some time with the brightness begotten by itself, according as those words can be believed and to some extent understood in connection with divine and spiritual and incorporeal and unchangeable things, for I hear that your friends have corrected them. Or is it, perhaps, untrue that they once said that the Father existed at some time without the Son, as if the eternal light existed without the brightness which it begot? If the Son of God was born of the Father, then the Father has now ceased to beget; and if He ceased, He began; but if He began to beget, there was a time when He was without the Son. But He never was without the Son, because His Son is His wisdom, which is the brightness of eternal light. Therefore, the Father begets from all eternity and the Son is born from all eternity. Here, again, we have to fear the idea of an imperfect begetting, hence we do not say He was born, but He is born. Bear with me, I beg of you, in these limitations of human thought and language, and let us take refuge together in the help of the Spirit of God, speaking through the Prophet: 'Who shall declare his generation?'[49]

Meanwhile, I ask you to look carefully whether the divine Scripture says anywhere of different substances that they are one. And if no mention is made except of things which evidently belong to one and the same substance, what reason have we for rebelling against the true Catholic faith? But if you find this written anywhere about different substances, then

47 Wisd. 7.24,25,27.
48 Wisd. 7.26.
49 Isa. 53.8.

I shall be forced to look for another passage from which I can show you that *homooúsion* is rightly used of the Father and the Son. For, if those who either do not know our Scriptures or do not study them thoroughly, yet who believe that the Son is of the same substance with and equal to the Father, should say to others who refuse to believe this, although they believe that God the Father has an only-begotten Son: 'Was God unwilling to have a Son equal to Himself or was He unable? If He was unwilling, He is jealous, if He was unable, He has no power: to believe either of these alternatives about God is sacrilegious'—in this case I do not know what they could say if they wanted to avoid saying something senseless and completely fatuous.

Here, then, is my belief. I have expressed it for you as best I could. Much more could be said and there could be a more detailed discussion, but I am afraid that what I have said may be an intrusion on your public duties. However, I wanted this to be written down to my dictation and I have also taken the trouble to sign it with my own hand, which, indeed, I would have been willing to do before if the agreement between us had been kept. But now I certainly think that you have no right to say that I was afraid to state my belief to you, since I have not only stated it but have signed it in writing, so that no one can say that I either said what I did not say or that I did not say what I said. Do this yourself if you are not looking for judges who will bow down to you before your face, but for those who will exercise their own freedom in judging your written words. If you fear a false accusation—a word I would never have dared to use if you had not said it—you are free not to sign your statement, for I have not wanted your name to be written in this letter of mine so as not to go against your wish.

It is easy for anyone to win a victory over Augustine. You decide whether the victory goes to truth or applause; it is not mine to say anything except that it is easy to win a victory over Augustine, and how much easier for anyone to seem to have won over him or, if he does not seem to, at least to have the reputation of it! It is easy, but I do not want you to think it is anything great; I do not want you to seek credit as for something great. For when men notice the great passion of your heart in this affair, many will be glad of the chance to make friends with so powerful a man by a few shouts of 'Good! Good!' I will not say that if they do not curry favor or if they express a contrary sentiment they will have to fear an enemy, which would be a silly and senseless thing to do—still, most men are like that.

Do not, therefore, try to see how a victory can be won over Augustine, who is only one man, such as he is, but see, rather, whether a victory can be won over *homooúsion,* not the mere Greek word which can easily raise a laugh among the unintelligent, but that doctrine which is expressed thus: 'I and the Father are one,' and: 'Holy Father, keep them in thy name whom thou hast given me, that they may be one as we also are one.'[50] And, likewise, a little further on He says: 'Not for them only do I pray but for them also who through their word shall believe in me; that they all may be one as thou, Father, in me and I in thee, that they also may be one in us, that the world may believe that thou hast sent me. And the glory which thou hast given me, I have given to them that they may be one as we also are one, I in them and thou in me, that they may be made perfect in one.'[51] Notice that as often as He says: 'that they may be one,' He does not at any time say: 'that they and we may be one,' but: 'as thou and I are one so they also may be one in us,' because, as they whom He wished to make partakers of one eternal life were of one and the same substance, so it is said of the Father and the Son: 'We are one,' because they

---

50 John 10.36; 17.11.
51 John 17.20-23.

are of one and the same substance and they are not partakers of eternal life, but they are pre-eminently eternal life itself. According to the form of servant, He could have said: 'I and they are one,' or 'We are one', but He did not say that because He wished to show that His and the Father's substance was not the same as theirs. If He had said: 'that thou and they may be one as thou and I are one,' or: 'that thou and I and they may be one as I and thou are one,' no one of us would refuse to admit the possibility of saying 'they are one' even of different substances. But now you see how that is not so, because He did not say so, and by often repeating what He said He called it strongly to our attention.

You find, therefore, in Scripture a certain unity of different natures, as we have shown above, but we add and understand what unity we mean as when we say that of one soul and body there is or there are one living being, and one person and one man. If you find in Scripture the expression 'they are one' used without any qualification, except as referring to those who are of one substance, you will be fully justified in demanding that we produce other passages from which we can prove *homooúsion*. There are, indeed, many others, but meantime meditate on this one and lay aside your zest for rivalry, that God may be favorable to you. It is not a good thing for a man to overcome a man, but it is good for a man to be willingly overcome by truth, just as it is an evil thing for a man to submit to truth unwillingly. For truth must necessarily prevail, whether we deny or admit it. Pardon me if I have spoken too freely—it was not to dishonor you, but to defend myself. I have relied on your seriousness and prudence, because you can measure how great necessity you imposed on me of answering you. If I have been wrong in this, pardon me this, also.

I, Augustine, have put my signature to this writing which I have dictated and reread.

239. *Augustine to the same Pascentius*[1]

If you say that you have declared your belief to me and that I have refused to declare my belief to you, as I hear you do not refrain from saying, reflect, I beg of you, how untrue both statements are. For you have not been willing to declare your belief to me and I have not refused to declare my belief to you, but I wished to state it in such form that no one could say that I had either said something I had not said, or had not said what I did say. You would have stated your belief to me if you had said in what you disagree with us; if you had said: 'I believe in God the Father, who made the Son as His first creation before all other creation; and in the Son, neither equal to the Father nor like Him, nor true God; and in the Holy Spirit made by the Son after the Son.' This is what I hear that you say, and if, perhaps, it is not true that you say it, I would prefer to know that from you. But if it is true that you say it, I wish to know how you defend your belief from Scripture. You said just now that you believe 'in God the Father almighty, invisible, immortal, not begotten by anyone, and from whom are all things; and in His Son, Jesus Christ, God, born before all ages, by whom all things were made; and in the Holy Spirit.' This is not your belief, it is the belief of both of us; provided you add that the Virgin Mary brought forth this same Son of God, Jesus Christ, which we both believe; and any other truths which we agree in professing. If you had been willing to state your belief, you would not have stated this one which we both share, but that other one in which we differ from you.

I would say this to your face, if our words were taken down as we had agreed. But, as you refused to do this, saying that you were afraid of false charges on our part, and as you went back after lunch on the agreement which you had

---

1 There is no formula of address.

consented to in the morning, why should I say what you could turn to any sense you wished and declare that I had said it, while I would have nothing to show what I had said or how I said it? Do not, then, boast any longer that you had stated your belief, but I had not stated mine, because there are men who notice that I am the one to have confidence in my belief, since I was willing to have it written down, while you were not, because you were afraid of a probable false charge. In that way you would have been ready to deny it, if objection were made that you had said something contrary to our belief. See what you have made men think of you! But, if you were not going to deny what was objected to, why did you not want your words written down, especially as you had wanted prominent men to be present at our talk? Why, in your desire to avoid a false charge, did you fear the stylus of the secretaries, but not the testimony of important men?

However, if you want me to state my belief, as you say that you have stated yours, I can say very briefly that I believe in the Father and the Son and the Holy Spirit. But if you want to hear some special detail in which you differ from me, I believe in God the Father and the Son and the Holy Spirit, not calling the Father the Son or the Son the Father, or the Spirit of both of them either the Father or the Son; yet the Father is God and the Son is God and the Holy Spirit is God, and the Father and Son and the Holy Spirit are one only God, eternal and immortal of His own proper substance, as He is the only God eternal and immortal in virtue of that divinity which is before all ages. If this does not satisfy you and you would like to hear from me how this belief is based on holy Scripture, read that longer letter that I sent to your Benignity. If you have no time to read it, neither have I time to waste in bandying words with you. However, as far as God gives me the ability to dictate or to write to you, I can answer any point you wish by dictating or by writing.

I, Augustine, have signed my name to this writing dictated and reread by me.

240. *Answer of Pascentius to Augustine*[1]

I had hoped that you, my dearest brother, would give up the pattern of your former error, and now I marvel that you still persist in it, as the letter which you sent me proclaims. For your Worthiness is like a thirsty man, parched with great heat, who finds muddy water and wallows in it, but if he finds clear, cool water and drinks it, it does not do him much good, because his heart and soul are covered with mud. Finally—I say it with all due respect to you—the pattern of your Excellency's belief is like a tree, bent and knotted, with nothing straight about it, an offense to the sight of the eyes. Your Holiness wrote me that the Father is God, the Son is God, the Holy Spirit is God, but one God. How can there be one God from three? Is He, perhaps, one triple Person, called by this name? If you had been willing and had confidence in your own profession of belief, you would have sat down with me and with your fellow bishops, with a pure and peaceful spirit, and you would have discoursed on the things of God which have to do with glory and spiritual grace. What use is there in writing back and forth what does not edify us?

---

1 There is no formula of address.

241. Augustine to Pascentius[1]

Your letter can neither stir me to return your abuse nor keep me from replying. What you wrote would trouble me if it proceeded from the truth of God instead of from the power of man. You said that my pattern of belief 'is a tree, bent and knotted, with nothing straight about it, an offense to the sight of the eyes.' What would you say against me if I had gone back on the agreement we had made together in the morning, and in a very easy subject and one to my liking had set up a bent rebuttal full of knots of difficulty? You would not have concluded that I had wallowed in muddy water but, what is worse, that I was drowned in the drunkenness of perfidy if I had not come back after lunch the same as I had retired before lunch. But look, now, have you not written something and done it willingly, and have you feared any false charge? You could do the same with the rest, so that there might be something for us and others to examine and judge. As to your saying that I believe in a triple Person in God, if you had condescended to read the other, somewhat longer, letter that I sent you, and if you had been willing to answer what was said in it, perhaps you would not have said this. Nevertheless, take this very point, that I am supposed to believe in a triple Person in God; you have both dictated it and sent it to me without fear of any false charge. See how you have proved the truth of what I say, that your reason for not wanting to dictate your words as we had agreed when we were together was not your fear of a false charge, but your lack of confidence in the truth of what you said. And now, as it has suited you to dictate a letter asking whether I believe in a triple Person in God, I answer that I do not so believe; His form is one because His Godhead, if

1 There is no formula of address.

I may so speak, is one, and therefore He is one God: Father and Son and Holy Spirit.

I ask you to be so kind as to answer me briefly how you interpret what the Apostle says: 'He that is joined to a harlot is made one body, but he that is joined to the Lord is one spirit.'[2] He says that bodies joined together, even of different sex, are one body, and although the human spirit cannot possibly say: 'I and the Lord are one,' yet, when it is joined to the Lord, it is one spirit; how much more He who said with perfect truth: 'I and the Father are one,'[3] because He is inseparably joined to the Father, is one God with the Father —if this word 'joined' is admissible when we speak of the divinity, because never at any time was He or could He be separated by any distance! Answer this: Do you like to call it a double spirit when he who is joined to the Lord is one spirit? If you do not like that, then I did not say that God the Father and Son and Holy Spirit is a triple God, but one God. However, if you are willing for us to speak face to face, I would be grateful to your Worthiness and your Benevolence. But, as you have now had the kindness to write me one letter, and have done it willingly, be so good as to write me another[4] saying that we will dictate what we are going to say, and I will not disappoint your desire, so far as the Lord helps me. For, if 'you write and I write' does not edify us, how can 'you say, I say' be edifying, when we find nothing to read and analyze after the noise of words?

I, Augustine, have dictated this and have signed it after having reread it. Let us refrain from wrangling, let us not waste our time, let us give our attention preferably to the question at issue between us.

2 1 Cor. 6.16,17.
3 John 10.30.
4 Pascentius did not write again, according to Possidius (*Life* 17).

242. *Augustine to the excellent lord, his deservedly honored and cherished Elpidius*[1]

That is another question which one of us is wrong in his belief and understanding of the Trinity. I am very grateful to you for trying to reclaim me from error because you think I am wrong, although you have never met me. May God reward your kindness in this and grant you to know what you think you do know, for it is a difficult matter, as I see it. And I ask you not to think I am demeaning you when I ask for you this great gift of understanding, for I fear that a presumption of supposed knowledge may alienate from your ears, not true precepts, perhaps, which I would never take upon myself to give you, but certainly my good wishes, which, unlearned as I am, I may form for you—for they are to be received as a sign of friendship, not of superior skill—and that you may be angry with me because I have not praised you as a wise man instead of being grateful that I have asked wisdom for you. However, if I, bearing as I do the burden of episcopal rank, am willing to embrace your Benevolence for having, as you write, been so kind as to send me[2] even across the sea to Bonosus and Jason, men of great learning, in order to bring back rich fruits from their arguments, and for having taken the trouble, in your kind solicitude, to send me a clever and forceful writing by one of your bishops, in order to remove the clouds of error from me, how much more reasonable is it for you to take in good part my having asked the Lord God to grant you what can be given by no human strength or resources! For the Apostle says: 'Now we have received not the spirit of this world but the Spirit that is of God: that we may know the things that are given us from God; which things also we speak, not in the

---

1 Another Arian correspondent.
2 That is, one of Augustine's letters or treatises.

learned words of human wisdom, but in the doctrine of the
Spirit, comparing spiritual things with spiritual. But the
sensual man perceives not these things that are of the Spirit
of God, for it is foolishness to him.'[3]

I would greatly prefer to ask you, therefore, if that is
possible, to what extent a man is to be called sensual, when
if we rise above him we may rightly rejoice to have attained
in some part of us those truths, perhaps, which remain
unchangeably above the human mind and understanding.
We must be on our guard lest, when we hear that the Son
is equal to the Father, we think that is something without
sense, because we are still acting as the sensual man of whom
it is said that the things that are of the Spirit of God are
foolishness to him. It is true, however, that the Majesty
which is exalted above all things can be conceived of by
spiritual beings, but can be defined by none; nevertheless,
according to my way of thinking, it is easy to see that He
by whom all things were made and without whom nothing
was made was not Himself made. For, if He was made by
Himself, He existed before He was made, so that He might
be made by Himself, which is certainly as ridiculous a thing
to say as it is futile to think. But, if He was not made by
Himself, then He was not made at all, since whatever was
made was made by Him; 'All things were made by him and
without him was made nothing.'[4]

I wonder that so little attention is paid to what the
Evangelist wanted to convey so explicitly that he would allow
no one to misunderstand, for he was not content with saying:
'All things were made by him,' but he added: 'and without
him nothing was made.' As for me, although I am slow and
the eye of my mind is still too much weakened by darkness
incompletely removed to behold the incomparable and un-

3 1 Cor. 2.12-14.
4 John 1.3.

utterable perfection of the Father and the Son, I accept with the greatest ease what the Gospel lays down as a foundation, not to make us comprehend the Divinity thereby, but to warn us not to boast rashly that we do comprehend it. For, if all things were made by Him, whatever was not made by Him was not made. But He was not made by Himself; therefore, He was not made. We are compelled by the Evangelist to believe that all things were made by Him; we are compelled by the same Evangelist not to believe that He was made. Likewise, if nothing was made without Him, He is therefore nothing, because He was made without Him. If it is sacrilegious to think that, it remains for us to confess that He either was not made without Himself or that He was not made. But we cannot say that He was not made without Himself, for, if He made Himself, He was already in existence before He was made, and, if another by whom He was made received help from Him in making Him, He nonetheless existed before He was made, so that He might be made with His own help. It remains, then, that He was made without Himself. But, whatever was made without Him is nothing. Therefore, He is either nothing or He was not made. And if He was not made and nevertheless is the Son, without doubt He was born.

'How,' you say, 'could the Son of God be born of the Father alone and be equal to Him of whom He was born?' I am not now able to declare that and I yield to the Prophet saying: 'Who shall declare his generation?'[5] If you think this is to be referred to the human generation by which He was born of a virgin, look into yourself and ask your soul whether the Prophet would dare to declare the divine generation if words failed him for the human one. 'Do not say that He is equal,' you say. Why not? when the Apostle said it:

5 Isa. 53.8.

'He thought it not robbery,' he says, 'to be equal with God.'[6] For, although he did not make clear that equality for a human mind not yet purified, he nevertheless put down in words what the purified soul can discover in reality. Let us devote ourselves to cleansing our heart, so that from it may come the sight by which we may be able to see those things; 'Blessed are the clean of heart,' He says, 'for they shall see God.'[7] Thus, by passing beyond the cloudy images of the sensual man we shall come to that unclouded purity by which we may see what we see cannot be said.

If I had time and if opportunity were given me to answer individual points in the treatise which you kindly sent me, I think you would recognize that the more anyone of yours thinks he is uncovering pure truth, the less he is clothed with the light of truth. To pass over other details and recall this one alone for the present, which I especially groaned over, who could bear to hear them say that they are uncovering pure truth, having divested it of all its wrappings, when the Apostle Paul says: 'We see now through a glass in a dark manner, but then face to face.'[8] If anyone were to say "We see pure truth,' there would be nothing more blind than that presumption of sight, but he did not say 'We see,' but 'We uncover,' which makes it seem not only as if truth were open to the perception of the mind, but as if it were also encompassed by the power of human speech. There are many things which can be said of the unutterableness of the Trinity, while itself cannot be expressed—otherwise, it is not unutterable— and by these words we understand that it cannot be expressed. But now I think my letter has exceeded the bounds of moderation, although you had warned me to write briefly. However, as you were so kind as to appeal to the tradition

6 Phil. 2.6.
7 Matt. 5.8.
8 1 Cor. 13.12.

of the ancients, if you will take the trouble to recall the
length of some of Cicero's letters—for you mentioned him,
too, in your letter—I shall not seem boorish to you.

243. *Augustine gives greeting in the Lord to his beloved lord and most dearly cherished brother, Laetus*[1]

I have read the letter which you sent to the brethren, in
which you indicated that you would like a letter from me,
and I long to comfort you because your apprenticeship[2] is
being assailed by many temptations. I grieved for you, brother,
and I could not refrain from writing, nor could I refuse to
satisfy your desire as well as my own, because I saw that I
owed it to you as a duty of charity. If, then, you claim to be
a recruit of Christ, do not leave the camp in which you have
to build that tower[3] of which the Lord speaks. If you stand in
it and fight with the weapons of the word of God, no temptation can reach you from any side. When you hurl your weapons from there against the Enemy, they fall on him with
crushing weight, and those aimed at you glance off from
that strong defense. Reflect also that, although our Lord Jesus
Christ is our king, He reminded us that kings called their
soldiers from that company in which He deigned to become
our brother, and that every single one ought to be fit, with a
following of 10,000 soldiers, to go to war with the king who
has 20,000.

But notice what He said shortly before He pronounced
the warning parables of the tower and the king: 'If any
man come to me and hate not his father and mother and

---

1 A gentleman who had entered religious life and was tempted by his
mother to abandon it for worldly reasons.
2 The word used by Augustine, *tirocinia,* means the training period of a
young soldier.
3 Cf. Luke 14.28.

wife and children and brethren and sisters, yea and his own
life, he cannot be my disciple; and whoever doth not carry
his cross and come after me cannot be my disciple.' Then
He goes on: 'Which of you, having a mind to build a tower,
doth not first sit down and reckon the charges that are necessary to finish it, lest, after he hath laid the foundation and is
not able to finish it, all that pass by and see it begin to say:
"This man began to build and was not able to finish?" Or
what king going to make war against another king doth not
first sit down and think whether he be able with ten thousand
to meet him that with twenty thousand cometh against him?
Or else whilst the other is yet afar off, sending an embassy
he desireth conditions of peace.' And He made clear the
purpose of those parables by saying: 'So likewise every one
of you that doth not renounce all that he possesseth cannot
be my disciple.'[4]

Therefore, the charges necessary for building the tower and
the strength of 10,000 against the king who has 20,000 mean
nothing else than that each one should renounce all that is
his. The first part of the speech is in agreement with its final
conclusion. The part where He says that each one should
renounce all that he possesses includes the admonition that
he should 'hate his father and mother and wife and children
and brethren and sisters, yea and his own life also.' For all
these are his personal possessions which often ensnare him
and prevent him from attaining not those private, transitory
gains of time, but the universal ones which remain forever.
The very fact that a certain woman is now your mother is a
sure proof that she is not mine. Therefore, it is a temporal
and transitory thing—and you see that it has now passed—
that she conceived you, bore you in her womb, brought you
forth and nourished you with her milk. But, inasmuch as she
is a sister in Christ, she belongs to you and to me and to all

4 Luke 14.26-33.

who have been promised a heavenly inheritance with God
for our Father and Christ for our Brother in the same kinship
of love. These are eternal goods, these are spoiled by no
deterioration of time, these are the more confident objects of
our hope, because we are told that their attainment is not a
matter of private but of universal privilege.

You can recognize this in the case of your own mother.
For, what made her free you from the entanglement in which
you were just now, and turn you back and set you going
when you were slowed down in your intended course, but
the fact that she is your own mother? But the fact that she is
a sister to all who have God for Father and the Church for
Mother does not detract anything from you any more than
it does from me or all the brethren who love her not with a
private love as you do in your home, but with a universal
love in the household of God. And thus your being joined to
her by the bond of fleshly relationship should make it possible
for others to share in your lot by speaking to her more
familiarly and finding her door more widely open for counsel,
so that this very private and personal love for you may be
killed in her, lest she think it more important that she brought
you forth from her womb than that she was brought forth
with you from the womb of the Church. What I have said
of your mother is to be understood of any other relationship.
Let each one also think this about his own life, that he may
hate in it that private affection which is undoubtedly transitory
and may love in it that union and sense of sharing of which
it was said: 'They had one soul and heart toward God.'[5]
Thus, your soul is not your own, but is shared by all the
brethren whose souls are also yours, or, rather, whose souls
form with yours not souls, but one soul, the single soul of
Christ, of which the psalm says that it is delivered from the

---

5 Cf. Acts 4.32.

hand of the dog.'⁶ From this it is an easy step to contempt of death.

Let parents not be angry that the Lord gives us command-ment to hate them, since He commands the same about our own life. For, as we are commanded in this passage about our life, to hate it as we do our parents for Christ's sake, so what the Lord says in another place about our life can be very aptly applied to our parents, also: 'He that loveth his life,' He says, 'shall lose it.'⁷ I will also make bold to say: 'He that loveth his parents shall lose them.' It is true He there speaks of our life when He says 'shall hate' as He says here 'shall lose.' But this precept by which we are enjoined to lose our life does not mean that a man should kill himself, which would be an unforgivable crime, but it does mean that he kill in himself the earthly attachment to his life which makes him take pleasure in this present life to the detriment of the life to come—for this is the meaning of 'shall hate his life' and 'shall lose it'—while in the same admonition He speaks most openly of the profit of gaining one's life when He says: 'He that loseth his life in this world shall find it unto life eternal.'⁸ In like manner, it is proper to say of parents that he who loves them loses them, not in the manner of murderers, but that with the spiritual sword of the word of God he kills his carnal affection for those who try to bind both themselves and their offspring with the fetters of this world, and by striking and killing with faith and confidence he brings that to life in what makes them brothers, whereby in common with their earthly children they acknowledge God and the Church as their eternal parents.

And now the zeal for truth and the desire of recognizing and understanding the will of God in the holy Scriptures

6 Ps. 21.21.
7 John 12.25; Matt. 10.39; 16.25; Mark 8.35; Luke 17.33.
8 Cf. John 12.25.

urges you on, the duty of preaching the Gospel urges you on. The Lord gives the signal for us to stand guard in camp, to build the tower from which we may be able to discern and ward off the Enemy of our eternal life. The heavenly trumpet of Christ urges the soldier on to battle and his mother holds him back. Certainly, she is not like the mother of the Machabees[9] or even like the Spartan mothers,[10] of whom history relates that they used to rouse their sons to warlike contests more keenly and more fervidly than the trumpet call could do, as they urged them to shed their blood for their earthly fatherland. For the mother who will not allow you to retire from worldly cares in order to learn life shows plainly how she would allow you to give up the world entirely in order to meet death if need arose.

But what does she say or what argument does she adduce? Is it, perhaps, those ten months in which you lay in her womb, and the pangs of birth and the burden of bringing you up? This is what you must kill with the sword of salvation; this is what you must destroy in your mother that you may find her unto life eternal. Remember that you must hate this in her if you love her, if you are a recruit of Christ, if you have laid the foundations of the tower, that the passersby may not say: 'This man began to build and was not able to finish.'[11] That is earthly affection and it still has the ring of the 'old man.'[12] Christian warfare bids us destroy this earthly affection both in ourselves and in our kindred, but not, of course, to the extent that anyone should be ungrateful to his parents or should mock at the list of their services to him, since by them he was brought forth into this life and cherished and fed. A man should always pay his filial duty, but let these things keep their place where higher duties do not call.

---

9 2 Mach. 7.1-6; 20-29.
10 Plutarch, *Mor. Lacaenarum apophth.*
11 Luke 14.28.
12 Eph. 4.22; Col. 3.9; Rom. 6.6.

Mother Church is also the Mother of your mother. She begot you both in Christ, she formed you in her womb of the blood of martyrs, she brought you forth to everlasting light, she nourished you with the milk of faith, and she still nourishes you by preparing stronger food, because it revolts her that you are still crying for the food of an infant without teeth. This Mother, present in the whole world, is shaken by such varied and manifold attacks of error that even sons born out of due time do not shrink from warring on her with unbridled arms. She suffers also because through the cowardice and sloth of men in many places her members grow cold and therefore less able to cherish her little ones. And whence does she seek just and due help if not from other sons and other members, of whom you are one? Will you turn your back on her need to heed carnal words? Do your ears not ring with her strong complaints? Does she not show you a dearer womb and heavenly breasts? Think, too, that her Spouse took human flesh that you might not be attached to carnal things; think that all the things with which your Mother reproaches you were undertaken by the eternal Word that you might not be subject to them; think of His humiliations, scourging, death, 'even the death of the cross.'[13]

Conceived of such seed and begotten to a new life from such a union, you languish and waste away with longing for the 'old man!' Did your Commander not have an earthly Mother? When in the midst of His heavenly tasks it was announced to Him that she was there, He answered: 'Who is my mother? and who are my brethren? and stretching forth his hand towards his disciples'[14] He said that no one belonged to His kindred except the one who would do the will of His Father. To be sure, He graciously included Mary herself in this number, for she was doing the will of His Father. Thus, the name of mother which they had announced to Him as

---

13 Matt. 20.19; Mark 10.34; Luke 18.32-33; John 19.1-3; Phil. 2.8.
14 Matt. 12.47-50; Mark 3.32-35; Luke 8.20-21.

His private and personal possession He rejected, because it was an earthly name when compared to heavenly kinship, and, referring that same heavenly kinship to His Apostles, He showed again the bond of relationship by which that Virgin was bound to Him, together with all the saints. And lest error should find some support from that salutary authority with which He taught us to despise earthly affection for our parents by saying, as some did, that He had no Mother, He charged His disciples on another occasion not to say that they had a father on earth,[15] but just as it is certain that they had fathers, so He showed that He had a Mother, while at the same time He gave His disciples an example of contemning such relationship by His rejection of earthly kindred.

Are these considerations interrupted by the words of your mother, and do you find a place in your thought for the reminder of her bearing and nourishing you that you might be born and raised as another Adam from Adam and Eve? Look, rather, look at the second Adam. But, no, let your mother's earthly benefits to you find place here, although she enumerates them to weaken your heart; let them indeed have their place; do not be ungrateful, pay your duty of gratitude to your mother, repay earthly favors by spiritual ones, temporal by eternal ones. But she does not wish to follow you? Let her not hinder you. She does not wish to be converted to a better life? Beware, lest she pervert you and drag you down to a lower one. What difference does it make whether it is a wife or a mother, when a man has to guard against Eve in every woman? For that shadow of filial affection came from the leaves of that tree with which our first parents covered their nakedness after the curse. And whatever she sets forth in her words and suggestions as a duty of charity so as to turn you away from the brotherly and true charity of the Gospel comes from the craftiness of

15 Matt. 23.9.

the Serpent and the duplicity of that king who has 20,000 men, which we are taught to overcome with 10,000, that is, with the simplicity of heart with which we seek God.[16]

Turn, rather, to these teachings, my very dear friend: take up your cross[17] and follow the Lord. For, when I noticed that you were being slowed down in your divine purpose by your preoccupation with domestic cares, I felt that you were being carried and dragged by your cross rather than that you were carrying it ahead of you. That cross of ours which the Lord commands us to carry, that we may be as well armed as possible in following Him, what else does it mean but the mortality of this flesh? It makes us suffer now until death is swallowed up in victory.[18] Therefore, this cross must itself be crucified and pierced with the nails of the fear of God,[19] for we should not be able to carry it if it resisted us with free and unfettered limbs. There is no other way for you to follow the Lord except by carrying it, for how can you follow Him if you are not His? 'But they that are Christ's have crucified their flesh with the vices and concupiscences.'[20]

If, however, your own wealth contains some of your family's property—in the management of which it is neither right nor proper for you to be involved—it should indeed be handed over to your mother and the members of your household. If you have decided to distribute such possessions to the poor that you may be perfect, the poverty of your own should hold first place with you: 'For if any man have not care of his own,' says the Apostle, 'and especially of those of his house, he hath denied the faith and is worse than an infidel.'[21]

---

16 There is a play on words here between simplicity (singleness) and duplicity (doubleness) and between 10,000 taken as a unit and 20,000 which is twice as much.
17 Matt. 16.24; Mark 8.34; Luke 9.23.
18 1 Cor. 15.54.
19 Ps. 118.120.
20 Gal. 5.24.
21 1 Tim. 5.8.

With things like this requiring attention, if you have left us to free your neck from their burden so as to bind it with the fetters of wisdom, how are you harmed or how are you turned aside by the tears of your mother, of corporeal source, or by the news of a runaway slave or of the death of maid-servants, or the precarious health of your brothers? If there is in you a well-founded charity you will know how to prefer the greater to the lesser, to be moved to pity so that the poor may have the Gospel preached to them[22] and that the bountiful harvest of the Lord[23] may not fall prey to birds[24] through lack of harvesters, and to have your heart ready to follow the Lord's will in whatever way He has determined to deal with His servants, whether by chastising or by sparing them. 'Meditate upon these things, be wholly in these things, that thy profiting may be manifest to all.'[25] I beg of you, be on your guard not to cause your good brothers greater grief by your sluggishness than you formerly gave them joy by your eagerness. I think it superfluous to commend them as you wished in my letter—it would be as if anyone had wished to commend you to me in the same manner.

244. *Augustine gives greeting in the Lord to his truly and deservedly dear lord and esteemed brother, Crisimus*[1]

A rumor has reached me—God grant it may not be so!—that you are greatly troubled in mind and I marvel much that a Christian soul like your Prudence should make so little of the thought that the state of earthly affairs cannot possibly

22 Matt. 11.5; Luke 7.22.
23 Matt. 9.37,38; Luke 10.2.
24 Matt. 13.4; Mark 4.4; Luke 8.5.
25 1 Tim. 4.15.

1 A layman who had suffered temporal adversity and was much dejected in consequence.

weigh in the balance against the heavenly destiny on which
our heart and hope should be fixed. Man of wisdom, surely
your whole good was not in those things which you now
see lost to you! Or did you fancy them so great a good that
their loss darkens your mind with excessive sadness, as if its
light were of earth and not of God? I have heard—and as
I said, God grant that what I heard is untrue!—that you
wanted to do away with yourself, and I would prefer to
believe that this neither entered your mind nor issued from
your lips. Nevertheless, because you are so troubled that this
could be said of you, I have been gravely concerned about
you, and I thought this little word in a letter might comfort
your Charity, although I would not doubt that the Lord our
God speaks better words in your heart, for I know with what
devout eagerness you have always listened to His word.

So, then, my dearest brother in Christ, lift up your heart,
our God is neither lost to His own nor will He lose them,
but He wishes to warn us how perishable and uncertain are
the things men love too much, so that they may free themselves from the bonds of covetousness through which things
entangle us and drag us along, and that we may accustom
our whole love to run to Him in whom we need fear no
losses. It is He who exhorts you through my ministry to
reflect manfully that you are a faithful Christian, that you
were redeemed by the Blood of One who taught us not only
as eternal Wisdom, but also as a human Presence, to despise
the prosperity of this world with sobriety and to bear its
adversity bravely, promising a reward of happiness which
no one can take from us. I have also written a word to the
count,[2] a man of rank, and I leave it to your judgment to
have it delivered, for I doubt not that the one who does
deliver it, be he bishop or priest or anyone else, cannot fail
you.

---

2 The identity of the count cannot be established, because the date of
this letter was not ascertained by the Maurists.

*245. Augustine and the brethren who are with me give
greeting in the Lord to the beloved lord, my
revered brother and fellow priest, Possidius,[1] and
the brethren who are with you*

You had better consider what to do with those who refuse
to submit than how to prove to them that what they are
doing is not allowable. But the letter of your Holiness has
found me exceedingly busy and at the same time the very
early return of the bearer has allowed me neither to fail to
reply nor to answer properly those points on which you consulted me. Still, I should not like you to make any impulsive
regulation forbidding the use of jewelry or fine clothing,
except that those who are neither married nor desirous of
being married ought to be thinking about how to please
God. But worldly people think of worldly things: if husbands,
how to please their wives; if wives, how to please their
husbands.[2] However, it is not seemly for women, even married ones, to uncover their hair, since the Apostle commands
them to veil their heads.[3] As to the practice of painting their
faces[4] to make themselves more pink and white, I doubt that
even their own husbands care to be deceived, and husbands
are the only men for whom women are allowed to deck themselves out, and that through indulgence, not command. The
true and unique adornment of Christian men and women is
a good character, not lying paint, or even gold or the
ostentation of fine apparel.

The wearing of amulets[5] is an accursed superstition; among

---

1 Cf. Letters, Vol. 2, p. 166 n. 2.
2 1 Cor. 7.32-34.
3 1 Cor. 11.5,6.
4 A practice denounced by many early Christian writers—Tertullian,
Cyprian, Ambrose, Jerome—and even by some pagan ones as Plautus
and Ovid.
5 A pagan survival, they were usually worn to cure or ward off disease,
and the practice was common at that time.

these we include the earrings worn by men on the top part of the ear, hanging down one side; they are not worn to please men but to serve devils. Who could expect to find in Scripture particular prohibitions of every kind of abominable superstition, when the Apostle says in general: 'I would not that you should be made partakers with devils,'[6] and again: 'What concord hath Christ with Belial?'[7]—unless, perhaps, that his having named Belial and forbidden the company of demons in general is a license for Christians to sacrifice to Neptune,[8] because we do not read any special prohibition about Neptune. Meanwhile, let those unhappy people be warned not to excuse their sacrilegious acts if they refuse to yield to more wholesome precepts, for they would thus involve themselves in deeper guilt. But what is to be done with them if they are afraid to take off their earrings and they are not afraid to receive the Body of Christ while wearing the Devil's livery?

I cannot assume responsibility for ordaining anyone baptized in the Donatist sect; it is one thing to do it if you are compelled, another to advise you to do it.

246. *Augustine to Lampadius*[1]

On the problem of fate and chance with which your mind is deeply troubled, as I noticed when I was with you, and now have more certain and satisfactory assurance in your letter, I ought to write you a book as an answer. But the Lord will grant me to explain it to you in a way suitable to you and to the safeguarding of your faith; for it is no slight

---

6 1 Cor. 10.20.
7 2 Cor. 6.15.
8 His cult seems to have been popular in North Africa.

---

1 He is mentioned only here.

evil to be led by perverted opinions, not only to commit sin under the enticement of pleasure, but also to excuse it and thereby turn away from the remedy of confession.

There is something, however, that I must let you know at once and in brief: that all the laws and all the basic principles of control, praise, blame, encouragement, fear, reward, and all forms of punishment by which the human race is ruled and regulated are completely undermined and overthrown and denuded of every vestige of justice if the cause of sin is not in the will. How much more right and just is it, therefore, for us to denounce the errors of astrologers[2] than to be forced to condemn and reject divine laws and even the management of our own household! This is something the astrologers themselves do not do, for when one of them has sold his foolish forecasts to wealthy men, and presently turns his eyes from his ivory tablets to the regulation of own household, if he finds his wife too forward in jesting, not to mention looking too freely out the window, he reproves her, not only with words, but even with blows. Yet, if she should say to him: 'Why do you beat me? Beat Venus if you can; she is the one who makes me do it,' his concern is no longer what fantastic words he can make up for the deception of strangers, but what justifiable blows he can inflict for the correction of his own household.[3]

When anyone, then, upon suffering reproof, throws the blame on fate and refuses to be censured because he says he was compelled to do what he is accused of doing, let him enter into himself, let him observe the same principle toward his household, let him not chastise a thieving slave, or com-

---

2 *Mathematicus* was a word that took an adverse meaning in post-Augustan Latin. In *Confessions* 4.3, Augustine confesses to having consulted astrologers. He never lost his attraction for numbers and frequently gave them mystical meanings in his interpretations of Scripture.

3 This sentence is a good example of Augustine's fondness for rhyme and assonance; he has *componat—imponat; verba—verbera.*

plain of an insolent son, or threaten a troublesome neighbor. Does he 'act justly in doing any of these things if all those from whom he suffers injury are under the compulsion of fate and have no personal guilt in the matter? If, however, acting under his personal right and his responsibility as head of the house, he encourages those who are temporarily under his authority to do good, prevents them from doing wrong, commands them to submit to his will, honors those who obey his nod, punishes those who make light of him, shows gratitude to those who do him favors, hates the ungrateful, shall I expect him to argue against fate when I find him expressing himself not in words, but in deeds to the extent that he almost seems with his own hands to break all the counters of the astrologers over their heads? If your eager desire is not satisfied with these few words, and you want a book on this subject which you can read more at length, you will have to wait until I have some free time, and beg God to deign to grant me both the leisure and the ability to satisfy your mind on this question. However, I shall be more eager to do it if your Charity does not weary in writing often to remind me, and also if you will answer this letter and let me know what you think of it.

247. Augustine gives greeting in the Lord to the beloved lord, his son, Romulus[1]

Truth is both sweet and bitter. When it is sweet it spares us; when it is bitter it cures us. If you do not refuse the draught which I offer in this letter, you will prove the truth of what I say. I pray that whatever insults you heap on me may do you no harm as they do me none, and that the injustice which you do to the wretched and the poor may do you as

1 An influential man apparently engaged in tax-farming.

much harm as it does to your victims. They work for time only, but look what treasure you are heaping up 'against the day of wrath and revelation of the just judgment of God, who will render to every man according to his works.'[2] I call upon His mercy to chastise you here, as He knows how to do, rather than reserve you for that day when there will be no longer a chance of amendment, and I ask that as He has given you His fear[3]—my reason for not despairing of you— He may open your understanding and make you see what you are doing, that you may be shocked and may repent. These acts seem to you slight and almost of no account, but they are so great an evil that, if once your avarice were brought under control and you allowed yourself to reflect, you would water the earth with your tears that the Lord might have mercy on you. On the other hand, if I am unfair in making this demand of you that wretched, needy men should not have to pay twice what they owe, when farm workers have paid their overseers, subject in their turn to their overlord and doing his bidding—and he cannot say that he did not receive it—if, then, I am unfair because it seems unjust to me that men who are hard put to pay once should have the tax extorted from them twice over, do what you like; but if you see that it is unjust, do what befits you, do what God commands and I ask.

I ask you not so much for their sake, but for your own—as He whom I fear knows—to 'have pity on your own soul,' as it is written, 'pleasing God.'[4] And now, indeed, what is needed is not to ask you but to reprove you, for this also is written: 'Such as I love, I rebuke and chastise.'[5] But for my part, if I had to petition you on my own behalf, I would probably not do it, but as I have to petition you for your own sake,

2 Rom. 2.5,6.
3 Jer. 32.40; Bar. 3.7; Mal. 2.5; Eccli. 36.2.
4 Eccli. 30.24.
5 Apoc. 3.19.

I ask you, if you are angry, to spare yourself, to be favorable to yourself, that He whom you petition may be favorable to you. I sent you word on Saturday while you were at lunch not to go away until you had seen me. You sent back word that you would do that. You rose on Sunday, and, as I have heard, you came to church, you prayed, you went away, and you refused to see me. May God forgive you. What else shall I say to you except that He knows what I desire. But I know that, unless you amend your life, He is just. When you spare yourself, you also spare me, for I am not so wretched or so far removed from the mercy of Christ that my heart is not pierced with a most grievous wound when those whom 'I have begotten in the Gospel'[6] act in that manner.

Again you will say: 'I did not tell them to give money to Ponticanus,'[7] and the answer is: 'But you told them to obey Ponticanus, and they could not have distinguished how far to obey him and how far not to obey, especially as he demanded what they knew they owed. They should have had a letter from you to show to the overseer if he made demands contrary to your intention, and they should have read to him that they were not obliged to pay unless they had a letter from you to that effect. For, if at any time you gave verbal orders that they were not to pay anything to the overseer, it is much that they should remember it, it is much that you yourself should remember whether you really gave orders, or whether you gave orders to them or to others or to all, especially now, as you have heard that payment was made to a second overseer, and that the money itself is safe, and you were not displeased at their paying it.' But when I said: 'What if he had pilfered it, would they have had to pay it again?' you began again to show displeasure at their paying it. And although you had often told me that you had never

6 1 Cor. 4.15.
7 Evidently the overseer or steward of the estate which owed the tribute.

delegated your authority to either Valerius or Aginesis,[8] when a question suddenly arose about the wine, because they were obliged to report if it began to turn sour, and you were told that he was away, I suppose what you told me so often has slipped your mind—you said that they had to report to Aginesis and act as he directed. Thereupon I said: 'But surely you do not usually delegate your authority to them,' and you answered: 'But Aginesis has a letter from me,' as if it were the ordinary thing for those whom you directed to do something to read a letter from you to the farm workers, so that they may believe they are acting by your orders. But, as they usually see the overseers so instructed by you, they surely do not believe that they would venture to presume anything unless they had your authority for it. Therefore, in the midst of these uncertainties, if it is not clear what you command, and they have nothing stable to hold to unless they have a letter from you, which is to be shown to all, then they should not comply when they have to pay anything unless your letter is displayed.

But what is the use of arguing so long with you and burdening your busy life with words, when, perhaps, in consequence, you will be angry at what I have said and you will want to take it out on these poor men? It will be counted as a good work for them that they suffer your anger because I say such things to you out of regard for your salvation, but I do not want to speak too harshly to you, lest you think I say such things not because I fear for you, but out of a malicious will. 'Fear God if you do not wish to be led astray; I call him to witness upon my soul'[9] that I fear more for you when I say this than I do for those for whom I seem to be interceding with you. If you believe this, thanks be to God; if you do not believe it, my consolation is what the

8 Two more overseers.
9 2 Cor. 1.23.

Lord said: 'Say: Peace be to this house, and if the son of peace be there, your peace shall rest upon him; if not it shall return to you.'[10] May the mercy of God protect you, my lord and most dear son.

248. Augustine gives greeting in the Lord to Sebastian,[1] his holy and esteemed lord and most sweet brother in honor with Christ

Although the sweet bond of charity does not in any way allow you to be absent from my mind, and I reflect unceasingly on your holy conduct and conversation, you have done a good deed and I thank you for having raised our spirits appreciably by sending us written assurances of your bodily welfare. But I felt in your letter that disgust has seized upon you because of sinners forsaking the law of God,[2] for you live in the spirit of which it is written: 'I beheld the transgressors and I pined away.'[3] That is a holy sadness and, if I may say so, a happy suffering to be afflicted by but not involved in the sins of others, to grieve over them, not to cleave to them, to have one's heart contracted by regret, not attracted by desire.[4] This is the persecution suffered by 'all who will live godly in Christ Jesus,'[5] according to that penetrating and truthful saying of the Apostle. For what else persecutes the life of the good but the life of the wicked, not by forcing them to imitate what displeases them, but by making them grieve

---

10 Luke 10.5,6.

1 Called a monk by Possidius, but the end of the letter shows that he was the abbot of a monastery.
2 Cf. Ps. 118.53.
3 Ps. 118.158.
4 Another striking example of rhyme and assonance: *maerere—haerere*; *contrahi—attrahi*.
5 2 Tim. 3.12.

over what they see, since the wicked man, by living an evil life in the sight of the devout man, wounds his feelings without wresting consent from him? For the secular powers often and for a long time spare the wicked from corporal punishment and relieve some of them from their harassments, but the hearts of holy men never have any respite until the end of the world from the sinful conduct of men. It is thus we have the fulfilment of what the Apostle said, as I cited it, that 'all who will live godly in Christ suffer persecution,' and their suffering is more bitter in proportion to its inwardness, until a man passes over the deluge where the ark shelters the raven and the dove.[6]

But, my brother, cling to Him from whom you have heard the words: 'He that perseveres to the end, he shall be saved;'[7] 'Join thyself to the Lord—that thy life may be increased in the latter end.'[8] I know that joy of heart is not lacking to our good brothers. Add to this the promises of God, faithful, vast, sure, eternal, and the unshakeable, indescribable reward of His mercy, and see how truly you can sing to the Lord: 'According to the multitude of my sorrows in my heart, thy comforts have given joy to my soul.'[9] Send our letter to brother Firmus.[10] The brothers and sisters who are with us join with me in returning greetings in the Lord to your Holiness, and the family of God which is governed by your ministry.

As you are safe, pray for us, beloved and holy brothers.[11]

I, Alypius, do most earnestly greet your Sincerity and all those who are joined to you in the Lord, and I ask you to consider this letter as mine, for although I could have written another of my own, I preferred to subscribe to this one so that one page might bear witness to our close union.

---

6 Gen. 8.6-12.
7 Matt. 10.22; 24.13; Mark 13.13.
8 Eccli. 2.3.
9 Ps. 93.19.
10 One of this name occurs as letter-bearer in Letters 115, 134, 191, 194.
11 In another handwriting.

*249. Augustine gives greeting in the Lord to his most cher-
ished lord, his most dear brother in honorable
sincerity, his fellow deacon, Restitutus*[1]

Brother Deogratias,[2] a faithful friend, has made known to
me the ardor which betrays the pious flame of your heart,
being, as you know,. a sharer in the same. Read Tychonius[3]
whom you know well, not that you will approve everything
he says, for you know well what you have to guard against in
him. It seems to me, however, that he has dealt vigorously
with this question, and has solved it; namely, how the bond
of unity is to be preserved if we have to tolerate abuses and
even accursed deeds which, perhaps, we are not able to correct or stamp out. However, in using his writings, we have
only to have recourse with upright intention to the primary
sources of the divine Scriptures, and there we can see how
few passages and examples of conduct he has adduced as
testimony on this matter, and how impossible it would be
for anyone to adduce them all, unless he were willing to
transcribe practically all the pages of the holy books into his
writings. There is hardly one which does not warn us interiorly, in that communication of sacraments by which we
are initiated into life eternal, that we should be peaceable
with them that hate peace[4] until our prolonged sojourning has
passed by with lamentation and, in the strength of Jerusalem,
our eternal mother, we enjoy the most secure peace with the
abundance in her towers[5] of true brothers, of whom we now
mourn the scarcity among many false ones. But what is the
strength of that city if not its God, who is our God? You

---

1 Cf. Letter 105, Vol. 2, p. 198 n. 8.
2 Letter 102 (Vol. 2, p. 148) is addressed to a priest of Carthage of
this name. Because of the absence of date for this letter, it is not
possible to say whether this is the same person.
3 Cf. Vol. 2, p. 70 n. 40.
4 Ps. 119.6.
5 Ps. 121.6-8.

see, therefore, in whom alone peace exists both for individual men who war with each other when they are not with Him, even though no external scandal arises, and for all in general who may love each other in this life and may be joined by the bonds of a faithful friendship, but are not fully and perfectly united either by physical presence or by agreement of minds. Let your heart be strengthened in the Lord and do not forget us.

250. Augustine gives greeting in the Lord to his beloved lord and revered brother and fellow priest, Auxilius[1]

That honorable man, our son, Count Classicianus,[2] has written me a letter complaining bitterly that he has suffered the injury of excommunication from your Holiness, claiming that he came to the church with a small retinue of attendants befitting his rank and made an agreement with you that you would not put his salvation in danger by favoring those who swore falsely on the Gospel, asking for help against a breach of faith in the very house of faith itself. He says that then, while thinking of what wrong they might have done, they left the church of their own accord, they were not forcibly ejected from it, and for this reason your Reverence was so angry at him that he and his whole household were struck with the sentence of excommunication,[3] which was made final by being put on the ecclesiastical records. After reading his letter I was not a little upset and, with agitated thoughts flooding through my heart in a great storm, I could not

---

1 A young and inexperienced bishop who had pronounced a sweeping sentence of excommunication.
2 That is, he was a member of the *comitatus*, or court, of the Roman vicar of Africa.
3 This had the effect of cutting him off entirely from the Church and sacraments, as well as from communication with other human beings.

refrain from speaking to your Charity so that, if you have a
statement on this matter, based on sure reasoning or on the
testimony of the Scriptures, you would be so kind as to
instruct me also how it can be right to excommunicate a son
for his father's sin, or a wife for her husband's, or a slave
for his master's, or even anyone not yet born in the house,
if he happens to be born at the time when the whole house
is under the excommunication and he cannot be saved, even
when in danger of death, by the laver of regeneration. For
this is not a corporal penalty such as we read of when certain
scoffers at God were put to death together with all their
followers, although these had not shared in their impiety.
For then, mortal bodies, destined in any case to die sometime,
were destroyed to inspire terror in the living, but this is a
spiritual penalty which effects what is written: 'Whatsoever
you shall bind on earth, it shall be bound also in heaven';[4]
it binds souls of which it is written: 'The soul of the father
is mine, and the soul of the son is mine, the soul that sinneth,
the same shall die.'[5]

It may be that you have heard of certain well-known priests
who excommunicated one or other sinner with his household.
But possibly, if they were questioned, it would be found that
they could give an adequate reason for it. As for me, if anyone
asks me whether it is right to do it, I do not know what I
should answer him; I have never dared to do it, not even
when I was very deeply moved by the inhuman acts of certain
men against the Church. However, if the Lord has perhaps
revealed to you how it can be done without wrong, I do not
despise your youth and your inexperience of ecclesiastical
office. Here I am, though I am an old man and have been
a bishop for so many years, more than ready to learn from a
young man, a colleague of scarcely a year, how we can

4 Matt. 18.18; 16.19.
5 Ezech. 18.4.

render a just account to either God or men if we have inflicted a spiritual punishment on innocent souls for the crime of another, from whom they derive no original sin as we do from Adam, 'in whom all have sinned.'[6] The son of Classicianus, it is true, contracted from his father the stain of the first man's sin, which was to be expiated by the sacred waters of baptism, but who doubts that any sin which his father committed after he begot him, in which he had no share, has nothing to do with him? Consequently, if one soul goes out of the body without baptism because of the severity which has excommunicated the whole household, the physical death of uncounted persons, if innocent men are dragged from the church and killed, cannot be compared to that loss. If, then, you can give a reason for this, pray furnish me with it, but if you cannot, how is it possible for you to do something through an impulsive reaction of your mind for which you can give no valid excuse if one were asked of you? I have said this much, although our son Classicianus admits having done something which might seem to you a just reason for the punishment of excommunication. But if the letter he sent me was truthful, he was not the only one in his household who deserved to be chastised with that punishment. However, I am not treating with your Holiness on that point. I am only asking that you forgive him when he asks for pardon, if he acknowledges his guilt, but if you are wise enough to discover that he has committed no wrong, since it was quite right for him to claim in the very house of faith itself that faith should be kept and not violated in the place where it is taught, do what a holy man ought to do, and if it has befallen you as a man to experience what the man of God says in the psalm: 'My eye is troubled through indignation,' cry out to the Lord: 'Have mercy on me, O Lord, for I am weak,'[7] that He may

6 Rom. 5.12.
7 Ps. 6.8,3.

stretch out His right hand to you and quell your anger and
calm your mind to see and do justice. For so it is written:
'The anger of man worketh not the justice of God.'[8] Do not
think that because we are bishops a sinful emotion cannot
sweep over us; consider, rather, that because we are men we
live a most dangerous life amid the snares of temptation.
Remove, then, those ecclesiastical censures which you invoked
perhaps in a state of agitation, and let that affection which
you had for him when he was a catechumen be restored
between you; give up your quarrel and call peace back, so
that a man who is a friend of yours may not be lost and the
Devil who is your enemy may not gloat over you. The mercy
of our God who hears my prayer is able to bring it to pass
that my grief on your account may not be increased, but
healed at its source, instead. May He govern you by His
grace and rejoice your youth which has not despised my
old age.

250A. Fragment of a letter of Augustine to Classicianus[1]

I greatly desire, with the Lord's help, to take up in our
council and, if need be, to write to the apostolic see questions
concerning those who bind under excommunication a whole
household, that is, many souls, because of one person's sin,
my special object being that no one should depart from the
body without baptism; also, whether it is our duty to drive
from the church persons who take refuge there in order to
break faith with those who have given bail for them. In this
manner, a decision may be made and strengthened by unani-
mous authority concerning the course we should follow in these

---

8 James 1.2.

1 There is no superscription.

cases. This I may say without indiscretion, that, if any one of the faithful is unjustly excommunicated, it will do more harm to him who commits than to him who suffers the injustice. For the Holy Spirit, abiding in the saints, through whom each one is bound or loosed, does not inflict unjust punishment on anyone; indeed, it is through Him that charity which dealeth not perversely[2] is poured forth in our hearts.[3]

251. Augustine gives greeting in the Lord to Pancarius,[1] his beloved lord and deservedly honored son

Inasmuch as the priest Secundinus was not disliked by the people of Germanicia[2] before your Reverence arrived, I do not know how it happens that they are now ready to accuse him of all sorts of crimes, as you have written, my beloved lord and deservedly honored son. However, we cannot possibly disregard the objection they seem to make against the priest, if, indeed, those who make the objection are Catholics, for we neither can nor should accept the charges of heretics against a Catholic priest. Hence, in this matter let your Prudence first establish that there are no heretics where there were none before your arrival, and we shall hear the case of the priest as it deserves to be heard. I urge you, however, as your welfare and good name are very dear to us, and as the people of Germanicia are under our humble charge, to be so kind as to adduce with confidence the concessions which you

---

2 1 Cor. 13.4.
3 Rom. 5.5.

1 He is addressed by the ecclesiastical title *Religio tua,* but it does not otherwise appear that he was a cleric.
2 A town in proconsular Africa which must have been in Augustine's diocese.

won from our glorious emperors, as well as the business you transacted before competent judges, so that all may be informed that you are not acting irregularly. In this way, the poor people who are involved in the case, which you and your supporters are carrying on for possession of the property, may not again be worn down and become so completely dejected as to be utterly undone. At the same time, I recommend that the house of the priest in question should not be looted or destroyed, for we have had news about his church that some persons or other want to pull it down, but I do not think that this can possibly be allowed by your Reverence.

252. Augustine gives greeting in the Lord to the beloved lord, Felix,[1] his deservedly honored and esteemed brother

Your reverence knows how careful the Church and the bishops have to be to protect the interests of all men, but most particularly of wards. Consequently, after receiving your letter and a copy of the letter of the honorable man, our brother,[2] I neither could nor should entrust the girl to anyone at random, especially as he had confided her to the care of the Church,[3] beloved lord, deservedly honored and esteemed brother. Therefore, I await his coming and, if any action is to be taken, I will consider it in his presence and will do whatever the Lord directs me to do.

---

1 One of the guardians and the uncle by marriage of the unnamed girl whose marriage prospects are discussed in the following four letters.

2 Evidently another guardian, called *vir spectabilis,* that is, some kind of public official. The supposition made by Migne that this refers to the pagan suitor of the girl is hardly tenable.

3 It was not unusual for the clergy to take on the duties of guardianship for orphans.

*253. Augustine gives greeting in the lord to his holy and
revered lord, Benenatus,[1] his cherished brother
and the brethren who are with you*

The man through whom I greet your Holiness is one
whose faith and true devotion to the Church give us joy. He
wanted to go to your Benignity with my letter, my beloved
lord and revered brother. And since I have heard what you
are thinking of doing, if it is true—and I wonder if it is
true—you know how you should provide for the Catholic
Church as father and bishop, and not enter into dealings with
any unreliable person[2]—if, however, as I said, what I heard
is true—but, rather, with a Catholic household, through
which the Church may be able to escape adversity and find
a faithful protector.

*254. Augustine and the brethren who are with me give greet-
ing in the Lord to the holy and revered lord,
Benenatus, his cherished brother and fellow priest
and the brethren who are with you*

The girl about whom your Holiness wrote me is so disposed
that, if she were old enough to choose, she would not marry
anyone. But, in truth, she is of such an age that, even if she
had an inclination to marry, she ought not yet to be given
or betrothed to any man. Over and above this, my dear lord
and revered brother Benenatus, God gives her His protection
in the Church to shield her from unprincipled men, not to

---

1 Bishop of Tugutiana, who had suggested marriage of the orphan girl,
a ward of the Church, to a pagan. This letter is written in what is
either a studied obscurity or an incoherent haste.
2 Rusticus (cf. Letter 255), father of the pagan suitor favored by
Benenatus.

allow me to hand her over to whomever I choose, but to prevent her from being carried off by an unsuitable person. The proposal which you have taken the trouble to make is not personally distasteful to me, if she is really going to marry, but at present, although I am more hopeful that she will carry out her announced intention, I do not know whether she will marry, because she is of an age where her expressed wish to become a nun might be the light whim of a chatterer rather than a solemn undertaking of religious profession. Besides, she has a maternal aunt, whose husband is our honorable brother, Felix,[1] and when I had conferred with him—for I neither could nor should have done otherwise—he agreed without reluctance, or, rather, he showed himself pleased, but he expressed a not unreasonable regret that they had received no written announcement of the plan, as was their right in view of the friendly relationship. Perhaps, too, her mother will come forward—which up to now she has not done—and her wish, I think, should naturally prevail over all others in the matter of handing over her daughter, unless the girl is by that time of an age which will give her a legitimate right to choose for herself what she wants to do. Your Sincerity should also consider this point, that if complete and uncontested authority over her marriage were vested in me, and if she, also, supposing she were old enough and willing to marry, should entrust herself to me, with God as my judge, to be given to the one I chose, then I declare, and I speak truly, I am satisfied with the condition you suggest, provided that under God's judgment I should not repudiate a better one. But whether a better one will turn up is, of course, uncertain. Therefore, your Charity can see how many considerations concur to make it absolutely impossible for me to promise her to anyone.

1 Cf. Letter 252.

255. *Augustine gives greeting in the Lord to the esteemed lord, Rusticus,[1] his deservedly respected and cherished brother*

Although I wish nothing but good to you and all your household, and not only the blessings of happiness in the present life, but also those which belong to eternal life in the world to come—in which you have not yet been induced to believe—nevertheless, my dear lord and esteemed son, I have written to my holy brother and fellow bishop, Benenatus, what seemed sufficient about my sentiments regarding the girl whose hand you are asking, namely, that I would not yet venture to make any promise. You surely know that even if it were in my unchallenged power to arrange a marriage for any girl, we cannot give a Christian maiden to anyone but a Christian; yet, if you were not willing to make any such promise to me about your son, who, I hear, is a pagan, with much greater reason ought I not to make any contract of marriage for this girl, for the reasons which you will be able to read in the letter to my aforementioned brother. And that would hold not only if I held the promise about your son which I spoke of, but even if I had the joy of knowing its accomplishment.

---

1 Father of the young man who wished to marry the girl. It will be noted that the girl herself had nothing to say about the choice of her husband. Marriage at that time was arranged by the parents or guardians of the young people in question.

256. Augustine gives greeting in the Lord to the deservedly revered lord, Christinus,[1] his sincerely cherished and much desired brother

Your letter gave me the news that you were longing for my letter, but brother James came as a better equipped witness of your longing affection for me because he told me, out of his own experience, more pleasant things about you than that poor little page could tell. I congratulate your Benignity and I give thanks to the Lord our God, whose gift it is, for your Christian heart, my deservedly revered lord, sincerely cherished and much desired brother. You ask me to seek you in letters, but I seek you in heart's affection which surpasses all letters, and I know that you understand well where I seek you. As far as reading my letters is concerned, I am more afraid of meeting blame at your hands for my garrulousness than desire for my speech. I will say this much, and if you reflect on it in long-continued meditation you will feel its wisdom: On the pathway to God easy and fruitful things are avoided through cowardly fear, but on the way of the world hard and fruitless things are borne with toil and labor. May you flourish and advance safely in Christ, deservedly revered lord, sincerely cherished and much desired brother.

---

1 From the title Benignity he would seem to be either a cleric or a layman of high position. The latter seems the more probable supposition, from the type of spiritual advice offered.

257. Augustine to the excellent lord, his deservedly honored and cherished son, Orontius[1]

I thank your Excellency for having taken the trouble to write me an advance notice of your coming, and for having sent me a greeting before the meeting,[2] so that I might enjoy hearing you before I see you, and might look forward to your long-desired acquaintance the more eagerly and ardently because of the foretaste, so to speak, of epistolary comfort, which I have savored with a greater pleasure and gratitude, my excellent lord, deservedly honored and cherished son. I return the compliment of this answer which is due to your deserts and to your thoughtful courtesy, rejoicing in your good health and praying that it may continue. But in asking an answer from my insignificance and claiming it by right of having made the first advances in kindness, you added these words: 'If, however, I can deserve it of such holiness.' I venture to hope that it will please your Prudence not only to praise the source of that holiness—and, if I am anything, it is because I have drunk of it according to my little measure —but to partake of it with us, that God, who is incomparably and unchangeably good, may restore your noble mind by His grace as He created it by His power. May almighty God keep you safe and make you happy, excellent lord, deservedly honored and cherished son.

---

1 The title Excellency makes him a layman of rank and the tone of the letter bears this out.
2 The letter abounds in puns and figures of sound, and is written in an artificial style which indicates a certain strain on the part of the writer.

258. Augustine gives greeting in the Lord to the deservedly cherished lord, Marcianus,[1] *his dear and longed-for brother in Christ*

I have torn myself away from my many duties, or, rather, I have slipped away and, so to speak, stolen myself away from them to write to you, my oldest friend, although I did not have you as a friend so long as I did not possess you in Christ. You know, of course, how friendship was defined by Tully, 'the greatest writer of the Roman tongue,' as someone[2] called him. He said, and he spoke with perfect truth: 'Friendship is the agreement on things human and divine, joined with kindliness and love.'[3] You used to agree with me at one time, my dear friend, on things human, when I coveted the enjoyment of them as people commonly do, and you sailed with me on a favoring wind to the pursuit of things of which I am now ashamed, or, rather, along with the rest of my admirers of that time—and you were among the chief of them—you filled the sails of my ambitions with the wind of praise. But on the side of divine things, of which no light of truth shone upon me at that time, certainly our friendship was deficient in the greater half of that definition, for it was an agreement only on things human, not divine, although it was joined with kindliness and love.

And after I stopped wishing for those things, you still continued with persistent kindliness to wish my welfare on a mortal plane and my success in that material prosperity which the world prays to attain. Thus, there was between us that kindly and affectionate agreement about things human. So I now can scarcely express in words how much I rejoice over you when the one whom I had so long regarded as a friend

---

1 An early friend and admirer of Augustine, not mentioned elsewhere.
2 Lucan, *Pharsalia* 7.62,63; quoted also in Letter 143.
3 Cicero, *Laelius de Amicitia* 6.20.

in a limited way I regard as a friend indeed. The agreement on things divine has been added as well, and you who formerly shared your temporal life with me in a most agreeable friendliness are now beginning to join me in the hope of eternal life. Now, however, there is no disagreement between us even on things human, because we value them according to our knowledge of things divine, so as neither to give them more importance than their measure justly requires, nor to do an injury to their Creator, the Lord of things heavenly and earthly, by casting them away with undue contempt. Thus it happens that there can be no full and true agreement about things human among friends who disagree about things divine, for it necessarily follows that he who despises things divine esteems things human otherwise than as he should, and that whoever does not love Him who made man has not learned to love man aright. Hence, I do not say that now you are fully my friend whereas you were only partially so before, but, so far as reason goes, you were not partially my friend so long as you did not maintain a true friendship with me in things human. And as to things divine, through which the human are rightly valued, you were not yet my comrade either, because you still had a strong aversion for them after I had begun to savor them.

I hope you will not be offended and that it will not seem senseless to you that at a time when I was passionately attached to the vanities of this world, although you seemed deeply devoted to me, you were not yet my friend, for then I was not even a friend to myself, but an enemy. Indeed, I loved iniquity, and that is a true statement because it is divine, as it is written in the sacred books: 'He that loveth iniquity hateth his own soul.'[4] Therefore, when I hated my own soul, how could I have as a friend one who wished me those things in which I allowed myself to be my own enemy?

4 Ps. 10.6.

'But when the goodness and kindness of God our Saviour appeared, not according to my deserts but according to his mercy,'[5] how could you be my friend when you were a stranger to it, when you were completely ignorant of the source of my happiness, and you did not love in me that in which I had already been made a friend, as it were, to myself?

Thanks be to the Lord, therefore, that He has been so good as to make you at last a friend to me! For now there is between us an 'agreement on things human and divine joined with kindliness and love' in Christ Jesus our Lord, who is our truest peace. He summed up all the divine pronouncements in two commandments when He said: 'Thou shalt love the Lord thy God with thy whole heart and with thy whole soul and with thy whole mind,' and 'thou shalt love thy neighbor as thyself. On these two commandments dependeth the whole law and the prophets.'[6] In the first of these there is agreement on divine things; in the second, on human things, joined with kindliness and love. If you are with me in holding firmly to these two commandments, our friendship will be true and everlasting, and it will unite us not only to each other, but also to the Lord Himself.

That this may be so I urge your Gravity and Prudence to begin now to receive the sacraments of the faithful; this is proper for one of your age, and I think it is consistent with your conduct.[7] Remember what you said to me as I was leaving, quoting a line from a comedy of Terence, and, indeed, a very apt and useful one: 'This day now introduces another life, it requires another code of conduct.'[8] If you were sincere in saying this, as I ought not to doubt that you were, you now are certainly living such a life that you are

---

5 Cf. Titus 3.4,5.
6 Matt. 22.37,39-40; Mark 12.30-31; Luke 10.27; Deut. 6.5; Lev. 19.18.
7 To do this he would have to be baptized, which he was probably trying to postpone, as Augustine himself had done.
8 Terence, *Andria* 189.

worthy to receive the remission of your past sins in the saving waters of baptism. For there is no other at all except the Lord Christ, to whom the human race can say:

'Under thy guidance if some trace remain
Of ancient guilt of ours, it shall be unavailing made
And free the earth from never-ending fear.'[9]

Vergil confessed that he borrowed this from the Cumaean, that is, the Sybilline prophecy, and it is possible that the prophetess, too, heard in spirit some tidings of the one Saviour which she had of necessity to proclaim. These words, whether they be few, or perhaps many, I have written in spite of pressing duties, for you, my deservedly cherished lord, my dear and longed-for brother in Christ. I long to receive your answer and to learn at the earliest moment that you have enrolled or are on the point of enrolling your name among the candidates[10] for baptism. May the Lord God in whom you have put your trust keep you here and in the life to come, my deservedly cherished lord and brother beloved and longed-for in Christ.

259. Augustine to his beloved lord and honored brother, Cornelius[1]

You have written asking me to send you a long letter of condolence, alleging that you are in deep grief over the death of your excellent wife, and you give as an example

---

9 Vergil, *Eclogues* 4.13,14.
10 The *competentes* were those preparing to receive baptism.

1 A widower given to dalliance, who had been a Manichaean with Augustine.

what St. Paulinus did for Macarius.[2] Your wife has indeed been admited to the company of faithful and chaste souls, and she neither cares for nor seeks human praise, but, since eulogies are delivered for the sake of the living, the first thing for you to do, if you wish to be comforted by hearing her praised, is to live such a life that you may deserve to be where she is. For I am sure that you do not believe she is where those other women are, who have either defiled the marriage bed with adultery, or, if free of any conjugal bond, have committed fornication. Therefore, when a man so utterly unlike her wants to flee grief by hearing her praised, that is not consolation but adulation. If you loved her as she loved you, you would have kept for her what she kept for you, and if you had died first it is unbelievable that she would have married anyone else. Should you not, then, refrain from seeking even one licit mate after her, if you are sincere in wishing to be consoled for your loss by hearing her praised?

You will probably say to this: 'Why are you so hard on me? Why do you berate me so harshly?' Lo, we have grown old hearing these words, while life is ended before it is mended. You want me to be indulgent to your fatal unconcern; with how much more propriety should you be indulgent to my anxiety, which is certainly full of pity if not of love! Tully inveighed against an enemy, and his preoccupation with the government of an earthly state was far different from mine, yet he said: 'I wish, conscript fathers, to be kind, but in the midst of these great perils to the state I do not wish to seem remiss!'[3] I have been appointed to the service of the eternal city, as minister of the divine word and sacrament, and how much more justly can I say—especially as you know what a friendly feeling I have for you—'I wish, brother Cornelius,

---

2 This could be Bishop Macarius of Magnesia, who flourished *c.* 400, or Macarius the Egyptian (d. 390), a monk of the desert.
3 Cicero, *In Catilinam* 1.2,4.

to be kind, but in the midst of such great perils to you and me
I do not wish to seem remiss!'

A horde of women lie down beside you, the number of
your concubines increases daily, and shall we bishops listen
patiently to the master, or, rather, the slave of that mob,
a man who indulges his insatiable lust with so many harlots,
when he asks of us, as if by right of friendship, praise for his
grief? When you were I shall not say a catechumen, but a
young man involved with me in a most deadly error[4]—I was
still younger—you corrected yourself of this evil by using a
finely tempered will, but after a short time you fell back
more basely than before, and afterward, in extreme danger
of death, you were baptized, but I shall not say you are one
of the faithful, for, as you see, I am now an old man, and a
bishop as well, and you have not yet amended your life. You
want me to console you on the death of your good wife, but
who is to console me on your more real death? Or is it because
I cannot forget your great services to me that I am to be thus
tortured by your conduct, thus despised and held for naught
when I bewail you to yourself? But I confess that my influence
is unavailing to correct or cure you; hearken to God, think
of Christ, listen to the Apostle when he says: 'Shall I then
take the members of Christ and make them members of an
harlot?'[5] If, in your heart, you spurn the words of a bishop
who is such a friend of yours, think of the Body of Christ in
your body. Finally, why do you keep on sinning by putting
off your conversion from day to day when you do not know
your own last day?

Now I will prove how much you long for praises of
Cypriana.[6] Certainly, if I were still in a school of rhetoric
selling words to my pupils, I would collect my fee from them

---

4 That is, Manichaeism.
5 1 Cor. 6.15.
6 The deceased wife.

in advance. I wish to sell you the praises of your most chaste
wife; give me first, as fee, your chastity. Give, I say, and
receive. 'I speak a human thing because of your infirmity.'[7]
I think that Cypriana does not deserve that you should prefer
the love of your concubines to her praises, which you will
certainly do if you choose to remain in that love rather than
to secure her praises. Why do you want to extort this from
me by merely asking for it, when you see that what I ask is
for your good? Why do you beg as a suppliant what you
could command if you were compliant? Let us send offerings
to the spirit of your wife: you send imitation of her, I send
praise of her. Although, as I said above, she does not seek
praise from men, she does seek, even in death, your imitation
of her, and she seeks it in proportion to her love for you—so
unlike her—during her life.

If that proud and wicked rich man of whom the Lord
speaks in the Gospel,[8] who was clothed in purple and fine
linen and feasted sumptuously every day, who, when he was
paying the penalty of his evil deeds in hell, did not deserve
to obtain his request of a drop of water from the finger of
the poor man who had lain neglected at his gate, remembered
his five brothers and asked that the poor man, whose rest he
saw from afar in Abraham's bosom, be sent to them lest they
also come into that place of torments, how much more does
your wife remember you! How much more does she, who is
chaste, wish that you may not come to the punishment of
adulterers, if the proud man wished that his brothers might
not come to the punishment of the proud! And when a
brother does not wish to be united to his brothers in evil, how
much less does your wife, established in good, wish her husband to be separated from her in evil! Read this place in the

---

7 Rom. 6.19.
8 Luke 16.19-28.

Gospel: 'The voice of Christ is loving: trust in God.'[9] You grieve, no doubt, because your wife is dead, and you think that if I praise her you will be consoled by my words. Learn what you will have to grieve over if you are not to be with her. Ought you to grieve more because she has not yet been praised by me than I should because she is not loved by you? Surely, if you loved her you would want to be with her after death, where you certainly will not be if you continue to be what you are. Love, then, the one whose praise you demand, lest I justly refuse what you hypocritically demand.

May the Lord grant us to rejoice over your salvation, beloved lord, honored brother.[10]

260. *Audax*[1] *gives greeting in the Lord to Augustine, his truly renowned lord, and father worthy of being esteemed and honored with every kind praise*

I am grateful to your Blessedness for your willingness to receive my attempts at literary expression, for the boldness[2] of good confidence is given to sons when it is bedewed with rain from the fount of their father. Therefore, I appealed to you, dear bishop, not in order to receive a stingy drink offering[3] from your generous heart, but to draw copiously from the great river of your riches. I craved the treasure of wisdom, but I received less than I wished, although one should not call less a gift bestowed by Augustine, the oracle

---

9 Quoted incompletely from the verse of Paulinus of Nola found at the end of Letter 32 (cf. Vol. 1, p. 123). The beginning of the line has the Gospel words 'His yoke is sweet' (Matt. 11.30).
10 In another handwriting.

1 A foppish and affected dabbler in things spiritual and literary who made greedy demands on Augustine's time.
2 He puns on his name, *audax*, 'bold.'
3 A libation offered to pagan gods consisted at most of a few drops.

of the Law, the consecrator of justice, the restorer of spiritual glory, the dispenser of eternal salvation. The universe is as well known to you as it is marked with your fame, you are as well known to it as you are praised by it. Therefore, I pray to feed on the flowers of wisdom and to be refreshed with draughts from the living fount. Grant to my eager desire what is beneficial to both of us. For the budding foliage of the half-stripped oak can grow green if it wins the boon of being gradually revived by your flowing streams. So I promise the presence of my lowliness, not so much by my pen as by my prayer, if I can set my eyes on the writing of your Reverence. May the divine mercy protect you for unnumbered years, revered lord.

Why with such paltry speech did earth's fount flow for me?
Did it then look for hearts less worthy of its streams?
Though from your waters every mind may drink, and all
May hope full speech to her in God's defense, it gives
Sweet streams to some whom faith awaits impaled on
 Cross of Christ.

261. *Augustine gives greeting in the Lord to the beloved lord, Audax, his brother greatly esteemed and desired in Christ*

Your short letter, with its pressing demand for a long letter from me, was not displeasing to me; on the contrary, it gave me pleasure, not that I could easily satisfy your greedy appetite, but I do congratulate your Charity because what you ask is good, although you are not asking it of the right person. It is not the ability to write you a long letter which fails me, but the leisure, deeply immersed as I am in Church cares from which I can scarcely secure a few little drops of time

for relief, either to think out something, or to dictate what
seems to me more pressing and more likely to be useful to
many, or even to recover the bodily strength needed for this
state of servitude. There is no dearth of words with which
many a page could be filled, but as to your request for that
same profusion of speech from me, I answer that I am not
the right person for that. You said that you craved a treasure
of wisdom but that you had received less than you wished,
while I myself with mendicant prayer ask my daily alms of
it and hardly get it.

How am I an oracle of the Law, when what I do not
know of its broad and hidden recesses is far more than what
I know, when I have not the ability to enter or penetrate its
manifold windings and shady retreats as I wish, and I know
myself to be none other than unworthy? Moreover, what
kind of consecrator of justice am I, when it is such a great
favor for me to be consecrated myself? And as to your calling
me a restorer of spiritual glory, pardon me, but you do not
know much of the one to whom you speak; indeed, up to now
I am so far restored in that glory that I confess I am ignorant
not only how near I come to it, but even whether I shall come
to it at all. It is true that I am a dispenser of eternal salvation
along with my other innumerable fellow servants. 'For if I
do this thing willingly, I have a reward, but if it is against
my will, a dispensation is only committed to me,'[1] and to
be a dispenser of that salvation by word and sacrament is
not at all the same as to be a partaker of it. For, if it were
not dispensed by good men, the Apostle could not rightly say:
'Be ye followers of me as I also am of Christ.'[2] Again, if it
were not dispensed by bad men, there would be no one of
whom the Lord could say: 'Whatsoever they say, do ye, but

1 1 Cor. 9.17.
2 1 Cor. 11.1; 4.16.

according to their works do ye not, for they say and do not.'[3]
There are, then, many dispensers through whose ministry we
attain eternal salvation, but 'it is required among dispensers
that a man be found faithful,'[4] and among the faithful ones
—may He who is not deceived include me in this number!—
'one is after this manner, another after that,'[5] 'according as
God hath divided to every one the measure of faith.'[6]

And so, my dearest and sweetest brother, may it rather be
the Lord who feeds you with the flowers of wisdom and
refreshes you with draughts from the living fount. If you
think that any boon can be conferred on your most devout
zeal by my poor effort—for I understand that you are capable
and I see that you are in earnest—you should turn your
attention to some other works of mine, which are collected
in many volumes, rather than to hope to receive by letters
what could satisfy your craving. Or at least come and receive
in person what I can give you, for I think you do not show
yourself to us because you do not want to; but what great
thing is it for a man like you, not tied by duty to any one
place, to come to us, with the Lord's help, whether to stay
with us for a long time, or to return after having spent at
least a little time here?

See, now, what you wrote in the third of your five verses
has almost happened, and you have a letter from me which
is more full of speech than eloquent. By the way, in your
fifth and last line there are seven feet. Did the number escape
your ear or did you want to find out whether I still remembered how to distinguish meter—something a man who
used to be keen about such things might by now have for-

---

3 Matt. 23.3.
4 1 Cor. 4.2.
5 1 Cor. 7.7.
6 Rom. 12.3.

gotten because of having made progress in later times in ecclesiastical literature?

I have no copy of the psalter translated from the Hebrew by holy Jerome. We have not translated it, but we have corrected some faulty places in our Latin copies by comparing them with the Greek.[7] In this way we have perhaps made it into something more suitable, but still not such as it ought to be. We are still making corrections, by comparison of copies, of details which escaped our notice at that time, and which are pointed out by readers. So we want you to bring that perfect version with you.

262. Augustine gives greeting in the Lord to his daughter, the devout lady, Ecdicia[1]

After reading your Reverence's letter and questioning the bearer on the points that remained to be asked, I felt a very deep regret that you had chosen to act so to your husband that the edifice of continence which he had begun to rear should have collapsed into the melancholy downfall of adultery by his failure to persevere. If, after making a vow of chastity to God and carrying it out in act and in disposition, he had returned to carnal intercourse with his wife, he would have been a source of grief, but how much more is he to be grieved over now that he has plunged headlong into a deeper destruction by breaking every bond and committing adultery in his rage at you, ruinous to himself, as if his perdition were a more savage blow at you! This great evil arose from your not treating him in his state of mind with the moderation you should have shown, because, although

---

7 Cf. Letter 71 (Vol. 1, p. 324).

---

1 She is not otherwise known.

you were refraining by mutual consent from carnal intercourse, as his wife you should have been subject to your
husband in other things according to the marriage bond,
especially as you are both members of the Body of Christ.[2]
And, indeed, if you, a believer, had had an unbelieving
husband,[3] you ought to have conducted yourself with a
submissive demeanor that you might win him for the Lord,
as the Apostles advise.

I say nothing of the fact that I know you undertook this
state of continence, contrary to sound doctrine, before he
gave consent. He should not have been defrauded of the
debt you owed him of your body before his will joined yours
in seeking that good which surpasses conjugal chastity. But
perhaps you had not read or heard or considered the words
of the Apostle: 'It is good for a man not to touch a woman,
but for fear of fornication let every man have his own wife
and every woman have her own husband. Let the husband
render the debt to his wife and the wife also in like manner
to the husband. The wife hath not power of her own body,
but the husband; and in like manner the husband also hath
not power of his own body but the wife. Defraud not one
another except by consent, for a time, that you may give
yourselves to prayer and return together again lest Satan tempt
your for your incontinence.'[4] According to these words of
the Apostle, if he had wished to practice continence and
you had not, he would have been obliged to render you the
debt, and God would have given him credit for continence
if he had not refused you marital intercourse, out of consideration for your weakness, not his own, in order to prevent
you from falling into the damnable sin of adultery. How
much more fitting would it have been for you, to whom

2 Eph. 5.30; 1 Cor. 6.15.
3 1 Cor. 7.13.
4 1 Cor. 7.1-5.

subjection was more appropriate, to yield to his will in rendering him the debt in this way, since God would have taken account of your intention to observe continence which you gave up to save your husband from destruction!

But, as I said, I pass over this, since, after you had refused to agree to render him the conjugal debt, he agreed to this same bond of continence and lived in perfect continence with you for a long time. By his consent he absolved you from your sin of refusing him the debt of your body. Therefore, in your case, the question at issue is not whether you should return to intercourse with your husband, for what you both vowed to God with equal consent you ought both to have persevered to the end in fulfilling. If he has fallen away from this resolution, do you at least persevere in it with constancy. I should not give you this advice if he had not given his consent to this course. For, if you had never obtained his consent, no lapse of years would have excused you, but, if you had consulted me however long afterwards, I should have made you no other answer than what the Apostle said: 'The wife hath not power of her own body, but the husband.' By this power he had already given you permission to practise continence and, for himself, undertook to practise it with you.

But there is a point which, I am sorry to say, you did not observe, because you should have given way to him all the more humbly and submissively in your domestic relationship since he had so devotedly yielded to you in so important a matter, even to the extent of imitating you. For he did not cease to be your husband because you were both refraining from carnal intercourse; on the contrary, you continued to be husband and wife in a holier manner because you were carrying out a holier resolution, with mutual accord. Therefore, you had no right to dispose of your clothing or of gold or silver or any money, or of any of your earthly property without his consent, lest you scandalize a man who joined you in vowing higher things to God, and had continently abstained from what he could demand of your body in virtue of his lawful power.

Finally, it came about that, when scorned, he broke the bond of continence which he had taken upon himself when he was loved, and in his anger at you he did not spare himself. For, as the bearer of your letter described it to me, when he found out that you had given away everything or almost everything you possessed to two unknown wandering monks,[5] as if you were distributing alms to the poor, he cursed them and you with them, and alleging that they were not servants of God but men, who creep into other people's houses, leading you captive[6] and plundering you, he indignantly threw off the holy obligation he had assumed with you. For he was weak and, therefore, as you seemed the stronger in your common purpose, he should have been supported by your love, not exasperated by your boldness. For, even if he was perhaps slower in being moved to almsgiving on a more liberal scale, he could have learned that also from you, and if he had not been affronted by your unexpected extravagance but had been won over by the dutifulness he expected from you, you could have done together even this which you rashly did of yourself, and much more prudently, in more orderly and honorable fashion, with union of hearts. Then there would have been no insult for the servants of God—if, however, they were that—who received such a quantity of goods from a woman they did not know, another man's wife, in the absence and without the knowledge of her husband. Then God would have been praised in your works, which would have been accomplished in such trustful partnership that not

---

5 That is: not attached to any monastery. They seem to have been plentiful in Africa, and were reprobated by Augustine in *De opere monachorum* 28.36. The Rule of St. Benedict called them *gyrovagues* and warned sternly against them.

6 2 Tim. 3.6.

only the most perfect chastity, but even glorious poverty,
would have been observed by you jointly.

But now see what you have done by your ill-advised haste.
For, although I should think charitably about those monks
by whom he complains that you were not edified, but robbed,
and should not readily side with a man whose eye is troubled
through indignation[7] against those who were perhaps servants
of God, was the good you did in refreshing the bodies of the
poor by too lavish alms as great as the evil by which you
turned the mind of your husband from so good a purpose?
Or should the temporal welfare of anyone be dearer to you
than his eternal welfare? If, on considering the wider aspect
of mercy, you had postponed the distribution of your goods
to the poor to avoid being a stumbling-block to your husband,
thereby causing him to be lost to God, would not God have
credited you with more abundant alms? Besides, if you
recall what you gained when you won your husband to the
service of Christ in a holier chastity with you, understand
what a grave loss you suffered through that almsgiving of
yours, a loss greater than the heavenly gains of which you
dreamed. For, if the breaking of bread to the hungry[8] has
such consideration here, how much more must we believe
there is for the mercy by which a man is rescued from the
Devil, going about like a raging lion seeking whom he may
devour![9]

However, when I say this, I do not mean that if our
good works prove a stumbling-block to anyone we should
think of leaving them off. The case of strangers is different
from the case of persons bound to us by any tie; the case of
believers is not the same as that of unbelievers; the case of
parents toward children differs from that of children toward

7 Ps. 6.8.
8 Isa. 58.7.
9 1 Peter 5.8.

parents; and, finally, the case of husband and wife (which is
the one especially considered in the present circumstances)
differs from the others, and the married woman has no right
to say: 'I do what I please with my own property,' since she
does not belong to herself, but to her head, that is, her
husband.[10] For 'after this manner,' as the Apostle Peter says,
'certain holy women who trusted in God adorned themselves,
being in subjection to their own husbands; as Sara obeyed
Abraham, calling him lord, whose daughters' he says 'you
are,'[11] and he was speaking to Christian, not to Jewish,
women.

And what wonder that a father did not wish the son of
both of you to be stripped of his means of support in this
life, not knowing what state of life he would follow when he
began to be a little older, whether it would be the profession
of a monk or the ministry of the Church or the obligation of
the married state? For, although the children of holy parents
should be encouraged and trained for better things, 'every
one hath his proper gift from God, one after this manner,
another after that,'[12] unless, perhaps, a father is to be blamed
for showing foresight and caution in such matters, although
the blessed Apostle says: 'If any man have not care of his
own and especially of those of his house, he denieth the
faith and is worse than an infidel.'[13] But when he spoke of
almsgiving itself he said: 'Not that others should be eased
and you burdened.'[14] Therefore you should have taken counsel
together about everything; together you should have regulated
what treasure is to be laid up in heaven and what is to be
left as a means of support for yourselves, your dependents
and your son, so that other men be not eased and you

10 Eph. 5.23.
11 1 Peter 3.5,6; Gen. 18.12.
12 1 Cor. 7.7.
13 1 Tim. 5.8.
14 2 Cor. 8.13.

burdened. In making and carrying out these arrangements, if any better plan happened to occur to you, you should have suggested it respectfully to your husband and bowed obediently to his authority as that of your head. In this way all who prize common sense, whom the news of this good way of life could reach, would rejoice at the fruitfulness and the peace of your household, and your enemy would be turned back, having nothing evil to say of you.

Moreover, if in the matter of almsgiving and bestowing your property on the poor, a good and great work about which we have precise commandments from the Lord, you ought to have taken counsel with your husband, a believer, and one who was observing with you the holy vow of continence, and not to have scorned his will, how much more necessary was it for you not to change or adopt anything in your costume and garb against his will—a matter on which we read no divine commands! It is true we read that women should appear in decent apparel and that the wearing of gold and the plaiting of hair[15] and other things of the kind which are usually put on either for idle display or to add allurement to beauty are deservedly reproved. But there is a certain matronly costume, appropriate to one's position in life, distinct from the widow's garb, which may be fitting for married women of the faith and which does not offend religious decorum. If your husband did not want you to lay this aside so that you might not flaunt yourself as a widow[16] during his lifetime, I think he should not have been driven to the scandal of a quarrel with you, with the result of more harm from your disobedience than good from any act of self-denial. For, what is more incongruous than for a woman

15 1 Tim. 2.9; 1 Peter 3.3.
16 This was a special dress of dark color, not unlike a religious habit, which distinguished widows, and was often conferred by the bishop. These women lived a retired and religious life and performed many charitable works for the Church.

to act haughtily toward her husband about a humble dress,
when it would have been more profitable for you to display
beauty in your conduct to him rather than stand out against
him in a matter of mourning garb? Even if it had been a
nun's dress that attracted you, could you not have assumed
it with better grace if you had submitted to your husband
and received his permission than you showed in presuming
to put on widow's dress without consulting him or deferring
to him? And if he absolutely refused his permission, how
would your purpose have suffered? Perish the thought that
God should be displeased at your wearing, in your husband's
lifetime, the dress, not of Anna[17] but of Susanna.[18]

But, if he who had begun with you to prize the great good
of continence had wished you to wear the dress of a wife, not
a widow, he would not thereby have obliged you to put on
an unbecoming adornment, and, even if he had forced you
to it by some harsh requirement, you could still have retained
a humble heart under proud attire. Surely, in the time of the
patriarchs the great Queen Esther feared God, worshiped
God, and served God, yet she was submissive to her husband,
a foreign king, who did not worship the same God as she did.
And at a time of extreme danger not only to herself but to
her race, the chosen people of God, she prostrated herself
before God in prayer, and in her prayer she said that she
regarded her royal attire as a menstruous rag,[19] and God
'who seeth the heart'[20] heard her prayer at once because He
knew that she spoke the truth. But as for you, if your husband
had remained steadfast in the plan of life he had undertaken
with you, and had not rushed into sin because he was offended by you, you had in him a husband who was not

---

17 The prophetess of Luke 2.36-38, a type of holy widowhood.
18 Cf. Dan. 13.1-63. She was a type of chaste matron. St. Ambrose praises
   both women in *De. Vid.* 4.21-25.
19 Esther 14.16.
20 Prov. 24.12.

only a believer and a worshiper with you of the true God,
but even a man of continence who was certainly not un-
mindful of your joint resolution, and who would not have
forced you to deck yourself with the ornaments of vanity
even though he obliged you to wear the garb of a matron.

As you have seen fit to consult me, I have written this,
not with the intent to break down your virtuous resolution
by my words, but because I am grieved at your husband's
conduct which is the result of your reckless and ill-considered
behavior. You must now think very seriously about reclaiming
him if you truly want to belong to Christ. Clothe yourself
with lowliness of mind and, that God may keep you in
constancy, do not scorn your husband in his fall. Pour out
devout and continuous prayers for him, offer a sacrifice of
tears as if it were the blood of a pierced heart, write him
your apology, begging pardon for the sin you committed
against him by disposing of your property according to what
you thought should be done with it, without asking his advice
and consent; not that you should repent of having given it
to the poor, but of having refused to let him share and direct
your good deed. Promise for the future, with the Lord's help,
that if he will repent of his shameful conduct and resume
the continence which he has abandoned, you will be subject
to him in all things as it befits you to be: 'If peradventure
God may give him repentance and he may recover himself
from the snares of the devil by whom he is held captive at
his will.'[21] As for your son, since you brought him forth in
lawful and honorable wedlock, who does not know that he
is more subject to his father's authority than to yours? Therefore, his father cannot be denied custody of him whenever
he learns where he is and makes a legal demand for him.
Consequently, your union of hearts is necessary for him,
also, that he may be reared and trained in the wisdom of God.

21 Cf. 1 Tim. 2.25,26.

*263. Augustine gives greeting in the Lord to the most
religious lady, his daughter, Sapida*[1]

I accept the gift which you wished me to receive, made by
the good and devoted labor of your hands, because I see that
you are in need of comfort, and I did not wish to add to
your sorrow, especially as you imagined that it would be no
slight solace to you if I were to wear the tunic which you
made for your brother, a holy minister of God, who has left
the land of the dying and stands in need of no perishable
things. I have therefore done as you wished, and have not
refused to your love for your brother this act which you
thought might be some kind of comfort, however slight. I
have accepted the tunic you sent and at the time of writing
this to you I am beginning to wear it. Be of good heart, but
make use of much better and greater consolations so that
the dark cloud drawn round your heart by human weakness
may yield to the sunshine of God's authority, and live in such
constancy that you may live with your brother, since your
brother has died only that he may live.

It is indeed a cause of tears that you do not see your
loving brother, a deacon of the Church at Carthage, who
revered you greatly for your mode of life and profession
of sacred virginity, as you used to see him going in and out,
performing his liturgical duties briskly, and that you do not
hear from him those admiring words which he poured out
with a devoted, respectful, and courteous affection for the
sanctity of your sisterly attachment. When these thoughts
recur and the force of habit makes its demands, the heart is
pierced and tears come forth like heart's blood. But let the
heart be lifted up and the eyes will be dry. Yet the loss of
those things which you grieve over, which have come to the

---

1 A consecrated virgin of Carthage.

end of their temporal course, does not mean the destruction of that affection with which Timothy[2] loved and still loves Sapida; it remains and is preserved among his treasures and is hidden with Christ in the Lord.[3] Do those who love gold lose it when they store it away? Do they not feel more secure about it, as far as that may be, when they keep it shut up from their eyes in safer coffers? Does earthly covetousness think it keeps a thing more safely if it does not see what it loves, and does heavenly charity grieve as if it had lost what it has sent before it to the celestial storehouses? Recall that you are called Sapida,[4] and savor 'the things that are above where Christ is sitting at the right hand of God,'[5] who deigned to die for us that we, the dead, might live, and that death itself should not be feared by man as if it were destined to consume man, nor should any of the dead for whom Life died be mourned as if he had lost life. These thoughts and others like them are divine consolations for you, which should make human sadness turn away with shame.

I do not mean that we should be angry at the sorrow of mortals for their dear dead, but the sorrow of believers should not be of long duration. If, then, you have been sorrowful, let that now be enough and 'be not sorrowful even as the Gentiles who have no hope.'[6] Now, the Apostle did not forbid us to be sorrowful when he said this, but 'to be sorrowful even as the Gentiles who have no hope.' For Martha and Mary, loving and faithful sisters, wept for their brother Lazarus who was to rise again, although at the time they did not know that he was to return to this life.[7] The

2 Migne suggests that this Timothy may be the deacon mentioned as letter-bearer in Letter 110.
3 Col. 3.3.
4 As an adjective, *sapida* means 'savory,' and also 'wise.'
5 Col. 3.2,1,
6 1 Thess. 4.12.
7 John 11.19,33,35.

Lord Himself wept, too, for the same Lazarus whom He was to raise to life, doubtless to allow us by His example— although He did not give a commandment—to weep over our dead, also, whom we believe destined to rise to the true life. Not without reason does Scripture say in the Book of Ecclesiasticus: 'Shed tears over the dead and begin to lament as if thou hadst suffered some great harm,' but a little further on it says: 'And comfort thyself in thy sadness, for of sadness cometh death, and the sorrow of the heart overwhelmeth strength.'[8]

My daughter, your brother lives in the spirit and sleeps in the flesh; 'Shall he that sleepeth rise again no more?'[9] God, who has received his soul, will restore it to his body, which He has not taken away to destroy, but has only delayed to restore. Therefore, there is no reason for long-continued sadness, because there is a more powerful motive for everlasting joy, since not even the mortal part of your brother which is buried in the earth will be lost to you. That body in which he was visible to you, through which he spoke to you and conversed with you, from which his voice issued forth as well known to you as his face when seen, so that he was always recognized by you, even though not seen, wherever you heard his voice—all these things have been withdrawn from the senses of the living that the absence of the dead may cause us grief. But, since they will not be lost for eternity, where 'a hair of your head shall not perish,'[10] and since, though laid aside for a time, they will be restored so as never again to be laid aside, but changed instead for the better and made strong, certainly there is greater reason for congratulation on our hope of a limitless eternity than for sorrow over the reality of too fleeting time. The Gentiles do not have this

8 Eccli. 38.17,19.
9 Ps. 40.9.
10 Luke 21.18.

hope, 'not knowing the Scriptures nor the power of God,'[11] who is able to restore what is lost, to raise what is dead to life, to revive what has rotted away, to gather together what is scattered, and thereafter to preserve forever what was corruptible and finite. He promised to do this, and He gives as guarantee the promises He has fulfilled; let your faith speak of this to you, since your hope will not be disappointed even though your love may be put to the test. Reflect on these thoughts, console yourself more effectively and more truly with them. For, if it bring some consolation to you that I am wearing the garment which you had woven for your brother, since he could not wear it, how much more should you be comforted that he for whom it was made is in need of no perishable garment, but is clothed in an imperishable one, even that of immortality!

264. Augustine gives greeting in the Lord to the honorable and distinguished servant of God, Maxima,[1] worthy of praise among the members of Christ

Much as your holy zeal delights us, it also saddens us in turn, because you inform us that your province[2] is greatly endangered by poisonous and deadly errors. But, as it was foretold that those things were to be, we should not wonder that they arise but watch that they do not hurt us. God our Deliverer would not allow these things to arise if it were not to the advantage of His saints to be trained by temptations of this

---

11 Matt. 22.29; Mark 12.24.

1 A pious lady who was disturbed at the inroads of error into her province.
2 It is suggested that this may have been Spain where, according to Orosius, 'deadly doctrine killed more souls than the swords of barbarians killed bodies.' Cf. Letter 166.

kind. For, those who neglect to convert and amend themselves while they are in this life, and who stubbornly refuse to be taught, win for themselves by their perverse will the punishment of present blindness and future eternal punishment. Nevertheless, as these make a bad use of the good things of God, 'who maketh his sun to shine upon the good and bad, and raineth upon the just and the unjust,'[3] who shows His patience by calling them to repentance while they 'treasure up to themselves wrath against the day of wrath and revelation of the just judgment of God,'[4] and as they also make a bad use of His goodness and patience, that is, the good things of God, so long as they are not converted, so, on His side, God makes a good use of their bad deeds, not only to serve His justice which will repay them as they deserve at the end, but also that His saints may be tried and rewarded. Thus, the good advance and are approved and made known through that very malice of the bad, as the Apostle says: 'For there must be also heresies that they also who are approved may be made manifest among you.'[5]

For, if God made no good use even of evil for the advantage of His elect, He who brought such great good even from the crime of Judas by having us redeemed by the Blood of Christ, He might either have allowed those whom He foreknew as evil not to be born, or He might have quenched their life at the very outset of their wickedness. But He allows them life so long as He knows that it is useful and sufficient to warn and train His holy household. Therefore, He comforts the sorrow they cause us because He relieves us of the very sorrow we feel for them, but when they persist in their perversity He makes it press heavily on them. The joy which we feel when any of them is converted, turned

3 Matt. 5.45.
4 Rom. 2.5.
5 1 Cor. 11.19.

to a better life, and joined to the company of the saints can
be compared to no joy in this world. Therefore, it is written:
'Son, if thou be wise, thou shalt be wise to thyself and thy
nearest, but if thou turn out evil thou alone shalt drink of
the evil,'[6] because when we feel joy for the faithful and the
just, their good conduct benefits both them and us, but when
we feel sadness for the unfaithful and unjust, their malice and
our sadness harm them alone, but it greatly helps us with
God when we feel sorrow and compassion for them, when in
proportion to that sorrow we lament and pray. I wholly
approve and praise you, honorable servant of God, worthy
of praise in Christ, for the sorrow over such persons and the
watchfulness and care against them which you expressed in
your letter, and, since you insist on it, I encourage and advise
you with all my strength to walk constantly in the right way,
to be simple as a dove in your compassion toward them,
but wise as a serpent[7] in guarding against them, and to strive
with all your might that those who belong to you may be
steadfast in the true faith with you, or, if any have gone
astray in anything, that they may be brought back to the
true faith.

Now, concerning the human nature which was taken by
the Word of God, when 'He was made flesh and dwelt
among us,'[8] I should make some correction if I found anything wrong or distorted in what you believe. Believe, then,
as you do believe, that in that humanity the Son of God
took our whole nature, that is, both a rational soul and mortal
flesh, without sin. He shared in our infirmity, not in our
iniquity, that by the infirmity He had in common with us
He might loose the bond of our iniquity and bring us to His
justice, drinking death from our cup, pouring out life from

---

6 Prov. 9.12 (Septuagint).
7 Matt. 10.16.
8 John 1.14.

His. But, if you have any of their writings in which they affirm what is contrary to this belief, be so kind as to send it to me so that we may not only profess our belief, but may, as far as possible, refute their unbelief. Without doubt, they attempt to support this false and wicked belief of theirs by some proofs from the divine Scriptures. In this it must be pointed out to them how wrongly they understand the sacred books which were written for the salvation of believers, as if someone were to do himself a grievous harm with surgeon's instruments, which are certainly not meant to wound, but to heal. We have labored and we still labor, as far as the Lord allows us, against various errors which require refutation. If, by any chance, you wish to have copies of our works, send people to copy them for you, God has willed that you may easily do that as He has given you the means.

265. Bishop Augustine gives greeting in the Lord to the devout lady, Seleuciana,[1] a servant of God worthy of honor in the love of Christ

I have read your letter with pleasure at the news of your health, and I am making no delay in answering what you wrote. In the first place, I am surprised that your Novatian[2] friend should say that Peter was not baptized, when shortly before you wrote that he said the Apostles were baptized. Where he got the idea that among the baptized Apostles Peter was not baptized I do not know, and I am sending you

---

1 From the address she would seem to have been a woman living a religious life either as a consecrated virgin or a widow.

2 The heresy and schism of Novatianism appeared after the persecution of Decius (249-252). Its adherents called themselves 'the pure' and refused reconciliation to those who had apostatized under torture. They even tried to claim that the Church had no power to remit mortal sin.

a copy of your letter, in case you have none, so that you may examine it more carefully and give me an answer to what I have found in your letter. Unless your secretary either heard it wrong or wrote it wrong, I do not know what kind of heart he could have had to say that Peter was not baptized when he said that the Apostles were baptized.

In saying that Peter did penance we have to take care not to think that he did it as those who are properly called penitents now do it in the Church. Who could bear it that we should think the first of the Apostles was numbered among such penitents? He repented of having denied Christ, as his tears show, for so it is written that 'he wept bitterly.'[3] For they had not yet been strengthened by the Resurrection of the Lord and the coming of the Holy Spirit who appeared on the day of Pentecost, nor by that breath which the Lord breathed on them after He rose from the dead when 'He breathed upon their face, saying: Receive ye the Holy Spirit.'[4]

Hence, it is correct to say that when Peter denied the Lord the Apostles had not yet been baptized, not, indeed, with water, but with the Holy Spirit. For, after He rose again and conversed with them, He said: 'John indeed baptized with water but you shall be baptized with the Holy Spirit whom you shall receive not many days hence unto Pentecost.'[5] It is true some versions have 'you shall begin to be baptized, but whether it says 'you shall be baptized' or 'you shall begin to be baptized' does not affect the matter. For in some copies we find 'you shall baptize' or 'you shall begin to baptize,' but these are faulty texts which are easily proved wrong from the Greek versions. But, if we say that they were not baptized with water, it is to be feared that we may put them seriously in the wrong and may give men some ground for despising

---

3 Matt. 26.75; Luke 22.62.
4 John 20.22.
5 Acts 1.5. The last words are not found in the Vulgate.

baptism, which is so far from deserving contempt that the apostolic teaching commends it, and the centurion Cornelius and those who were with him were baptized, even though they had already received the Holy Spirit.[6]

As the just men of old were guilty of no sin if they were not circumcised, but after God commanded that Abraham and his posterity should be circumcised[7] it was a grave sin if it was not done, so also before the Lord Christ[8] gave holy baptism instead of circumcision of the flesh as a sacrament of the New Testament in His Church, and said very plainly: 'Unless a man be born again of water and the Holy Spirit, he cannot enter into the kingdom of heaven,'[9] we do not have to inquire when a man was baptized; but when we read that certain ones in the Body of Christ, which is the Church,[10] belong to the kingdom of heaven, we must understand that this applies only to the baptized, unless it happens that the pressure of persecution has come upon those who refused to deny Christ and they have been put to death before they were baptized, in which case the shedding of their blood substitutes for baptism. But is it possible to say this of the Apostles, who had such ample time in which to be baptized that they even baptized others? Not everything that happened is found written in the Scriptures; the fact of some happenings is proved from other sources. The time of the Apostle Paul's baptism is recorded, but there is no record of when the other Apostles were baptized, yet we must understand that they had been baptized. Thus, the time when the people of the Churches of Jerusalem and Samaria were baptized is recorded, while the time when the other people of the Gentiles to

6 Acts 10.47.48.
7 Gen. 17.10-14.
8 A suggested lacuna has been excised at this point by Goldbacher.
9 John 3.5.
10 Col. 1.24.
11 Acts 9.18.

whom the Apostles sent Epistles is not recorded, yet we can surely not doubt that they were baptized because of those words of the Lord: 'Unless a man be born of water and the Holy Spirit, he cannot enter into the kingdom of heaven.'

Two statements are, however, made about the Lord, both that He baptized more than John and that He 'himself did not baptize but his disciples,'[13] so that we may understand that He Himself did indeed baptize by the presence of His majesty, but not that He baptized with His own Hands. He instituted the sacrament of baptism, but the ministry of baptism belonged to the disciples. Therefore, when the Evangelist John says in his Gospel: 'After these things Jesus and his disciples came into the land of Judea and there he abode with them and baptized,'[14] and when he speaks of Him a little later, and says: 'When Jesus therefore understood that the Pharisees had heard that Jesus maketh more disciples and baptizeth more than John (though Jesus himself did not baptize, but his disciples), he left Judea and went again into Galilee,'[15] we know that it was when He went from Jerusalem with His disciples into the land of Judea and abode there with them that He baptized, not personally, but through His disciples, whom we understand to have been already baptized either with the baptism of John or, more credibly, with the baptism of Christ. For He would not have shunned the ministry of baptism so that He might have His servants baptized through whom He would baptize others, since He did not shun that memorable service of humility by which He washed their feet, and when Peter asked Him to wash not only his feet, but also his hands and his head, He replied: 'He that is washed needeth not but to wash his feet but is

12 Acts 2.41; 8.12.
13 John 4.1,2.
14 John 3.22.
15 John 4.1-3.

clean wholly,'[16] from which we conclude that Peter had been baptized.

What you wrote in your letter about the Novatian saying that the Apostles gave penance instead of baptism is not clearly expressed. If by saying 'instead of baptism' he means that sins are remitted through penance, he has some ground for what he says. Such penance can be effective if one sins after baptism. But, since he denies that there is opportunity for penance to be given after baptism when he says, as you wrote, that penance alone comes before baptism, we are given to understand that, when he said the Apostles gave penance instead of baptism, he means that they gave it before baptism and that those to whom it was given were not baptized afterward, because the sacrament of penance was a substitute for baptism. I have never heard any Novatian say that. Examine carefully, therefore, whether he may not, perhaps, be involved in some other error and may either be pretending to be a Novatian or imagining that he is one. However, if the Novatians do say this, I am unaware of it; what I know is that whoever says it differs radically from the rule of Catholic faith and the teaching of Christ and the Apostles.

Men do penance before baptism for their former sins so that they may be baptized, as it is written in the Acts of the Apostles, when Peter spoke to the Jews and said: 'Do penance and be baptized every one of you, in the name of the Lord Jesus Christ for the remission of your sins.'[17] Men also do penance in order to be forgiven, if after baptism they have sinned so grievously as to deserve excommunication, and in this manner those who are properly called penitents do it in all the Churches. It was of such penance that the Apostle

16 John 13.5-10.
17 Acts 2.38.

Paul spoke when he said: 'Lest when I come again, God humble me among you and I mourn many of them that sinned before and have not done penance for the uncleanness and lasciviousness and fornication that they have committed,'[18] for he wrote that to men who had already been baptized. We also have in the Acts of the Apostles the example of Simon,[19] previously baptized, who wanted to buy with money the power of conferring the Holy Spirit by the laying on of hands, and who was rebuked by Peter and told to do penance for this grave sin.

There is also the almost daily penance of the good and humble among the faithful by which we strike our breasts saying: 'Forgive us our debts as we also forgive our debtors.'[20] For we do not wish to be forgiven for what we doubt not was forgiven in baptism, but certainly we do wish it for those slight but frequent offenses which steal in on our human weakness, and which, if they were added together, would weigh us down and crush us as one great sin would do. What difference does it make to the shipwrecked whether the ship is swallowed up and sunk by one great wave, or whether the water, seeping by degrees into the hold and being disregarded and overlooked through carelessness, fills the ship and carries it down? This is our reason for being on guard by fasting, almsgiving, and prayers. When we pray: 'Forgive us as we forgive,' we show that we have sins to be forgiven, and when we humble our souls by these words we do not cease to do what may be called daily penance. I think I have given a brief but adequate reply to what you wrote; it remains that he whom you thought to win by sending me such a letter should not be obstinate.

---

18 2 Cor. 12.21.
19 Acts 8.18-23. This was Simon Magus.
20 Matt. 6.12; Luke 11.4.

*266. Bishop Augustine gives greeting in the Lord to the
excellent lady, Florentina,[1] his deservedly honored
and cherished daughter in Christ*

Your holy purpose and the 'chaste fear of the Lord, endur-
ing forever,'[2] which is entwined in your heart have roused
me to show my considerable interest in you, not only by my
prayers to God, but also by my advice to you. This I have
done more than once in the letters I sent to your Reverence's
mother, a lady I mention with due respect. As she was so
kind as to write me that you wished to receive a letter from
me first, and that you would not be silent but would set
forth your desire in answering it, I have finally done as you
wished, in case you had any need of my help, which I realize
that I owe, to the extent of my ability, as a free service to
your admirable study and that of all like you. Although I did
not learn it from you, I have complied with your wish, lest I
seem to be cruel in closing the door of assurance against you.
The next step is for you to set forth for yourself whatever you
want to ask of me, for either I know what you ask and I will
not say I do not, or I do not know it, but my ignorance will
not be a detriment to faith or salvation, and in that case I
will set you at ease about it by reasoning it out to the best of
my ability. Another alternative, to be sure, would be that I
do not know it but it is something that ought to be known,
and then I will either ask the Lord not to let me fail you,
for often the duty of sharing is the reward of receiving, or I
will answer so that you may know about this thing which
neither of us know.

I have made these prefatory remarks so as not to raise
your hopes of hearing with certainty whatever you ask of me,

1 A studious girl whom Augustine wished to help.
2 Cf. Ps. 18.10.

for then, when it did not come out that way, you might think I had acted with more boldness than prudence in giving you the chance to ask me anything you wished. I have acted thus, not as a finished master, but as one needing to be perfected with his pupils, excellent lady, daughter deservedly honored and cherished in Christ. Indeed, even in the subjects which, one way or another, I know, I am more anxious for you to be learned than to be in need of my learning, for we ought not to desire the ignorance of others in order to teach what we know, it surely is much better for all of us to be ready to be taught of God[3] what will certainly be perfected in that country on high when the promise will be fulfilled in us, that a man shall not say to his neighbor: 'Know the Lord, for all shall know him,' as it is written 'from the least of them even to the greatest.'[4] In teaching we must be especially careful to guard against the vice of pride, which is not the case with learners. Hence, the holy Scripture warns us of this when it says: 'Let every man be swift to hear but slow to speak,'[5] and when the Psalmist said: 'To my hearing thou shalt give joy and gladness,' he added immediately: 'that the bones that have been humbled shall rejoice.'[6] For he saw that humility is easily preserved in listening, whereas it is hard to do it in teaching, because the teacher must necessarily hold a higher position where it requires an effort for him to keep his footing without letting conceit steal in on him.

Do you see how dangerous it is for us of whom the world expects not only that we be teachers, but even that, men though we be, we teach divine truth? There is, however, an extraordinary comfort in our labors and perils when scholars like you make such progress that you reach the point of

---

3 John 6.45; Isa. 54.13.
4 Jer. 31.34.
5 James 1.19.
6 Ps. 50.10.

needing no man to teach you. In that peril we are not alone—for, compared with him of whom I am going to speak, what are we?—I repeat, we are not alone in that peril, but the famous Doctor of the Gentiles[7] bears witness that he was in danger, too, when he says: 'Lest by the greatness of my revelations I should be exalted, there was given to me a sting of my flesh,'[8] and the rest. Hence, also, the Lord Himself, our admirable Physician, prescribed for this swelling when He said: 'Be not you called Rabbi, for one is your Master, Christ,'[9] and the same Doctor of the Gentiles maintains the same idea when he says: 'Neither he that planteth is anything nor he that watereth, but God that giveth the increase.'[10] He who was the greatest among those born of women[11] remembered this and humbled himself the more,[12] declaring that he was unworthy to bear the shoes of Christ.[13] And what else does he show when he says: 'He that hath the bride is the bridegroom, but the friend of the bridegroom, who standeth and heareth him, rejoiceth with joy because of the bridegroom's voice.'[14] This is that hearing which I mentioned awhile ago in that passage of the psalm: 'To my hearing thou shalt give joy and gladness and the bones that have been humbled shall rejoice.'

Consequently, you must know that the less you need to learn anything from me or from any man anywhere, the more surely, more deeply, and more rationally do I rejoice in your faith, hope, and charity. However, when I was at your home and you showed the modesty befitting your youth, your good parents, who are both entranced with your serious

---

7 1 Tim. 2.7.
8 2 Cor. 12.7.
9 Matt. 23.8,10.
10 1 Cor. 3.7.
11 Matt. 11.11; Luke 7.28.
12 Eccli. 3.20.
13 Matt. 3.11; Luke 3.16; John 1.27.
14 John 3.29.

studies, were so kind as to enlighten me concerning the ardor you show for true piety and wisdom, and they very cordially asked me not to withhold my poor services in teaching you what you have need to know. I have, therefore, thought fit in this letter to exhort you to ask what you will, within the above-mentioned range of choice, so that I may not be useless to you by attempting to teach you what you know, provided you hold most firmly to the belief that, even though you may be able to learn something helpful from me, He who is the interior Master of the interior man will teach you and will reveal to your heart how true it is that, as it is said: 'Neither he that planteth is anything nor he that watereth but God that giveth the increase.'[15]

267. Augustine gives greeting in the Lord to the most religious and excellent lady, Fabiola,[1] his daughter worthy of praise in the charity of Christ

I have read the letter of your Holiness and, although it is an answer to mine, I feel impelled by the obligation of answering it. For you grieve over the pilgrimage through which we attain to rejoice forever with the saints, and you rightly give first place to the longing for our heavenly country where we shall not be separated by earthly distance, but shall rejoice always in the contemplation of the One. You are happy in dwelling faithfully on the thought of such things, happier in loving them, and you will be most happy in attaining them. But examine more carefully even now in what sense we are said to be absent, whether it is because we do not see each other in the flesh, or because our minds do not

---

15 1 Cor. 3.7.

---

1 It is known only that she lived far from St. Augustine.

give and receive communications from each other, that is, we do not converse. For I think, although separated in the flesh by long distance, if we could know each other's thoughts we should be more together than if we were in one place, looking at one another but sitting in silence, giving no sign by words of our inner feeling, showing our minds by no movement of our bodies. Hence you understand that each one is more present to himself than one is to another, because each one is better known to himself than to another, not by beholding his own face which he carries around without seeing it, unless there is a mirror at hand, but by beholding his own conscience which he sees even with his eyes closed. How great, then, is our life which is so prized!

268. Augustine gives greeting in the Lord to the members of Christ, his much loved and cherished lords of the holy congregation to which he ministers

The well-known and often-proved generosity of your Holiness has given me a confidence in our Lord Jesus Christ that makes me rely on it in absence as I have always rejoiced in it when present. Yet I am always with you in spirit, not only because the grace of our Lord Jesus Christ unceasingly pours out its fragrance, but also because you do not allow me who serve you in the Gospel to endure hardship. Our brother Fascius[1] was being pressed for payment of a debt of seventeen soldi[2] by the tribute-collectors, and, as he could not at that time find the wherewithal to acquit himself, he fled for refuge to Holy Church,[3] to avoid having to suffer corporal punish-

---

1 A layman of Augustine's congregation, who was liable to seizure and removal unless the bishop discharged the debt.
2 About thirty-five dollars.
3 That is, he took sanctuary.

ment. And as the collectors were obliged to depart and therefore could not give him an extension, they loaded me with the
bitterest complaints, demanding that I hand him over to
them or provide the means of giving them what they proved
was owing to them. I suggested to Fascius that I speak to
your Holiness about his necessities, but, held back by shame,
he begged me not to do it. So, being pressed by a greater
need, I accepted seventeen soldi from our brother, Mace-
donius,[4] which I at once paid on his behalf, with his promise
that by a certain day he would be able to meet his obligation.
He agreed that, if he was not able to meet it, an appeal
should be made for him to your brotherly compassion, which
you have always shown to the brethren.

And now, since he is not here, it remains for you to come
to the assistance, not of him, since in his absence no one can
put pressure on him, but of my promise, for my good name
is always dear to you. As the day on which he said he would
meet the debt is already past and gone, I do not know what
answer to make to the one who trusted his soldi to my good
faith, unless I do what I promised to do. As I had not been
notified of the matter by the day of Pentecost so that I might
have made an appeal at a time when there was a larger
attendance of you, I ask you to be so kind as to take this
letter as my voice and presence while God our Lord urges
and exhorts you in your hearts. You have put your trust in
Him and He never forsakes us while we fear Him and honor
His Name; in Him I am always united with you, although
in bodily presence I seem to have departed from you; it is
He who promises you the harvest of eternal life from that
seed of good works, as the Apostle says: 'And in doing good
let us not fail, for in due time we shall reap not failing.
Therefore whilst we have time let us work good to all men,

---

4 Not the Vicar of Africa in 414 who appears in Letters 152-155, but
evidently a layman of Hippo.

but especially to those who are of the household of the faith.'[5]
Since, then, he is of the household of the faith, a faithful
Christian, our Catholic brother, whose need I ask you to
supply, do what the Lord commands you to do, without
repining, without complaining, with joy and cheerfulness, for
your trust is in God, not in man, because He promises you
that nothing you do in mercy will be lost, but on that day you
shall receive it back with eternal usury.[6] And since the Apostle
himself says: 'Now this I say: he who soweth sparingly shall
also reap sparingly,'[7] you should understand that now is the
time, while we are still in this life, to be swift and eager to
purchase the gift of eternal life, for when the end of the
world comes it will be given only to those who have bought
it for themselves by faith before they were able to see it.

I have also written to the priests that if, after the contribution of your Holiness, there is a deficit, they are to make
it up from the treasury of the church, provided that you
make your offering cheerfully according to each one's inclination, for whether the money is given from yours or that of
the church, it is all God's, and your generosity will be much
more pleasing than the treasures of the church, as the Apostle
says: 'Not that I seek the gift, but I seek the fruit.'[8] Gladden
my heart, then, because I wish to rejoice in your fruits, for
you are the trees of God, which He deigns through the ministry of such as I am, to water with continual showers. May
the Lord preserve you from all evil both here and in the
world to come, my well-beloved lords and much desired
brothers.

---

5 Gal. 6.9,10.
6 Matt. 25.34-40.
7 2 Cor. 9.6.
8 Phil. 4.17.

269. *Augustine to his holy and revered brother and fellow priest, Nobilius*[1]

The ceremony[2] to which your brotherly affection invites me is so important that my will might drag my poor body to you if weakness did not hold it back. I might have come if it were not winter, I might have disregarded winter if I were young, for either the warmth of youth would have borne the rigor of cold or the warmth of summer would have tempered the chill of age. But as it is, my holy lord, saintly and revered brother and fellow priest, I cannot bear so long a journey in winter with the chill of advanced age which I carry about with me. I return the greeting owed to your merits, and I commend my own welfare to your prayers, asking the Lord myself that peace and prosperity may attend upon the dedication of so great a building.

1 Not otherwise known. This appears to be one of the last letters Augustine wrote and can be dated in the winter of 429-430.
2 The dedication of a church.

270. *To Augustine*[1]

When I traveled to the city of Leges some time ago, I was very much grieved at not being able to find all of you there. For I found half of you[2] and, so to speak, a part of your soul in my dearest Severus,[3] which made me feel somewhat joyful. I should have rejoiced perfectly if I had found the whole of you. Consequently, I was happy in the part of you that I found, and I was wholly sad on account of the part of you

1 There is no title of address. This anonymous letter was formerly attributed to St. Jerome, and was listed as No. 40 among his. The tone and style show that it could not have been his.
2 Cf. Letter 110 (Vol. 2, p. 243).
3 Bishop of Milevis; cf. Letter 97 n. 3.

that I could not see at all. So I said to my soul: 'Why art thou sad and why doest thou trouble me? Hope in God'[4] and He will make thy friend whom thou lovest present to thee. Hence, I trust in the Lord and I hope that He will gladden me with the sight of you. Oh, if love could be seen with the eyes! Certainly you would see how much of my love there is in you. It would either bring you great joy by being equal to your love, or, if it were greater, it would bring you a great eagerness to imitate it. Therefore, since I love you in the Lord, do you love the one who loves you, and use your ecclesiastical authority to urge others to love with you. As for your asking me in your letter to pray for you, I might properly do it if I myself were free from sin, so that it would be lawful for me to pray for others. For that reason I urge you to pour forth constant prayers from your heart to the Lord for me, and to be mindful of your profession by setting before your eyes that day on which 'the just shall not fear the evil hearing,'[5] and therefore the just man shall not fear because he will not hear: 'Depart . . . into everlasting fire,' but: 'Come, blessed of my Father, receive the kingdom.'[6] May He who lives and reigns forever and ever lead us there. Amen.

---

4 Ps. 41.6.
5 Ps. 111.7.
6 Matt. 25.41,34.
7 Tob. 9.11; Apoc. 1.18; 11.15.

INDEX

INDEX

293

294

20; *De Genesi ad litteram, 3*: 365, 375; *4*: 279; *De Genesi contra Manichaeos, 1*: 67; *De gestis Pelagii, 3*: 169; *4*: 114, 214, 217; *De gratia Christiana et de peccato originali, 4*: 134; *De gratia et libero arbitrio, 5*: 63; *De haeresibus, 5*: 114; *De libero arbitrio, 1*: 116, 230; *3*: 150, 153, 375; *4*: 12, 22; *5*: 136; *De moribus ecclesiae Catholicae et de moribus Manichaeorum, 1*: 67; *De musica, 2*: 144, 147; *3*: 13; *De natura et gratia, 4*: 50, 98, 192; *De nuptiis et concupiscentia, 4*: 403; *5*: 22; *De peccatorum meritis et de remissione et de baptismo parvulorum, 3*: 339; *4*: 297; *De praedestinatione sanctorum, 2*: 158; *De quantitate animae, 3*: 375; *De spiritu et littera, 4*: 190; *De Trinitate, 3*: 152, 375; *4*: 83; *De vera religione, 1*: 90; *3*: 375; *Retractationes, 1*: 252, 385; *2*: 159; *3*: 151, 224, *4*: 6, 32, 141; *5*: 166; *Soliloquia, 1*: 7, 10, 332

Aurelius, Archbishop of Carthage, *1*: 68, 109, 117, 179; *2*: 300, 309, 365, 369, 376; *3*: 136, 270; *4*: 83, 94, 121, 132, 136, 289, 302, 403; *5*: 99

Auxentius, *5*: 191
Auxilius, *5*: 239

Badesitta, in Africa, *1*: 310
baptism, ceremony of, *2*: 135-137; grace of, *2*: 130; infant, *4*: 28, 89, 130, 137; of St. Peter, *5*: 276; validity of, *2*: 38, 99-103, 205
Barbarus, brother, *3*: 363
Barcelona, *1*: 66
Barnabas, monk, *2*: 349; *5*: 53
beauty, definition of, *1*: 9, 44
Benenatus, Bishop of Tungitana, *5*: 245, 247
bishops, hard duties of, *1*: 114; *2*: 11; precedence of, *1*: 299
body, resurrected, *2*: 122, 152; *3*: 218, 220, 230, 236, 238
Boniface, Bishop of Cataqua, *2*: 124, 129; *3*: 55, 150, 240, 279
Boniface, Count of Africa, *4*: 141, 190, 266; *5*: 101
Boniface, Pope, *5*: 32
Boniface, priest, *1*: 373, 376, 379
Bonosus, *5*: 215
bread, breaking of as recognition, *3*: 264; small loaves in token of charity, *1*: 70, 75, 117, 119
bribery, *3*: 299-301
Brutus, *3*: 43
Bulla, in Numidia, *1*: 312

Caecilian, Bishop of Carthage, *1*: 183, 186, 189, 194-198, 206, 213, 249, 373; *2*: 22-24, 68, 196, 200, 201, 215, 224, 227,

296

clerics, Donatist, received into Church, *1*: 302; as legal guardians, *5*: 244; punishment of, *1*: 313; requirements for, *1*: 301; versus monks, *1*: 301

Communis, monk, *1*: 320

Communion, daily, 1: 213, 254, 255; fast before, *1*: 258, 259

Concordialis, monk, *3*: 162

Consentius, 2: 294; *5*: 8

consequences, secondary, not willed, *3*: 295

Constantina (Cirta), in Africa, *1*: 134, 175, 207

Constantine, Emperor, *1*: 185, 199, 249, 370; *2*: 201, 202; decrees of, *2*: 23, 36, 68, 372; *3*: 141, 143, 144; *4*: 146

Cornelius, *5*: 253

Cornutus, priest, *4*: 347, 350

Councils, authority of: *1*: 52, 54, 255; of Bagai, *1*: 239; *2*: 33, 217; *3*: 141; of Carthage, *1*: 298, 303, 379; *2*: 33, 92, 97, 128, 367; *3*: 53, 136, 137, 141; *4*: 85, 121; of Hippo, *1*: 310, 372; of Milevis, *4*: 91; of Nice, *4*: 404; *5*: 33; of Sardis, *1*: 211; of Zerta, *3*: 136

Cresconius, monk of Hadrumetum, *5*: 62

Cresconius, tribune of coast guard, *2*: 256

Crisimus, *5*: 227

Crispinus, Donatist bishop of Calama, *1*: 238, 314; *2*: 29, 199

cross, mystical interpretation of, *3*: 113, 114, 201, 202; symbolism of, *1*: 280

customs, local, to be disregarded, *1*: 287; to be observed, *1*: 253

Cutzupitae, Donatist sect, *1*: 247

Cyprian, deacon, 1: 324, 332, 342, 420

Cyprian, bishop, *1*: 415

Cyprian, priest, 2: 55; *5*: 165

Cyprian, St., *1*: 411; *2*: 71, 87, 91-93, 98, 131, 222, 223, 225; *3*: 273; *4*: 28, 120; *5*: 76

Cypriana, wife of Cornelius, *5*: 255

Dardanus, Prefect of Gaul, *4*: 221

Darius, Count of Africa, *5*: 152, 153

Delphinus, of Bordeaux, *1*: 69

Delphinus, of Cirta, *3*: 57

Demetrias, granddaughter of Proba, 2: 376, 401; *3*: 266

Democritus, philosopher, 2: 274, 283, 287, 289; *3*: 14

Demosthenes, 2: 282

Deogratias, deacon, *4*: 81; *5*: 238

Deogratias, priest of Carthage, *4*: 81; *5*: 238

Deuterius, Donatist bishop of Macrimini, 2: 97; *5*: 179

Didymus, of Alexandria, *1*: 345, 364, 410

Diocletian, Emperor, *1*: 248

Dioscorus, physician, *5*: 140

Dioscorus, student, 2: 261, 262

Eusebius, Donatist bishop, *1*: 131, 135

Eusebius, of Caesarea, historian, *1*: 68, 364; *5*: 157

Eusebius, priest, *4*: 406

Eusebius, St., of Vercellae, *1*: 364

Eustochium, *4*: 73, 406

evidence, value of, *3*: 174, 176

Evodius, *1*: 127, 128, 386; *2*: 336; *3*: 354, 363, 374, 381, 382; *4*: 51, 94, 132; *5*: 70

excommunication, partial, *5*: 32; total, *5*: 239

Exodius, monk and bishop, *1*: 68

Fabiola, *4*: 5; *5*: 285

Fabricius, *2*: 185

faith, versus reason, *2*: 295, 302, 303

Fascius, debtor, *5*: 286

fasting, *1*: 139-157, 160, 253, 255, 283, 284, 314, 315

Faustus, messenger, *4*: 266

Faventius, tenant farmer, *2*: 256-259

Felicia, Christian virgin, *5*: 24

Felician, of Musti, *1*: 239-242, 250, 323, 371, 372; *2*: 33, 211, 213, 216, 218-220, 227-231; *3*: 141

Felicitas, mother superior, *5*: 36

Felix, Donatist, *1*: 182, 207

Felix, Bishop, *5*: 22

Felix, layman of Hippo, 1: 373

Felix, layman, *5*: 244

Felix, monk of Hadrumetum, *5*: 58, 62, 69

Felix, Manichaean priest, *1*: 385

Felix, of Aptunga, *1*: 183, 186, 192, 193; *2*: 24, 26, 200, 202, 373; *4*: 144, 145

Felix, of Nola, St., *1*: 182, 207, 378

Festus, *2*: 34

fifty, symbolism of, *1*: 284, 285

Figulina, church estate, *2*: 198

fire, blessing of, *1*: 79

Firmus, messenger for St. Jerome, *1*: 389, 390, 420; *4*: 73, 141, 288, 301, 401; *5*: 165, 167, 237

Firmus, rebel of Mauretania, *2*: 21

Flavian, prefect, *2*: 19

Flora, festivals of, *2*: 45

Florentina, *5*: 282

Florentinus, officer, *2*: 257, 259

Florentius, Bishop of Hippo Diarrhytus, *2*: 128; *3*: 153; *5*: 99

Florentius, monk, *5*: 167, 173

Florus, monk, *5*: 58, 68-70, 73, 74

food, offered to idols, *1*: 231

forgiveness, duty of, *3*: 44, 45

Fortunatianus, Bishop of Sicca, *3*: 224

Fortunantianus, priest of Hippo, *3*: 224

Fortuniantianus, priest of Tagaste, 1: 387

Fortunatus, Bishop of Cirta, *2*: 218, 260

Fortunatus, consecrated by Augustine, *1*: 218, 245

Fortunatus, Manichaean priest, *1*: 385

Fortunius, Donatist bishop of Cirta, *1*: 207, 209, 215

forty, symbolism of, *1*: 284

Gaius, *1*: 44

Galla, consecrated widow, *5*: 57

Gaudentius, Donatist bishop, *5*: 8

Gaudentius, monk, *2*: 241

Gavinianus, *5*: 139

Geliza, in Numidia, *1*: 187

Generosus, of Constantina, *1*: 245

Generosus, Governor of Numidia, *2*: 260

Genethlius, Bishop of Carthage, *1*: 217

Gennadius, physician at Carthage, *3*: 365

Germanus, *4*: 136

Gildo, *2*: 16

Glorius, *1*: 182, 207

God, fear of, *3*: 102, 107; foreknowledge of, *2*: 158; how we see, *2*: 52, 53; *3*: 179, 182, 184, 185, 188, 193, 200, 221, 223, 224, 228-230, 233, 236, 373; omnipresence of, *3*: 237; *4*: 229; and reason, *3*: 368-370; will of, *2*: 387, 388

government, provincial, *2*: 25

grace, *3*: 28, 58, 64, 67, 68, 72, 83, 98, 100, 114, 121, 122, 135, 163, 164, 168, 321, 325, 332, 339, 344; *4*: 95-97, 130, 193-208

Gracian, Emperor, *2*: 202

Grammaticus, *1*: 182

Gregory Nazianzen, *3*: 232, 236

Gregory, of Elvira, *3*: 232

guilt, proved by divine manifestation, *1*: 374, 377; lies in acceptance of evil by the will, *2*: 254

happiness, where found, *1*: 9, 10; *2*: 384

heaven-dwellers, heretical sect, *1*: 248

Heraclian, *3*: 270

heretics, use of force against, *2*: 56-75

Hermogenianus, *1*: 3

Heros, Bishop of Arles, *4*: 83

Hesychius, Bishop of Salona, *4*: 347, 350, 356

Hilarinus, citizen of Hippo, *1*: 373

Hilarinus, physician of Hippo, *1*: 181

Hilary, Bishop of Arles, *5*: 127, 129

Hilary, Bishop of Narbonne, *4*: 108

Hilary, Bishop of Poitiers, *1*: 78; *2*: 87; *4*: 119

Hilary, layman, of Gaul, *5*: 129

Hilary, layman, of Sicily, *3*: 318

Hippo, *1*: 49, 57, 70, 133, 243, 310, 371; *2*: 10, 12, 127; *3*: 53

Holiness, as title, *1*: 46, 49, 51, 71

301

Marcian, of Urga, 2: 190
Marcianus, 5: 250
Marcion, heretic, 1: 358
Marcionites, 2: 273; 5: 182
Marinus, Count of Africa, 3: 270, 272
Marinus, Donatist, 1: 249
Marinus, Mercator, 4: 191
Mark of Casphaliana, convert from Donatism, 2: 197
Martinianus, 5: 53
martyrs, of Sufes, 1: 237; self-made, 1: 203; 4: 155; true and false, 4: 149, 150; wrong commemoration of, 1: 99-101
Martyrius, 3: 56
Mass, act of worship, 3: 98; for dead, 3: 356; prayers of, 3: 250, 251; of thanksgiving, 3: 120; time of, on Holy Thursday, 1: 256; when offered, 1: 253
Mascula, in Africa, 1: 249
Maurusius, citizen of Hippo, 1: 295
Maxima, 5: 273
Maximian, Bishop of Bagai, 2: 29; 4: 168
Maximian, Donatist bishop, 1: 205, 213, 240, 243, 323; 2: 211, 213, 216-219, 227, 228, 231-233, 369; 3: 140-149; 4: 157
Maximian, Emperor, 1: 248
Maximianists, 1: 242, 250, 324, 372; 2: 17, 67, 80, 229, 230, 233, 273, 373
Maximinus, convert, 2: 198

Maximinus, Donatist bishop of Sinitus, 1: 58; 3: 136
Maximus, doctor, 4: 61, 68, 69
Maximus, grammarian, 1: 37, 39
Maximus, investigator, 2: 26
Maximus, letter-bearer, 2: 212
Maximus, priest, 2: 224
Megalius, primate of Numidia, 1: 169
Melania, junior, 2: 337, 348, 349; 3: 4, 15, 36; 4: 406
Melania, senior, 2: 108, 337, 403; 3: 5, 15
Melchiades, Pope, 1: 185, 193, 195; 2: 202
Memorius, Bishop of Capua, 2: 144
memory, 1: 13-15
Mercator, 4: 292
mercy, corporal works of, 2: 335
Milan, 1: 69, 199, 213
Milevis, Council of, 4: 91; bishops of, 4: 127
Minaeans (Nazarians), heretics, 1: 356
military service, how sanctified, 4: 268, 269
mind, effect of, on body, 1: 21
Monica, St., 1: 253
monks, not to leave diocese, 1: 311
Montanists, 5: 183
Montenses, Donatist sect, 1: 247
moon, phases of, 1: 266; symbolism of, 1: 268, 269
Moses, Law of, not binding on Gentiles, 1: 395-400

helped by fasting, 2: 401; manner, object, 2: 383; 3: 22; various words for, 3: 248-251
predestination, 4: 276, 277
Primian, Donatist bishop of Carthage, 1: 205, 250; 2: 211, 215-217, 219, 227, 229, 373, 374; 3: 140; 4: 79
Primus, subdeacon, 1: 136
Priscillian, 2: 294; 4: 3, 7; 5: 182-189
Priscillianists, 1: 162; 4: 13, 61
Priscus, Bishop, 5: 33
Privatus, monk, 2: 6; 3: 360
Proba, 2: 376, 402; 3: 3, 266
Probus, Sextus Anicius, 3: 266
Proculeianus, Donatist, 1: 126, 135, 136, 382; 2: 28, 198, 236
Proculus, Bishop, 5: 99
Profuturus, 1: 94, 169, 177, 328, 336; 3: 360
Prosper of Aquitaine, 4: 191; 5: 139
psalms, commentary on, 4: 51, 60; singing of, 1: 290
Publicola, convert, 1: 220, 225
Publicola, son of Melania, 2: 108, 337
Punic, as native tongue, 1: 315; 2: 9, 230; 5: 117; names in, 1: 38-41
punishment, lenient for Donatists, recommended, 3: 55; right of capital, 1: 230
Purpurius, 1: 87
Pythagoras, 2: 156, 283, 3: 28; 4: 3

Quintianus, deacon, 3: 277
Quintianus, priest of Carthage, 1: 309
Quintilian, Bishop, 5: 51
Quintas, deacon, 2: 107, 115
Quintus, priest, 3: 239
Quodvultdeus, 2: 241; 5: 112, 114, 116, 117

reason, and God, 3: 368-370
rebaptism, 1: 59, 63, 64, 131-136, 314; 2: 20, 33, 37, 92, 134, 205, 211, 231, 249
Regulus, 2: 341
Religianus, cleric, 5: 53
Renatus, priest, 4: 271
restitution, obligation of, 3: 296-302
Restitutus, Bishop, 2: 128, 228
Restitutus, deacon and convert, 2: 198; 5: 238
Restitutus, delegate to emperor, 2: 128
Restitutus, martyred priest, 3: 6, 53, 55
resurrection, of body, 2: 121-123, 149, 150; 4: 300; 5: 12
rhetors (sophists), 2: 270
Rogatian, Donatist, 2: 202
Rogatists, 2: 21, 66
Rogatus, 2: 56, 66, 218
Romanianus, 1: 13, 36, 75, 116, 117
Romanus, 1: 110, 111, 117, 181, 182, 219
Rome, primacy of, 1: 68, 187;

306

siege of, 2: 334, 359; 3: 304; 4: 4

Romulus, tax farmer, 3: 43; 5: 232

Ruferius, deacon, 3: 239

Ruferius, monk of Hippo, 2: 356

Ruferius, opponent of St. Jerome, 4: 4, 20

Rufinus (Calpurnius), opponent of St. Jerome, 1: 336, 337; 2: 185

Rufinus, deacon, 3: 239

Rufinus, official of Cirta, 3: 57

Rufinus, P. Cornelius, senator, 2: 185

rule, religious, of St. Augustine, 5: 38-51

Rusticanus, deacon, 2: 235

Rusticus, 5: 53, 255

Rusicada, in Numidia, 2: 21

sabbath, changed to Sunday, 1: 279; meanings of, 1: 143; seventh day: 1: 274, 275

Sabellians, 2: 273, 313

Sabinus, 5: 70

sacrament, meanings of word, 1: 261; validity among schismatics, 1: 303; 2: 36

sackcloth, symbol of penance, 1: 234

sacrifice, due to God alone, 2: 162; instinctive in man, 2: 159; origin and kinds of, 2: 159

Sallust, 2: 183; 3: 30, 42, 48, 299; 4: 19, 38, 72

salvation, before Christ, 2: 153-156; free gift of, 3: 256; outside Church, 2: 159

Salvius, Donatist of Membresa, 2: 229, 233

Samsucius, Bishop of Turris, 1: 134, 304; 2: 6, 14

sanctuary, right of, 2: 256

Sapida, virgin of Carthage, 5: 270

Sardis, 1: 211

Saturninus, city clerk, 2: 25

Saturninus, converted Donatist priest, 3: 147

Saturninus, priest, 1: 57; 4: 407

scandal, to be avoided, 2: 7

schism, effects of 1: 129

Scripture Holy, authority of, 1: 394; canon of 1: 310, 311; 5: 261; interpretation of, 3: 254; translations of, 1: 95, 326; varying Latin versions of, 1: 328, 419; quotations from or references to:

Acts, 1: 73, 110, 122, 156, 162, 164, 230, 288, 348-350, 352, 386, 395, 396, 398; 2: 19, 31, 32, 54, 61-63, 77, 99, 111, 169, 208, 215, 281, 307, 321, 324, 380, 401; 3: 32, 46, 84, 184, 196, 245, 247, 323, 351, 383, 388, 393; 4: 15, 56, 57, 64, 75, 139, 146, 163, 169, 170, 176, 209, 212, 225, 228, 229, 250, 253, 268, 275, 276, 303, 321, 337, 340, 347, 351, 355, 358, 374, 375, 388, 389, 396, 417; 5:

311

223, 274, 293, 311, 373, 397, 402; 5: 59, 81, 88, 104, 123, 164, 205, 226, 227, 266, 267, 269, 284

2 Timothy, 1: 137, 235, 251, 262, 263, 286, 417; 2: 104, 225, 327; 3: 149, 235, 264; 4: 129, 131, 172, 215, 228, 256, 290, 300, 310, 312, 352, 353, 357, 374, 376

Titus, 1: 133, 137, 182, 183, 292; 2: 86, 323, 352, 384; 3: 7, 111, 122, 257, 345; 4: 96, 241, 322, 329, 338; 5: 47, 50, 63, 187, 252

Tobias, 1: 153; 2: 390; 3: 118, 358; 5: 184, 188, 290

Wisdom, 1: 255, 266; 2: 114, 146, 296; 3: 3, 27, 73, 134, 154, 160, 216, 223, 253, 324, 338, 385; 4: 56, 63, 97, 110, 177, 178, 180, 190, 226, 231, 261, 264, 269, 273, 293, 329; 5: 20, 85, 90, 96, 97, 133, 206

Zacharias, 2: 341; 3: 196, 377; 4: 29, 280

Sebastian, abbot, 5: 236

Secudinus, priest, 5: 243

Secundus, primate of Numidia, 1: 184, 186, 188, 190, 191, 196, 206, 248; 2: 251; 5: 99

Secundus, relative of Purpurius, 1: 187

seeds, power of, 3: 25

Seleuciana, 5: 276

Seneca, 3: 291

senses, bodily, 3: 21, 22, 176

Septuagint, authority of, 1: 328, 419

Servilius, monk, 3: 360, 362

Severinus, Donatist bishop, 1: 243

Severus, Bishop of Milevis, 1: 117, 170, 181, 304, 306; 2: 8, 127, 238, 241; 5: 53, 289

sight, of God, 3: 214; mental, 3: 206, 209; versus belief, 3: 175, 177, 207; visual, 3: 173

Silvanus, Bishop of Cirta, 1: 196

Silvanus, primate of Numidia, 2: 365, 369, 376; 3: 136; 4: 127; 5: 30

Simplicianus, 1: 168

Simpliciola, consecrated virgin, 5: 51

sin, original, 2: 130, 134; 3: 334-338; 4: 15, 37, 278, 279

singing, in church, 1: 60, 290

Sinis, near Hippo, 2: 256

Sinitus, in Numidia, 2: 198

sins, equality of, in pagan philosophy, 2: 179; not equal, 4: 37

Sissinius, deacon, 1: 328, 329, 313

Sissinius, martyr, 3: 56

Sitif, in Mauretania, 2: 17; 4: 147

Sixtus, Pope, 4: 288, 301; 5: 59

Solus, civil servant, 2: 26

soul, born in sin, 4: 273, 278; immortality of, 4: 8; incorporeality of, 3: 357; 4: 8; no

Scriptural authority for any,
4: 281, 307-312; theories of origin of, *3*: 154; *4*: 13, 32, 120, 281; union of, with body, *3*: 85
Spes, monk, *1*: 374
Spirit, Holy, *4*: 82
Spondeus, son of Celer, *3*: 55
state, definition of, *3*: 43
stenographer, use of, *1*: 208
Stesichorus, Greek poet, *1*: 318, 362, 418
Stilicho, *2*: 124, 127, 200
Stoics, *2*: 193, 273, 277, 279-281, 286; *3*: 13; *4*: 3
substance, characteristics of, *1*: 27
Sufes, in Africa, *1*: 237
suicide, as martyrdom, *5*: 5, 6
Superius, centurion, *2*: 25
synods, calling of, *1*: 298

Tagaste, *1*: 13, 68, 70, 219; *2*: 219, 337
Taphnis, in Egypt, *2*: 336
Terence, *1*: 17, 76, 120, 416; *2*: 44; *3*: 38, 309, 316; *4*: 406; *5*: 252
Tertullian, *4*: 4
Thamugadi, *2*: 17; *5*: 4, 8
Theasius, Bishop, *1*: 386; *3*: 361
Themistocles, *2*: 274; *5*: 158
Theodore, African bishop, *1*: 302
Theodore, Arian bishop of Heraclea, *1*: 346, 364, 411

Theodore, deacon, *4*: 81
Theodore, letter-bearer, *2*: 212
Theodosius, Emperor, *2*: 127, 202; *4*: 403; *5*: 52
Theodotion, Ebionite, *1*: 363
Theoprepia, church of Donatists, *3*: 540
Therasia, wife of Paulinus, *1*: 66, 85, 87, 88, 109, 111, 219, 386; *2*: 106, 115, 317; *3*: 239; *4*: 19
Thiave, hamlet, *2*: 3
throne, bishop's, *2*: 235
Tibilis, town, *2*: 254
Tisigis, town, *1*: 184, 248
Timasius, monk of Hippo, *2*: 349; *4*: 50, 98, 111
Timothy, deacon, *1*: 304; *2*: 241
Titianus, monk, *4*: 81
Titianus, proconsul, *2*: 229
torture, use of, to secure evidence, *2*: 48, 195; *3*: 7, 9
tradition, source of truth, *1*: 252
traditors, 1: 183, 187, 190, 210, 239; *2*: 196, 201, 209
Trinity, doctrine of, *1*: 26, 29; *2*: 297, 306, 307, 309, 310, 313, 314; *4*: 54, 64, 83, 232
Tripoli, *2*: 80
Trismegistus, *5*: 175
Tubursicum, town, *1*: 207, 219
Turris, town, *1*: 134
Tychonius, *2*: 70, 96, 98, 181; *5*: 238

Urban, Bishop of Sicca, *3*: 150, 266; *5*: 152, 153

THE FATHERS
OF THE CHURCH

(A series of approximately 100 volumes when completed)

translated by L. Schopp
The Magnitude of the Soul
translated by J. McMahon
On Music
translated by R. Taliaferro
The Advantage of Believing
translated by L. Meagher
On Faith in Things Unseen
translated by R. Deferrari, M–F. McDonald

OCLC 856032

Volume 5:   SAINT AUGUSTINE   (1948)
The Happy Life
translated by L. Schopp
Answer to Skeptics *(Contra Academicos)*
translated by D. Kavanagh
Divine Providence and the Problem of Evil
translated by R. Russell
The Soliloquies
translated by T. Gilligan

OCLC 728405

Volume 6:   WRITINGS OF SAINT JUSTIN MARTYR   (1948)
The First Apology
The Second Apology
The Dialogue with Trypho
Exhortation to the Greeks
Discourse to the Greeks
The Monarchy or Rule of God
translated by T. Falls

OCLC 807077

Volume 7:   NICETA OF REMESIANA   (1949)
Writings of Niceta of Remesiana
translated by G. Walsh
Prosper of Aquitaine: Grace and Free Will
translated by J. O'Donnell
Writings of Sulpicius Severus
translated by B. Peebles
Vincent of Lerins: The Commonitories
translated by R. Morris

OCLC 807068

Volume 8:   SAINT AUGUSTINE   (1950)

The City of God (books 1–7)
translated by D. Zema, G. Walsh

OCLC 807084

Volume 9:   SAINT BASIL ASCETICAL WORKS   (1950)
translated by M. Wagner

OCLC 856020

Volume 10:   TERTULLIAN APOLOGETICAL WORKS   (1950)
Tertullian Apology
translated by E–J. Daly
On the Soul
translated by E. Quain
The Testimony of the Soul
To Scapula
translated by R. Arbesmann
Minucius Felix: Octavius
translated by R. Arbesmann

OCLC 1037264

Volume 11:   SAINT AUGUSTINE   (1957)
Commentary on the Lord's Sermon on the Mount
Selected Sermons (17)
translated by D. Kavanagh

OCLC 2210742

Volume 12:   SAINT AUGUSTINE   (1951)
Letters (1–82)
translated by W. Parsons

OCLC 807061

Volume 13:   SAINT BASIL   (1951)
Letters (1–185)
translated by A–C. Way

OCLC 2276183

Volume 14:   SAINT AUGUSTINE   (1952)
The City of God (books 8–16)
translated by G. Walsh, G. Monahan

OCLC 807084

Volume 15:   EARLY CHRISTIAN BIOGRAPHIES   (1952)
Life of St. Ambrose by Paulinus
translated by J. Lacy
Life of St. Augustine by Bishop Possidius

Life of St. Cyprian by Pontius
translated by M. M. Mueller, R. Deferrari
Life of St. Epiphanius by Ennodius
translated by G. Cook
Life of St. Paul the First Hermit
Life of St. Hilarion by St. Jerome
Life of Malchus by St. Jerome
translated by L. Ewald
Life of St. Anthony by St. Athanasius
translated by E. Keenan
A Sermon on the Life of St. Honoratus by St. Hilary
translated by R. Deferrari

OCLC 806775

Volume 16:   SAINT AUGUSTINE   (1952)
The Christian Life
Lying
The Work of Monks
The Usefulness of Fasting
translated by S. Muldowney
Against Lying
translated by H. Jaffe
Continence
translated by M–F. McDonald
Patience
translated by L. Meagher
The Excellence of Widowhood
translated by C. Eagan
The Eight Questions of Dulcitius
translated by M. Deferrari

OCLC 806731

Volume 17:   SAINT PETER CHRYSOLOGUS   (1953)
Selected Sermons
Letter to Eutyches
SAINT VALERIAN
Homilies
Letter to the Monks
translated by G. Ganss

OCLC 806783

Volume 18:   SAINT AUGUSTINE   (1953)

Letters (83–130)
    translated by W. Parsons

                                              OCLC 807061

Volume 19:   **EUSEBIUS PAMPHILI**   (1953)
    Ecclesiastical History (books 1–5)
    translated by R. Deferrari

                                              OCLC 708651

Volume 20:   **SAINT AUGUSTINE**   (1953)
    Letters (131–164)
    translated by W. Parsons

                                              OCLC 807061

Volume 21:   **SAINT AUGUSTINE**   (1953)
    Confessions
    translated by V. Bourke

                                         OCLC 2210845

Volume 22:   **FUNERAL ORATIONS**   (1953)
    Saint Gregory Nazianzen: Four Funeral Orations
    translated by L. McCauley
    Saint Ambrose: On the Death of His Brother Satyrus I & II
    translated by J. Sullivan, M. McGuire
    Saint Ambrose: Consolation on the Death of Emperor
    Valentinian
    Funeral Oration on the Death of Emperor Theodosius
    translated by R. Deferrari

                                         OCLC 806797

Volume 23:   **CLEMENT OF ALEXANDRIA**   (1954)
    Christ the Educator
    translated by S. Wood

                                       OCLC 2200024

Volume 24:   **SAINT AUGUSTINE**   (1954)
    The City of God (books 17-22)
    translated by G. Walsh, D. Honan

                                         OCLC 807084

Volume 25:   **SAINT HILARY OF POITIERS**   (1954)
    The Trinity
    translated by S. McKenna

                                         OCLC 806781

Volume 26:   **SAINT AMBROSE**   (1954)

Letters (204–270)
translated by W. Parsons

OCLC 807061

Rule for the Monastery of Compludo
General Rule for Monasteries
Pact
Monastic Agreement
translated by C. Barlow

OCLC 718095

Volume 64: THE WORKS OF SAINT CYRIL (1970)
OF JERUSALEM II
Lenten Lectures (Catcheses) 13–18
translated by L. McCauley
The Mystagogical Lectures
Sermon on the Paralytic
Letter to Constantius
translated by A. Stephenson

OCLC 21885

Volume 65 SAINT AMBROSE (1972)
Seven Exegetical Works
Isaac or the Soul
Death as a Good
Jacob and the Happy Life
Joseph
The Patriarchs
Flight from the World
The Prayer of Job and David
translated by M. McHugh

OCLC 314148

Volume 66: SAINT CAESARIUS OF ARLES III (1973)
Sermons 187–238
translated by M. M. Mueller

OCLC 1035149; 2494636

Volume 67: NOVATIAN (1974)
The Trinity
The Spectacles
Jewish Foods
In Praise of Purity
Letters
translated by R. DeSimone

OCLC 662181